Space Race

Space Race

**An inside view of the future
of communications planning**

Jim Taylor

John Wiley & Sons, Ltd

Copyright © 2005   John Wiley & Sons Ltd, The Atrium, Southern Gate, Chichester,
West Sussex PO19 8SQ, England

Telephone (+44) 1243 779777

Reprinted December 2005, January 2006

Email (for orders and customer service enquiries): cs-books@wiley.co.uk
Visit our Home Page on www.wiley.com

Other Wiley Editorial Offices

John Wiley & Sons Inc., 111 River Street, Hoboken, NJ 07030, USA

Jossey-Bass, 989 Market Street, San Francisco, CA 94103-1741, USA

Wiley-VCH Verlag GmbH, Boschstr. 12, D-69469 Weinheim, Germany

John Wiley & Sons Australia Ltd, 42 McDougall Street, Milton, Queensland 4064, Australia

John Wiley & Sons (Asia) Pte Ltd, 2 Clementi Loop #02-01, Jin Xing Distripark, Singapore
129809

John Wiley & Sons Canada Ltd, 22 Worcester Road, Etobicoke, Ontario, Canada M9W 1L1

Wiley also publishes its books in a variety of electronic formats. Some content that appears
in print may not be available in electronic books.

Library of Congress Cataloging-in-Publication Data
Taylor, Jim.
    Space race : an inside view of the future of communications planning / Jim Taylor.
        p.   cm.
    Includes bibliographical references and index.
    ISBN 13 978-0-470-09451-8 (cloth : alk. paper)
    ISBN 10 0-470-09451-6 (cloth : alk. paper)
   1. Communication in marketing.   2. Advertising.   3. Marketing.   I. Title.
    HF5415.123.T39 2005
    659.2—dc22

                                                              2005020004

British Library Cataloguing in Publication Data

A catalogue record for this book is available from the British Library

ISBN 13 978-0-470-09451-8 (HB)
ISBN 10 0-470-09451-6 (HB)

Typeset in 11/14 Bembo by SNP Best-set Typesetter Ltd, Hong Kong
Printed and bound in Great Britain by TJ International Ltd, Padstow, Cornwall, UK
This book is printed on acid-free paper responsibly manufactured from sustainable forestry in
which at least two trees are planted for each one used for paper production.

To Ali

Contents

Foreword xi

Preface xvii

Acknowledgements xxv

List of Interviewee Quotes References xxvii

Part I: Wanting to Fly 1

2000–2005 – a period of naivety and hope – a period of 'gold-rush' type sentiment – a period of 'unconscious incompetence'

1 **The Space Race** 3

A definition of communications planning, a review of the different approaches being practised, and an introduction to the players in the 'race' to occupy the territory

what is communications planning? – what the hell should we call it? – the three schools of practice – who are the players?

2 **Of Straw and Sponges** 19

The key reasons for adopting communications planning

being true to your annual objectives – interlinking communication channels and encouraging better use of them – first-mover competitive advantage

3 **Gravity** 43

The issues that are holding communications planning back

inability to prove it's better in ROI terms – agencies are culturally and structurally hide-bound to execution – clients are not sure how to do it or who should do it – politics – conservatism – not a clear enough understanding of the consumer – it's impossible to quantify ideas – client's mixed messages – conclusion

4 **Reviewing the Fleet** 57

A look at the different types of structural 'toe-dipping' that are currently being used by different clients and agency types

some clients have committed to it and want to control it – many agencies have committed to communications planning, irrespective of current client demand – communication independents – ad agency networks – media agency networks – integrated BTL agency networks – JVs – Nitro – and waiting in the harbour . . . – so where's the real action?

5 **Life Below Decks** 83

An assessment of the pros and cons of the different agency types in terms of their suitability to do communications planning, and a look at alternatives beyond 'agency'

media agencies – ad agencies – integrated BTL agencies – communication independents – four internal factors for change – a perfect agency structure – is 'agency' the only structure we should be thinking about? – how many winners will there be?

Part II: Learning to Fly 115

2005–2010 – a period of great pressure to be accountable – a period of realism, knuckling down to it – a period of 'conscious incompetence'

6 **A Slow Wind on the Water** 117

Developments 2005–2010

putting ROI at the heart of things – more emphasis on digital, direct and in-store communication – changes in media buying – what are the implications for agencies? – watching the wrong thing!

7 **The Soul Meter** 137

Technology as the change agent that allows communications planning to 'take off'

disruptive technology – the Soul Meter – who might create a Soul Meter? – conclusion

Part III: Cutting Through the Earth's Atmosphere 157

2010–2020 – the marketing machine phase – a period where data will become the dominant driver of communications planning – a period of 'conscious competence'

8 **The Dark Days of Data** 159

Developments 2010–2015: data driving communications planning

data storage and ownership – data use – general implications – management consultants – research agencies – media agencies and integrated BTL agencies – independence of execution? – communication independents – what about the ad agencies? – conclusion

9 **Antarctica** 181

Clients starting to want to own and do communications planning

bringing it all back home – the implications – conclusion

10 **The Twin Achilles' Heels** 203

Developments 2015–2020: ad agencies starting to split in two

production – ideas – ad agencies transforming – fusion – conclusion

Part IV: Weightlessness 223

2020 onwards – a period where ideas make a comeback; where
their ROI value is 'outed' – a period where communications
planning is liberated – a period of 'unconscious competence'

11 **2020 Vision** 225

A summary of where we end up at in 2020 and how each
of the players will have done over the period 2005–2020

those at the centre of things will be the big winners – how
will the individual players have fared over the years? – in
2020, what will life be like?

12 **Beyond 2020: The ROI of Snow** 237

A look at the future beyond 2020, where ideas start to drive
communications planning

Andorra – to summarise . . .

Last Words 245

Profile of Interviewees 251

References 267

Index 271

Foreword

This is the story of two groups in the world of marketing services, the engineers and the artists. It's the story of how they lose their power and respect, but then earn it back by combining forces and inventing something new, precious and powerful – a thing called *communications planning* – a thing *so* powerful that it shakes the foundations of the creators and transforms them into something new as well. It's a story whose ending is unknown, because it's still being written and will take decades to unfold.

However, if you have a stake in this story, and you're the impatient sort not inclined to wait, then you would do well to read Jim Taylor's terrific book that follows. Jim has taken on the gargantuan task of not just explaining what communications planning is, but also of predicting where it's headed, and what that will mean for the marketing services industry globally.

Further, he's the only one I know who has the guts (and the insights) necessary to make savvy predictions about how this story will eventually turn out, not just next year, but 20 years from now. Not only does he offer dates and numbers, he gives both at the same time – a fine quality in any prediction.

Jim addresses, and answers, these sorts of questions:

- Who will ultimately win when it comes to ownership of communications planning?

- Could media buying be unbundled from media strategy, the same way media services unbundled from the creative agency?
- Will creative development ever be unbundled from production and execution?
- Could we return, full circle, to a new kind of full-service agency in the future, and what sort of agency would this be?

Here's a bit of background to acquaint you with the territory that Jim knows so well.

In marketing, as in many other endeavours, there is an engineering dimension and an artistic dimension. These are the sorts of companies who have their roots in the engineering dimension:

- media agencies;
- research firms;
- management and marketing consultants;
- direct marketing experts;
- sales promotion shops;
- interactive and online specialists;
- search marketing firms;
- and, importantly, most clients (especially their powerful and expanding procurement departments).

The engineering dimension is the domain of quantitative research, ROI (return on investment) measurement, key performance indicators, budget setting and allocation, single-source tracking, econometric analysis, market modelling, media optimisation, database marketing, 'analytics' and so on. The engineering dimension employs this mechanical muscle to eke out usually small (though not insignificant) gains in communications performance. Typically, it takes large companies to compete effectively in the engineering domain because the tools are complex and costly, and only large firms can afford them.

By contrast, the artistic dimension has a very different orientation and approach to marketing problems. These are the sorts of companies who have their roots in the artistic dimension:

- ad agencies;
- production houses;
- directors' studios;
- communications planning agencies;
- branding experts;
- design and identity shops;
- public relations firms;
- store design and merchandising experts.

On the whole, companies in the artistic dimension have fewer tools and systems − at least, the really expensive kind. For some ad agencies, a cleverly labelled quadrant chart counts as a profound proprietary tool. Generally, it's not expensive to compete in this space. Although salaries for superstars in established firms are high, the cost and barriers for new entrants are low. *Anybody* can start an ad agency, and some days, it seems that just about everybody does.

However, even though they don't have the same tools as the engineers, the artists have one tremendous advantage over the engineers: the artistic dimension possesses the only known ability to produce giant, dramatic leaps in marketing performance (as opposed to the incremental gains delivered by the engineers). The secret to this power is simple. The artistic dimension is the domain of *ideas*.

While there are significant differences in how marketing engineers and artists look at the world, there are some deep continuities as well. For one thing, neither group is doing such a bang-up job these days. The power of marketing is eroding, and the traditional forms of marketing services on both sides of the divide are proving inadequate to the task of stemming the decline.

What makes matters worse is that both groups suffer from a lack of respect. Many media agency leaders would admit, perhaps off the record, that lack of respect from their creative brethren was a significant catalyst for driving the unbundling of media services from their ad agency parents in the first place.

In parallel, the ad agencies, never universally respected in the best of times, have seen public esteem and industry regard for their services erode at an alarming rate. In many pitches today, ad agencies don't even like to *call* themselves ad agencies, much less refer to their main product as ads. I am reminded of the remark by Jacques Seguela: 'Don't tell my mother I work in an advertising agency. She thinks I play the piano in a whorehouse.'

Clearly, we have entered a confusing era in marketing services. Viewed from one angle, it appears that the lines that divide marketing specialities are blurring. Viewed from another, it seems that the gaps separating them have never been wider. And yet, for communications planning to take seed and thrive, the gaps must be overcome – one way or another.

Sometimes it seems as if marketing services specialists come from different planets. Imagine two settings: the media agency and the creative agency, both at work on the client's new campaign.

At the media agency, specialists pore over analysis late into the night in order to offer carefully researched and analytically sophisticated rec-ommendations on how to gain market share. At the creative agency, a manager describes their process. 'Obviously, we work in advertising, but we rarely do research. We do what we like. Research-driven advertising has no heart, no soul. This year, I said to Lisa Prisco, our creative director, "Khaki!" A week later, she came back to me and said "Swing!".' (The true story and actual words behind one of the greatest campaigns of the 1990s, for Gap khakis.)

Bryan Millar, reminiscing about the Gap campaign, speculates how Chiat/Day might have sold the iPod campaign to Apple: 'So, they're Gap ads, but with iPods and, uh, we'll make them green.'

Both approaches have their merits. I won't reveal my opinion as to which is more fun. Nonetheless, looking to the future, it is clear that roles and responsibilities are changing. It is also certain that communications planning will play a central role in reviving the power of marketing services in the twenty-first century.

The ideal and most powerful marketing services agency of the future will be one that practises communications planning – one that figures out a way to integrate the left-brain orientation on analytics and ROI and the right-brain focus on ideas and creativity. Evolutionary science has taught us that evolution has no predetermined direction. What 'species' of marketing service firms will survive? Which will become extinct? Which will evolve into new forms? No one can say for sure.

The only certainty is (paraphrasing William Gibson), the future is here already. The only thing is, it's not evenly distributed yet.

Read Jim's book and explore that future.

Ken Sacharin, San Francisco, author of Attention

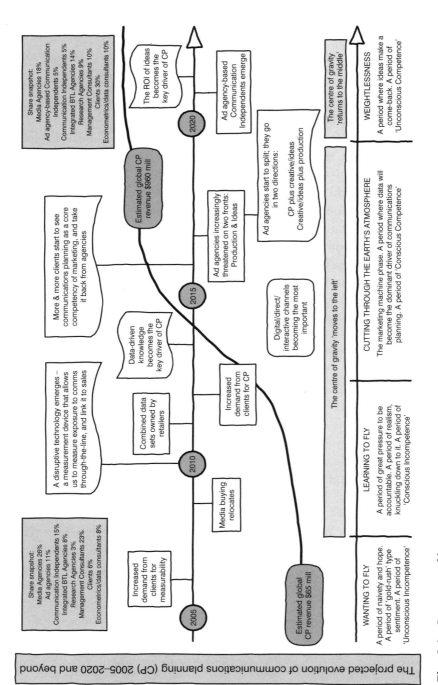

Fig. 0.1 Summary of key events.

Preface

There has been a blue haze over the communications industry for quite some time. Visit the Blue Mountains outside Sydney and you'll see the kind of thing I mean. Vaporised oil rising off the leaves of its eucalyptus forests makes this area of New South Wales one of the most highly combustible places on Earth. Every few decades, the oil-rich air of the tree crowns erupts with a ferocity that leaves fire-fighters helpless and destroys everything in its path. But the eucalyptus is not a suicidal plant; it depends on the intense heat of the fire to crack the nut that contains its seed so it can germinate and put down fresh roots.

Over the next decade the blue haze over the communications industry is likely to explode in just the same way. There will be a bonfire of the certainties. New technologies will throw up great plumes of flame. Safe old assumptions will be torched. The mighty trunks at the heart of the forest – TV, print, radio – will creak amid the heat. Mass audiences will splinter apart. The last remaining limbs of the old full-service agencies will crash to the earth. Obscure agencies once thought of as brushwood will burst into a raging blaze, while many creative giants of the past will be charred beyond recognition.

As we survey the flaming treescape of our industry, we will have to conclude that it is impossible to douse the flames. But we will be able to console ourselves with the thought that somewhere in the forest is the nut; though what exactly is inside it and how it will develop is open to debate. It seems highly unlikely that a new generation of full-service agencies will spring up – as unlikely as a new generation of trees being identical to the one that went before. So just what will come next?

It is my contention that inside the nut is a new idea – communications planning – and all indications are that it represents the catalyst for the future, for everyone involved in the industry, for communications agencies as well as their clients, be they brand owners/manufacturers or indeed retailers.

Communications planning is a simple enough idea. It is a strategic overview of how all available communications can best be used to help a brand meet its objectives as successfully as possible, and it happens prior to implementational briefing. It might sound like plain common sense, but in the past marketers got away with using intuition rather than strategy and displayed an unhealthy tendency to default to TV advertising as the answer to everything. But communications planning has no respect for the way things have always been done. If a planner can prove that a brand's best interests are served by ploughing its entire marketing budget into digital media, then that's exactly what will happen, even if it means ditching a long-running campaign – and the faithful agency that went with it. In short, it is highly disruptive!

The communications industry is in a period of structural and cultural turmoil, there's no getting around it. Agencies of all descriptions are seeing opportunity and threat in communications planning, in equal measure. Clients are wrestling with it, and with how to embrace it and adapt to it.

If you're an industry insider, it might seem that communications planning has been written about ad nauseam. Pick up the latest copy of the relevant trade press in your country – *Ad Age, Adweek, Marketing, Campaign* or *B and T Weekly* – and chances are you'll see it written about in some form. Much has been made of it in terms of media and ad agencies, and their relationship. But nearly all that has been written about it deals with its history, and why it's emerging. Virtually nothing has been written about the questions that are on everyone's mind, namely, where's this all going? Who will own communications planning? What will the future look like, once communications planning takes off?

If I am running an agency of some description, how might I best gear up for this future? What sort of investments should I make? How should I compete in the inter-agency game, how should I position myself? If I'm a brand owner, a CEO, a marketing director or indeed a trade marketing director, how important is communications planning for the growth of my brands? Should I give it to an agency or try to do it myself? How can I use it as a competitive advantage over my competitors – other brand owners or indeed the retailers I sell through?

So this book attempts to predict a future that is of critical interest to hundreds of thousands of individuals around the world. It looks at how the communications industry will evolve from now up until the year 2020.

This is no small task, because it is a slippery, complex subject. If it were easy, there would be no point in writing this book! And others would have worked out the answer already.

Is this book unique? Yes, it really is. It's the first time anyone has truly tried to predict the future of communications planning. The only other attempt to define it that I've ever seen was a paper written by Neil Dawson and Michael Ellyatt of TBWA/GGT (Dawson & Ellyatt, 2003). But that paper only really scratched the surface.

Who am I?

So who am I to try to tackle this? Well, I am a communications planner for starters. A practitioner of the discipline of communications planning. And I've been doing this for the last five years, at both a local market level as well as, more recently, an international level.

Let me explain further. I started my career as a media planner, working for full-service agencies like Ogilvy & Mather and McCann Erickson, in both the UK and South Africa. Twenty-odd years ago, these were the norm. Clients came to 'agencies' for everything, including media planning. But over the last 10 to 15 years, media planning and buying in nearly every country in the world have emerged from the 'full-service agency basement' to form so-called media independents and media dependents. These have gradually fused to become known simply as 'media agencies'.

So media has been unbundled, and it did this for a few reasons. First, as a way to aggregate media budgets to obtain the maximum leverage in buying – but in reaction to the initial consolidation of media selling points; secondly, because of the erosion of the commission system (switching to fee or simply cutting commission), which meant an agency could not afford 'nonessential' departments like media; and last, because within the full-service environment it was never given the respect it deserved, because the media strategy was all too often 'coloured' by the creative or laid hostage by the creative idea. It was also because within a full-service environment, the research and systems needed by media were never prioritised as highly as creative resource. So media nowadays is done by media agencies. The full-service agency has haemorrhaged, and is now a thing of the past in virtually every country in the world.

In my mind, media within the full-service agency was like a teenager. To grow up, to gain confidence, to express itself, it had to escape its parents. It had to leave home. Since separating from their 'parents', media agencies have evolved, grown in confidence and have even spawned a subspecies – a type of agency initially called media strategy agencies. Media strategy agencies were the first type of communication agency to divorce themselves of execution. In this case, they were divorcing themselves of buying, by setting up media strategy as an upstream function that demanded its own expertise and, indeed, objective independence.

In the last five or ten years, post full-service agency, things had started calming down. We were all starting to get used to the new world

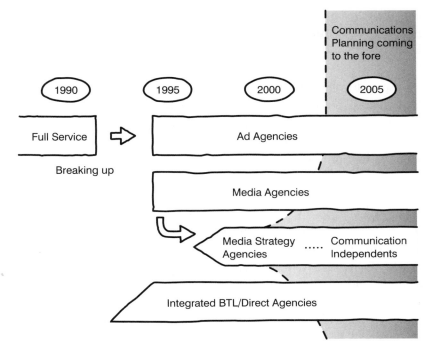

Fig. 0.2 Roughly what's been happening around the world to agencies.

order, and how to work together again. But then along came communications planning, to spoil the calm that was descending.

In 1998 I was working as the media director of Ogilvy & Mather in Cape Town – still a full-service agency – when I and a business director friend of mine called Peter Vogel decided to leave and start up a new agency. But not a 'normal' media agency; rather, one of the new subspecies I've just mentioned – a media strategy agency, called Nota Bene. It was the first media strategy agency in South Africa and the third in the world, after Michaelides & Bednash and Unity.

The agency thrived and evolved along with the times. When communications planning emerged on the world stage, it was only natural that we embraced it as an extension of media planning. In 2000, we won the communications planning business for FirstRand, a big bancassurance group. And in 2001, we won the Unilever communication channel planning business, in a joint venture with Initiative Media.

By the early years of the twenty-first century, agencies just like Nota Bene had started popping up all over the world. With the emergence of communications planning, they had an evolved function, and these agencies had now become known as communication independents – agencies that primarily did communications planning and were independent of execution.

Now by 2003 we'd sold Nota Bene to Tempus, which subsequently became part of WPP. And Nota Bene was doing more communications planning than media planning. It had become, in fact, probably one of the most advanced practitioners of communications planning in the world.

At this time, with Nota Bene well established, my young family and I decided to leave South Africa after 10 happy years there, to come back to the UK. So I left Nota Bene and relocated to 'head office', as it were, to Mediaedge:cia, a top-five global media agency – which is where I am now.

By then Mediaedge:cia had also started to practise communications planning actively, so I picked up where I'd left off in South Africa. And in the last two years, I've been responsible for driving communications planning at an international level, among international clients.

So in my career I've worked for full-service agencies, communication independents and media agencies, in that order. I've five solid years of communications planning experience under my belt, at a local market level and at an international level. I've got as much experience as anyone 'out there' in communications planning. So I hope that qualifies me to write this book!

Getting beyond 'me', how have I informed my opinions? Well, to kick off with, by talking to lots of people who are leaders in the marketing and communications industry and who are intimately involved in the subject.

I've spoken to a number of very senior brand owner clients. In the agency world, I've spoken to the leaders of ad agencies, media agencies, so-called integrated below-the-line agencies and communication independents. I've also spoken to management consultants, brand consultants, research agencies, media owners and econometricians. You'll find a profile of each of them at the back of the book.

These interviews and conversations offered me fantastic insights, and I'm deeply indebted to the individuals involved. I've included references to them throughout this book. But as you might suspect, none of them was able to offer me a concrete view of the future on a plate. And many of their opinions were contradictory.

What they did provide me with, however, were thoughts that became like boiling water. And just as boiling water rises up to become steam – to become something new – so too with these thoughts. In immersing myself in them and thinking about them for weeks and weeks and weeks, walking to and from work, these thoughts became something new.

OK, so now you're thinking: this guy is basically a media guy. He might have worked in some different organisations and in different places, but nevertheless, he is a media guy. So won't his opinion be prejudiced? Even if he has spoken to around 30 leaders in various corners of the communication industry, won't he be biased?

Well, when I first undertook this book, I made a very conscious decision to be as objective as humanly possible. Without an objective frame of mind, it would be impossible actually to see an outcome beyond self-interest. To this end, I have written this in my own time, and not company time. I've ploughed through the chapters during weekends and at 5 in the morning! It is very much my own book, not a company-endorsed book. I hope it achieves a balanced perspective.

One last word to the doubting Thomases. At the moment the communications planning marketplace is tiny. It's tempting to question whether it really exists or not. But have no fear, it's emerging, and it's going to be big.

I believe in the communications planning future.

Key points made here

- The communications industry is in a period of structural and cultural turmoil, based on the collapse of the full-service agency model and, more recently, the emergence of communications planning.
- Communications planning will be a big catalyst for change in future, but trying to predict the impact it will have on clients and agencies is very difficult and complex.
- This is the first real attempt to try to predict the future of communications planning.

Acknowledgements

First and foremost, I'd like to thank all of the many people I interviewed while writing this book. These individuals are not only leaders in their organisations, but individuals who, for one reason or another, know more about communications planning than most people – because their company is integrally involved in the subject and at the cutting edge of its development, or indeed because as individuals they have huge experience of actually doing it. So some are exceptionally 'big names', but also some are the 'experts' experts'.

To all of you, I'd like to thank you very much indeed for your time, for your honesty, and for your passion and support. I'm really indebted to you. It was a real pleasure to meet you and it made the exercise of book writing much more interesting and enjoyable. Thanks again for giving up so much of your time, and for all your diverse ideas and points of view. There's no doubt that it gave the book a much richer, more rounded perspective.

I'd also very much like to acknowledge four particular individuals . . .

Ken Sacharin, thank you for your friendship and thanks for writing such an interesting Foreword, when I know you were in the thick of it at the time with pitches at work.

Dave Evans, thanks for the inspiration.

Matthew Bull, an old friend from South Africa, thanks for your nice endorsement on the cover.

And Dawn Hudson, I'm very indebted to you for taking the time to read my manuscript and for your kind words on the cover as well.

I'd also like to acknowledge those people who supported me in the whole process: the guys at Wiley – Claire, Viv and Darren – for making the publishing process as smooth and painless as it turned out to be. Martin and Mary, for a quiet house to work in. Steve, Mel, Charlie and Tash at work; Charlie Hiscocks and Mark Sherrington from SABMiller; and indeed John Griffiths.

You all helped a lot, in different ways.

And last on a personal note, to my wife Ali and my darling kids Tom, Joe and little Amy: thanks for making this possible. Thanks for giving up so many weekends. I love you all very much.

To everyone – here's to the future.

Interviewee Quotes References

Paul Alexander: P. 15, 53, 98

Paul Baker: P. 144

Stephan Bruneau: P. 164, 184

MT Carney: P. 28, 40–1, 51, 53, 210

Will Collin: P. 15–16, 52, 85, 86, 89–90

Charles Courtier: P. 15, 76–7, 111–13

Jonathan Dodd: P. 93, 209

Nick Emery: P. 4, 183

Nigel Foote: P. 241

John Grant: P. 37, 77, 87, 90, 103–4, 111

Bruce Haines: P. 66, 213

Rob Hill: P. 39, 95, 186, 242, 246

Chris Ingram: P. 84, 108

Reg Lascaris: P. 192, 204, 211, 241

Kees Kruythoff: P. 22, 58, 168, 218

Richard M. Metzler: P. 48–9, 183, 189–90

George Michaelides: P. 52, 64, 96–7

Grant Millar: P. 117, 119, 167, 169, 190, 219

Guy Murphy: P. 29, 80, 87, 88

Damian O'Malley: P. 85, 86, 98–9

John Partilla: P. 56, 109, 194

John Preston: P. 90

Tony Regan: P. 85, 190, 212

Paul Shearer: P. 212

Martin Thomas: P. 67, 90–1, 93, 205–6
James Walker: P. 73, 89, 91, 105–6, 187–8, 219–20
Peter Walshe: P. 214
Rod Wright: P. 20, 62, 88–9, 91, 215–16

Part I
Wanting to Fly

2000–2005

A period of naivety and hope
A period of 'gold-rush'-type sentiment
A period of 'unconscious incompetence'

1
The Space Race

A definition of communications planning, a review of the different approaches being practised, and an introduction to the players in the 'race' to occupy the territory

People cannot abide an empty space. Think of our ancestors of 60 000 years ago stumbling out of northeast Africa and first setting eyes on the vast Eurasian steppes; or Columbus gazing at the western horizon; or a NASA scientist staring hungrily at the stars. Throughout history, human instinct has remained the same. When people see a space, they want to fill it. But we also seem to have an instinctive understanding that this is more than just an urge to fill a space: it is always a race. Whether we're talking about settling empty land or setting the standard in a new industry, humans seem to have an instinctive grasp of first-mover advantage. Reach the prize first and you have a far better chance of hanging on to it over the long term. That's why in business we have seen so many famous dogfights over technological standards. Think of Apple v Microsoft in computing, VHS v Betamax in home video, or the vicious war that is being waged over the next generation of mobile telephony today.

At the moment, there is also a dawning realisation that there is a huge empty space at the top of the communications industry. And it's not just any old space. This is a space that can deliver the helicopter view along with the money and the power that go with it. Indeed, it would seem that the communications industry is now engaged in a space race that will radically reshape its entire structure, in fact its very nature. And the most astute players have already realised that it will be played out over the very long term – perhaps as long as the next 15 years or more.

The space is communications planning. And all main agency types are involved in this race, in one way or another. When I spoke to Nick Emery, chief strategy officer of MindShare Worldwide, he underlined this:

All communications companies, no matter what they do, are trying to get into the communications planning business, however you define it. Everyone says it's the future of their business, although they come at it from different angles. For example, ad agencies come at it realising that they're not going to get enough revenue just from creativity, so they're going to need to find another source. Research companies come at it saying, we've got the data, why not interpret it?

Let's begin this book by attempting to stake out the territory.

What is communications planning?

The formal origins of communications planning can be traced back to around 1997 and the formulation of Ogilvy's 360-degree philosophy. Following on Ogilvy's heels, Unilever developed its 'fish' process, which later became the ABC process and within which communications planning as a discipline was created. In his book *Added Value*, Mark Sherrington, co-founder of Added Value and now global marketing director at SABMiller, writes:

A few years ago, Unilever decided to overhaul its whole approach to developing brand communication. It was a very comprehensive exercise led by a team of experienced senior managers, which Added Value supported in its own modest way. . . . Unilever's new approach stated that the means of communicating and connecting should be decided before the brief for the creative content was written. This may sound straightforward, but it is in fact a radical departure from what Unilever did before and what most big advertisers still do. It is also at odds with the way that most ad agencies work. (Sherrington, 2003)

Although these two companies were well ahead of the curve and were the formal pioneers in this area, other clients had also been 'doing it', informally, for even longer, but just hadn't made so much noise about it. This was particularly the case (and still is) with many business-to-business brands.

Debate and discourse about what exactly communications planning is has matured somewhat. I think we all now pretty much agree on what it broadly is. As was discussed in the Preface, communications planning is the discipline of developing a holistic plan, across marketing and trade marketing functions, that defines how a brand will communicate with consumers. It means planning the use of a client's communication across all marketing channels and disciplines, at times

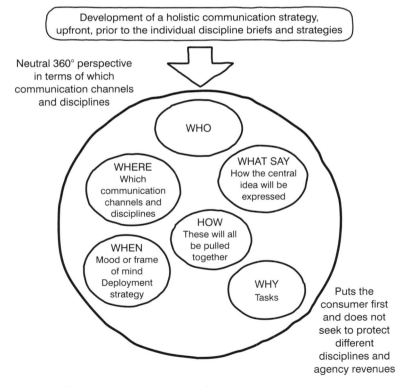

Fig. 1.1 What is communications planning?

even challenging the definition of established channels or inventing new ones. But it goes beyond simply selecting channels and allocating monies. It also means defining the brand proposition, identifying the best consumers to talk to and determining the best times to find them in the right frame of mind to hear the message. Ultimately, communications planning is about creating a 'big picture' for the consumer by weaving together every aspect of a brand's communications.

In other words, it is a fairly comprehensive vision of how to go to market, and it would normally express itself as a PowerPoint document running to 60 pages or so.

It is, self-evidently, planning that has a holistic, 360-degree perspective – in the sense that it is discipline and solution neutral. It puts the consumer first and does not seek to protect revenues specific to any one discipline or agency. In terms of the marketing process, it would normally happen immediately after marketing and trade marketing brand plans are signed off, and before any implementation is briefed out. It thus forms the link between the two – a springboard

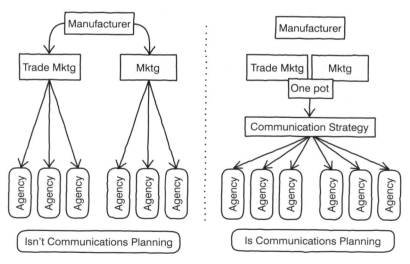

Fig. 1.2   Where does communications planning fit in?

from which to brief creative, media, PR, CRM, in-store promotions and so on.

But communications planning shouldn't be confused with a conventional 360-degree marketing solution. It differs because it treats all disciplines and channels objectively and doesn't prejudge, so it could result in a communications plan for the same brand and budget that uses four channels or twenty-four. It is also about more than 'integration'. What we call integration is what happens 'after the fact' − a search for a 'golden thread' linking proposition to creative to channel, *after* the channels have been chosen or, indeed, after the above-the-line executions have been created. Integration is what has been going on for many years by taking elements from advertising's executional idea through the line and exploiting it across the marketing mix. But this fails to exploit the potential of nonadvertising contact points and doesn't recognise that different communication channels work in very different ways.

What the hell should we call it?

Communications planning goes by more aliases than a villain in a Bond movie. At a global level, Unilever introduced the name 'communication channel planning'. Like many pioneers, its first-mover term has been widely adopted and communication channel planning is now almost a generic term in many countries − in Australia, South Africa, Asia and North America.

But Europe refuses to conform. In the UK in particular, the terms 'media neutral planning', 'total communications planning' and '360° planning' are all commonly used.

And then there are individual clients and agencies, who in the 'name fog' have given the discipline their own terms. For example, The Coca-Cola Company calls it integrated marketing communications.

On the agency side, TBWA, Fallon and Vizeum call it 'connections planning'. Zenith, Carat, Optimedia, OMD and Mediaedge:cia call it 'communications planning'. JWT calls it 'total branding'. BBH calls it 'brand engagement'. Millward Brown calls it 'channel neutral planning'.

Disagreement and debate on the name of a discipline generally happen very early on in its life (at birth). And moving the game on means getting past what it's called. So at a global level, we now need to get past this 'name' nonsense. We need to agree on one name . . .

If all the practitioners around the world were to vote on it democratically tomorrow, I think it would probably be called either 'communication channel planning' or 'communications planning'. There are advantages and disadvantages to both.

'Communication channel planning' is accurate, because the practice looks at how we combine communication proposition with channel. However, this name inevitably gets shortened to 'channel planning'. Although this has a nice ring to it, the real issue with this shortened name is that it can imply just thinking about which channels to use – which would be glorified media planning. Whereas in reality, what we're talking about is a much bigger thing involving more holistic thinking.

The upside of 'communications planning' as a name is its simplicity; the downside is that it is vaguer, and could refer to what ad agency strategic planners think they've been doing for donkey's years. But after all is said and done, I prefer 'communications planning' not because it's used by the company I work for, but simply because it's cleaner. It's easier to say and easier to talk about, without resorting to acronyms. It will better stand the test of time.

The three schools of practice

Communications planning is now undoubtedly a discipline in its own right, but there are still some important distinctions in how it's approached and done.

The first school of practice we could term 'purely technical'. This is really just about defining budget allocation splits between brands and geographies, as well as channels and disciplines. Several management consultancies like Accenture and Cap Gemini operate in this area. They use data and econometrics to build a model of past channel/ discipline response curves and performance and then use these to show how a client can optimise sales by using channels and disciplines more effectively and efficiently.

The clients who favour this approach tend to be organisations like telecommunications companies, banks and energy companies. Many of these are direct-response oriented in their communication and so need to maximise response to call centres. They have a fine-needle approach to moving money around, in almost real time. In fact, in extreme cases, their stock prices are actually affected by call-centre volumes and so they have to monitor the effectiveness of individual communication disciplines, channels and even vehicles.

A second school of practice we could term 'channel, consumer and brand'. This is all about understanding how communication channels, consumers and brands interrelate. It means identifying the most efficient means of reaching a consumer – which channels have the

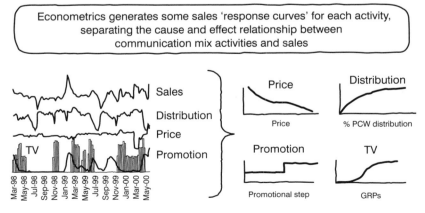

Fig. 1.3 The 'purely technical' approach.

biggest reach, or are the most accurate – and which channels are most effective in delivering a message, based on the communication tasks or the category dynamics.

To do this requires more than sales data. It relies on research – and even more importantly on insight. This research and insight need to delve into key consumer audiences and their passions. It needs to understand these audiences' relationships and interactions with different channels in the context of their lifestyle and motivations, taking account not only of how consumers use channels, but also how they think and feel about them. It also seeks to investigate the category, and how different channels influence attitudes and behaviours in that category, as well as how consumers see the brands within it.

In this area, there are now a raft of channel and discipline 'tools' in the market, proprietary media agency ones as well as industry-wide tools such as Integration's MCA©, TGI's Compose and Millward

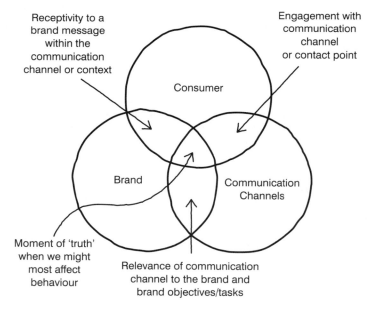

Fig. 1.4 The 'channel, consumer and brand' approach.

Brown's ChannelConnect, which all mix qualitative and quantitative research.

The third school of practice could be termed 'ideas first'. This is based on the belief that in today's complex marketplace, a brand needs a strong central idea. This idea will help engage consumers and differentiate the brand, as well as driving simplicity and focus in planning and activation (by answering many objectives at the same time) and ensuring 'brand-centric' planning. In a funny way, it is also about ROI, as ideas can sometimes (but not always) create big jumps in ROI.

This ideas-first approach requires more than bringing an idea to life. It involves a fair amount of rigour as well, because in essence it's about colliding a central idea with the things we just talked about in 'channel, consumer and brand'. It's similar to the second school of practice, in that it entails understanding and insight, but it accepts the idea of 'art' as a force in the strategy mix. It recognises that ideas are powerful and that they need to have a disproportionate emphasis over more academic factors, like channel performance versus task or accuracy versus target consumer. It also recognises that 'ideas' are the glue of planning and that without them it's very hard to build a unified, simple and bold plan. And it gets us beyond debates and arguments about which should come first, channel or content. In this case ideas precede and influence both channel and content equally. To put it simply, the central idea works 'top down', whereas the understanding of how communication channels, consumers and brands interrelate works 'bottom up'.

Not surprisingly, the ideas-first approach to communications planning predominates in agencies – ad agencies, communication independents, media agencies and direct-based agencies. But the balance between top down and bottom up varies slightly between them: the ad agencies are probably 80:20 in favour of ideas as the driver, the latter two probably about 60:40 in favour.

These three approaches can be plotted on a map, as three points in a triangle. This map, which I call the Strategy Map, is a very useful

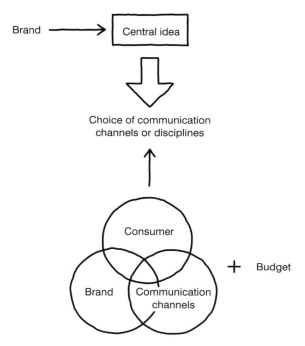

Fig. 1.5 The ideas-first approach.

way of understanding the macro trends and indeed the interrelation-ships of agency players, as you can see in Figures 1.6 and 1.7.

Communications planning might be a very new idea in some markets, but as we've seen, very different categories are embracing it in very different ways. There is no doubt that it is now emerging as a global phenomenon and it is my view that it will become the key com-munications discipline in all markets, even if this is not the case in your market today. All the principles of this book, if not the exact detail, will apply to all categories and all types of manufacturer.

Who are the players?

Ivan Pollard, a managing partner from The Ingram Partnership, describes communications planning by using an analogy with the movie business:

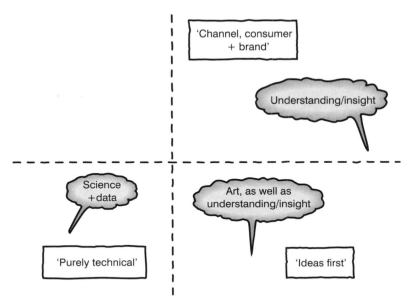

Fig. 1.6 The Strategy Map.

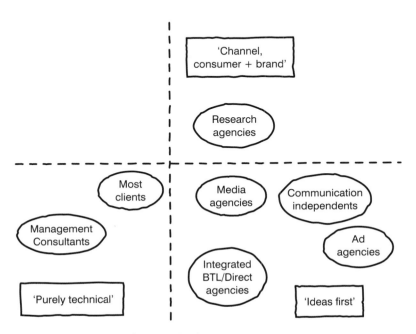

Fig. 1.7 Overlaying the organisations.

I think there is a developing role for someone in our world who is like a producer in a film company. Someone who has the vision, has the insight, and has the wherewithal to drive that through all the different ways of executing a piece of communication. And I think that responsibility lies, very simply, with whoever is willing to take it. In some ad agencies it's still strategic planners or creative people, in media agencies there's a growing trend for media people to be at the forefront of that, some clients are also trying to do it for themselves.

The question of who will take responsibility for communications planning is one that is central to this book. Ivan is right to point out that clients themselves may well attempt to fulfil the communications planning role. But while some clients may be tempted to do communications planning themselves, most at this stage are looking outside for communications expertise – as they have always done in the past. But who will rise to the challenge of providing it for them? In the current industry landscape, there are four main kinds of agency, each of whom would consider itself best suited for the job.

The media agencies think they are the most obvious candidates. They have the knowledge of how to connect brands to consumers through communication channels – something the ad agencies have lost to a large degree. For media agencies, communications planning is an extension of above-the-line planning to incorporate first below-the-line, then in-store, then digital and so on; it's a natural evolution. They also have a degree of rigour and econometric back-up, which enables them to recommend to clients how they should spend their money.

But the ad agencies feel they should be doing it. They believe that communications planning comes out of real insights and Big Ideas. In this regard, they still consider themselves supreme – their culture supports this notion – although both the below-the-line and media agencies are getting better in this area and might question that.

The integrated below-the-line agencies also see themselves doing communications planning as they think it needs to be all about changing consumer behaviour – and this, of course, is their heritage.

Finally, there are the communication independents. They see their key advantage as being independent of execution, which makes them more neutral than other agencies. What they might not play up enough, however, is their unique cultural perspective, which puts strategy over execution and embraces ideas and insight.

The truth is that none of these agency types really owns communications planning yet – and perhaps they never will. Perhaps it is simply too big a territory for any of them to claim convincingly. Certainly, this was the point of view of a number of people I spoke to.

Charles Courtier, worldwide executive chairman of Mediaedge:cia, based in New York, had this to say:

I don't think anybody in the marketing business owns 360 communications planning. I don't think media agencies own it yet. I don't think anybody else owns it either. It'll be different client by client, need by need, and skill set by skill set. The 360 degree strategic role could be played by any number of people.

And talking to Paul Alexander, vice-president, global advertising for the Campbell Soup Company, he also felt that no one agency type would ever 'have it':

I don't think any one type of agency can own communication channel planning in future because different categories and business models will look at it in very different ways. For one agency to be able to win is not very realistic. The best source of ideas and strategy may come out of where most money is spent. So if we were to choose to put 50% of our budget into the direct marketing, maybe a DM agency would be the best source of channel planning.

Will Collin, co-founder of communication independent Naked Communications, agreed that nobody owned it yet, but thought that the ad agencies probably shouldn't get it:

Ad agencies are painted into a corner by being experts in just one part of communications planning. As advertising becomes less important in consumers' lives, so advertising as a lever of influence in marketing is nothing like as critical as it used to be. This means that ad agencies are expert advisers and creators of something that is of dwindling importance. And because ads are no longer so important, it's almost not right that the lead strategy should sit within the ad agency. In effect, it's not right that the ad strategy should be the communication strategy.

We'll examine the respective claims of all these kinds of organisations in more detail later in the book. But before we do so, let's look more closely at some of the factors that are shaping the current business, media and communications environment.

◆

Key points made in this chapter

- There is now broad consensus on what communications planning is.
- Although there are myriad different names for it, I prefer to call it communications planning.
- There are three different approaches to doing it, which can be mapped on my Strategy Map:
  - Purely technical:
    - This is about defining budget allocation splits between brands and geographies, as well as channels and disciplines; using modelling that takes historical data and models it for the future.
    - Currently practised by management consultants and some clients (financial service, energy, telcos).
  - Channel, consumer and brand:
    - This is about understanding how communication channels, consumers and brands interrelate. It is about identifying the optimal time and place when the consumer is most open to the brand message and you can best affect consumer behaviour (the 'moment of truth').
    - In essence, it's about bottom-up 'channel, consumer and brand' considerations.
    - Currently practised by research agencies.

○ Ideas first:

- ■ This is about understanding that in today's complex marketplace, a brand needs a strong central idea. And this approach is about interrogating ways in which you can bring the idea to life; matched against considerations of how communication channels, consumers and brands interrelate.
- ■ In essence, it's about combining top-down 'ideas' with bottom-up 'channel, consumer and brand' considerations.
- ■ Currently practised by media agencies, integrated below-the-line agencies, ad agencies and communication independents; with different emphases on top-down versus bottom-up.

2
Of Straw and Sponges

The key reasons for adopting communications planning

Every summer in the English seaside town of Bognor Regis, there is a celebration of the absurdity of humans' attempts to fly. The annual Bognor Birdman competition features the astonishing sight of hundreds of people dressed as doughnuts, clergymen, sugar plum fairies and skateboarding cows hurling themselves off the end of the town's pier and flapping frantically before they splash into the sea below. If nothing else, it demonstrates that flying is counter-intuitive. 'If God had meant us to fly, he would have given us wings,' as they say.

But, approached from a scientific point of view, flying makes perfect sense. And so it's no surprise that the first people to get airborne were two intrepid French scientists called Pilatre de Rozier and the Marquis d'Arlandes. One afternoon in November 1783, a cynical crowd of several hundred gathered in a field just outside Paris and watched in amazement as their hot air balloon rose serenely into the sky. When it reached a height of approximately 90 metres, the two gentlemen doffed their hats to acknowledge the incredulous cheers below and then drifted off for a 25-minute flight across the city.

Rozier was a member of the distinguished French Academy of Sciences, and it was obvious to him that the balloon would rise as he had observed the phenomenon of convection many times before in the laboratory. So he and his colleague were quite confident in the success of their experiment, despite the potential for looking extremely foolish, to say nothing of the risk to their lives! Indeed, they took to the air armed with no more than a few bales of straw to feed their balloon's burner and some wet sponges to douse the flames should things get out of control.

Likewise, to those who can afford to take the lofty view of business, communications planning seems the theoretically obvious way to get a brand's communications off the ground. To many CEOs and senior clients who are slightly removed from the coalface, it seems a no-brainer. After all, it is perfectly logical to move from business strategy to marketing strategy to communication strategy to advertising strategy. Rod Wright, worldwide CEO of integrated BTL (below-the-line) agency TEQUILA\, explained it like this:

One of the big gaps in agency thinking has been how to flow down the line from business strategy to marketing strategy to communication strategy to advertising strategy. Ad agencies naturally skip straight from the marketing strategy to the advertising strategy – and they forget the communication strategy in between, which is the most important piece.

If only that logic were obvious to everyone. Unfortunately, the cynical crowd remains unconvinced. Several years after communications planning first emerged, there continues to be remarkably little genuine demand from clients for it. So what is it about this balloon that prevents it from rising? Is it still tethered to the ground? Is someone squeezing too much water from the sponge? Or are people just too timid to throw enough straw on the burner?

There are plenty of good, worthy reasons why communications planning should evolve quickly and be widely adopted. But perhaps the problem is that these reasons are all a little too worthy; and business doesn't respond well to 'worthy'. Rather, it responds to things like ROI and share price; it responds to crises and events that capture the imagination of a company. So maybe we need a crisis to really set the burner ablaze. Maybe someone should pour a little kerosene on it.

Because in marketing and communication, we are not really in a situation of crisis. People can still get away with doing things in the same old way, even if it is far from effective in driving brand growth. Marketing directors are unlikely to be criticised for not adopting communications planning, although they'll certainly get it in the teeth if their TV campaign is awful. It becomes a bigger company problem, with no ownership and no automatic responsibility. So nothing much happens.

In this chapter I want to try to sketch out for you the good, worthy reasons why clients should adopt communications planning – the straw that should be feeding the burner and getting this balloon to fly. Then in the next chapter, I'll look at a few of the wet sponges and tethers that are holding it back.

There are three key reasons for adopting communications planning as an approach; that is, developing a comprehensive up-front strategy before briefing implementation of any sort. These are:

1. Being true to your annual objectives.
2. Interlinking communication channels and encouraging better use of them.
3. First-mover competitive advantage.

Being true to your annual objectives

Communications planning is about being neutral and being directed by objectives. It's about being open to an outcome and not prejudging

Marketing has a habit of paying lip service to things. For years marketers have got away with paying lip service to ROI and there has been a tendency to do exactly the same with communication objectives. Every year brand communication objectives change, which surely means that the communications mix and the way it is used should change too. But all too often clients are tempted simply to default to what they did last year. If they are to be true to their objectives they should develop a communication strategy before briefing agencies, because how else can they logically do it? How else can they decide the splits between above-the-line (ATL) and PR, or direct marketing and sponsorship, for example?

So following communication objectives through to their logical conclusion is what communications planning is all about. There is no other way to be true to your marketing and communication objectives each year. It's an argument that is sitting there staring us in the face.

This point was underlined by Kees Kruythoff, chairman of Unilever Bestfood Robertson in South Africa, when I spoke to him:

Ten years ago, a) there were less communication channels, and b) we accepted 50% was wasted and we closed our eyes and just threw some money on it. But increased shareholder value pressure on businesses is driving continuous improvement in communication effectiveness. And communications planning as a discipline comes in here because it takes communication objectives and has an honest and detailed assessment of the most appropriate way to use communication to fulfil these. It is the logical way to be true to your marketing and communications objectives each year.

Interlinking communication channels and encouraging better use of them

Brands increasingly need to rely less on ATL and be more prepared to use multiple channels and disciplines to communicate

The demise of above-the-line communication has been widely discussed in the media for many years and it will continue to decline for many more. A basic reason for the diminishing importance of ATL – and TV in particular – is the recognition nowadays in marketing that consumers have different cognitive learning styles. This means that brands need to communicate with them in different ways – which means using multiple communication channels and disciplines.

This has always been the case, but until fairly recently the choice of channels and disciplines was far more restricted than it is now. In the last couple of decades, with new digital technologies emerging and the cost of producing content falling, channels of communication have proliferated at a staggering rate. Traditional communication channels have multiplied − in most countries now there are hundreds of TV channels, thousands of radio stations and magazines, newspapers with so many sections you could never possibly read them all and new forms of outdoor communication appearing all the time. This shows no sign of abating; on TV, for example, digital technology is driving the development of new terrestrial channels all the time.

New communication channels have also emerged: the internet, emails, computer games, mobile phones, web-linked kiosks, in-store TV plasma screens, together with new ways of using these channels. For example, we now have viral marketing using emails, and CRM (customer relationship management) and couponing on mobile phones. So, to quote Julian Saunders of The Joined-Up Company, 'Nowadays everything communicates, or tries to' (Saunders, 2004).

I'm sure we can all think of bizarre, ambient communication ideas that we've seen lately. The effect of all this clutter has been to ramp up the message volume being driven at consumers. Some of these new media are converging with older, traditional media forms: the living room is transforming with the advent of new mobile transponders of music, entertainment, games and movies. The computer is merging with the television, stereo and telephone. New convergence ideas like MP3 players in watches are also on the horizon. All in all, we've got incredible change happening in the area of communication channels.

And then as consumers, when we go in-store and become shoppers, we're also faced with proliferation, this time in brand choice.

In 2002 Sainsbury's in the UK introduced 9,000 new product lines and five new own-label sub-brands. Even within one category the choice can be overwhelming, typically . . . 83 different shampoos, 68 shower gels, 42 deodorants, 77 washing powders and 87 breakfast cereals. (Marketing, 2004a)

As consumers, we've also changed a lot. We're more educated and, as the famous brand marketing consultant John Grant has said, our IQs have actually (collectively) gone up. We're busier than ever and we're out of the home far more than we used to be.

As a result of all the proliferation and clutter and with consumer social changes, our relationship with mass media has changed completely, in particular with regard to TV. We consume less communication in general and what we do consume is increasingly out of home. Fewer of us spend less time sitting as an audience in front of the TV and the audience that is there is fragmented by channel proliferation and, more often than not, is actively trying to avoid ads.

A recent study by Yankelovich Partners in America found that 65% of people now feel 'constantly bombarded by ad messages' and that 59% feel that ads have very little relevance to them. Almost 70% said they'd be interested in products or services that helped them avoid ads. Many surveys in Europe concur and in markets like Spain and Italy, where there is particularly high clutter and particularly long ad breaks, TV ad avoidance is as high as 70% (Economist, 2004).

While technology has helped drive the channel and message prolif- eration, it has also come to the rescue of consumers in helping them avoid communication – and ads in particular. The humble TV remote control might have started the ball rolling here, but now we are seeing the effects of a far more sinister piece of technology in terms of its potential for ad avoidance – the PVR, or personal video recorder. This technology enables viewers to record up to 20 hours of pro- grammes on a hard disk, freeing them from the constraints of channel schedules and offering a clear advantage for a new active generation. Most controversially, the technology allows viewers to fast forward and so avoid traditional TV advertising altogether. In the US, PVRs have already started to make serious inroads. In the UK, although initial uptake has been slow (in early 2005 in the UK only 250 000 homes in the UK owned a PVR, representing less than 1% of all households), many industry sources expect this to change in the second half of the decade with penetration forecasts for 2010 ranging from 20–30% of households – or what is the cusp of a majority market.

Many agencies have done research looking at the possible implications of ad avoidance. For example, in Mediaedge:cia's MediaLab's study, when respondents were asked about their expectations of PVR behaviour during ad breaks while watching prerecorded programmes, 69% of respondents stated that they would zip through the ads. Other similar studies have put the figure at around 75%.

So PVRs look likely to force advertisers to rethink their approach. As a result, according to Lee Daley, chairman of Saatchi & Saatchi in the UK, 'we're looking at the death of the TV-comes-first model'. And what is spent in future on TV will have a different emphasis. It will no longer be just about spots (and hasn't been for some time); sponsorship of whole programmes will become more common. Alternative ways of advertising will develop – from product placement, advertiser-funded content and channels to more interactive advertising (to encourage viewers to 'opt in').

Fragmentation of TV audiences coupled with this increasing ability to avoid ads is starting to seriously diminish the importance of TV to marketers and agencies. And while TV still works, it doesn't work that well and it's ever more expensive to buy. In many markets – particularly in the US and western Europe – we're at a tipping point in terms of its importance.

If reaching consumers is now very complex, engaging with them is another matter altogether. Consumers are tuning out of communication. Even when they are technically 'seeing' a piece of communication, they are not really registering it. They are becoming ever more adept at not processing it. Attention levels to communication have declined drastically.

As I mentioned, consumers have become smarter in every way over the last 20 years. They are incredibly well informed. They are able to multitask, buying anything from any location, and choosing what communication channel they consume when they want, how they want. And they are much smarter and more sophisticated in their reactions to communication. They do not take brands at face value any more. They judge them not by what they say, but by how they behave.

Because of this, so-called below-the-line is becoming more effective, and more money is swinging into it. We've seen that companies can build extremely strong brands without above-the-line. Think of Starbucks, which is based on experiential marketing, or The Body Shop, which has created a phenomenally strong brand around supporting causes, or indeed Lipton Ice Tea, which has grown rapidly by using what it calls Visibility (which is point of consumption outdoor).

Or think about Red Bull, a brand and product I like a lot. I have never spoken to Red Bull, but I have really studied its communication around the world and I have surmised that when it launches its brand in a market, it does so in the following way. First, through mass sampling and promotions at clubs. Secondly, through the use of ambassadors: student brand managers and consumer education teams. Thirdly, through involvement in events that capture the hearts and minds of the target – usually, but not exclusively, through extreme and alternative sports. And last, through above-the-line, but only when a market is deemed mature.

So with Red Bull, above-the-line has been used to reinforce, not introduce; to amuse more than educate or entice. And the brand strength is the result of the balls it takes to create the sort of PR shown in the picture overpage: Felix Baumgartner on his way to becoming the first man to fly unassisted across the English Channel in 2003.

Consumers are flexing their muscles . . . and brands are increasingly meeting not creating needs. Dr Atkins popularised the 'low-carbohydrate' approach to weight loss that has been so popular. It has had a heavy impact on the sales of high-carbohydrate food such as potatoes, bread and pasta, leading many brands to invest in NPD

Fig. 2.1 Red Bull gives you wings! Reuters/Ulrich Grill

(new product development). In fact, Coca-Cola launched C2 in 2004 as a low-carbohydrate alternative.

Brand choice has also become increasingly political. The power of lobby groups such as the anti-Esso campaign (www.stopesso.com) has shown the sophisticated and powerful nature of twenty-first-century consumer campaigns where the internet is used to get the message across. What this all boils down to is that brands have entered a new era of engaging and influencing consumers. That might sound like a load of clichés, but it's true.

In the last ten years, the concept of 'influence' has become increasingly important. Broadly, this says that people rarely make decisions alone − rather, they are influenced by a range of sources; and that the basic role for communication is influence, not awareness.

Mark Earls from Ogilvy wrote a good paper on this subject called 'Advertising to the herd' (Earls, 2003). In it, he talks about humans as fundamentally herd creatures, not individualists. In other words, we often behave collectively in what we think, how we react to things and what we choose to buy. And if we accept this herd perspective, then we need to think about communication differently to how we've done in the past. We need to design it so that it will influence and be talked about by the herd.

Kate Watts from Chime Communications is also an advocate of influence, but from a slightly different perspective (Watts, 2003). Her thinking is quite simple. In the last couple of decades we have moved from an 'age of deference', where we still respected authority, to an 'age of reference', where we prefer to trust those with similar experiences to ourselves, those close to us, or media sources that have earned our respect. The implication of this is that we need to move away from traditional awareness-based models of communication.

What needs to replace these, in Kate's opinion, is an influence model. This is about coming at the consumer more subtly – about viral models, and targeting those who have a disproportionate influence. So there needs to be more use of communication disciplines that are about active brand engagement and stimulating third-party reference, and thinking fundamentally differently about how to plan communications, by developing a mindset based on finding interconnections between communication elements. So the concept of influence would indicate that we need to use communications channels and disciplines differently, and to think about them more holistically.

MT Carney, senior partner and worldwide planning director of Ogilvy New York, confirms that communication in today's environment needs to be more subtle and intelligent:

Nowadays with communication, you have to know how to start the conversation with consumers and bring it to a successful conclusion. It isn't us just asking a girl out for a drink. It's about getting her into bed as well. You need to know how to plan that conversation. Because the days when two tequilas and a hammer over the head did it are long gone. You need to be a little bit more intelligent about how you structure communication, through-the-line.

Communications planning encourages wider use of channels and disciplines, which is needed in today's marketplace; although this could also be achieved just with a savvy brand manager

All of these emergent trends help to clear the way for communications planning, but in themselves they are not a sufficient reason for it to move centre stage. There's a real tendency in all the talk about technology and social change to hype communications planning. In our rush as agencies to sell it to manufacturing clients, we tend to believe that the declining importance of above-the-line leads logically towards it. This is not the case. Yes, we have seen a real swing in the proportion of budget going into below-the-line. But this in itself does not make communications planning inevitable. For if the old approach was (and is) for marketers just to assume certain budget splits between channels and disciplines and then get on and brief executional agencies, then a swing to below-the-line or a different combination of channels and disciplines is something that can be done without recourse to communications planning. The budget splits can be changed in a vacuum, without a strategy to influence them. As Guy Murphy, deputy chairman of ad agency Bartle Bogle Hegarty, told me:

The decline of TV and ATL is not a problem that communications planning addresses. Isn't that rather just a buying problem? I think there's an awful lot of assumptioning going on.

So we need to be careful with our argument. Simply using more channels – or different ones – is not the same thing as communications planning.

Communications planning does, however, enable us to find interconnections between channels and disciplines and ensure that they all work in a genuinely orchestrated way

Communications planning is certainly not an arid technical science, although it may make use of sophisticated modelling and rigorous analysis. It is something that enables more focused, holistic, joined-up execution in the marketplace, and that enhances creativity, which in turn delivers more 'punch' for the money. Let's look at how finding interconnections between channels and disciplines makes it a catalyst for change in these three critical areas:

- It facilitates the interlinking of marketing and trade marketing communication.
- It allows the brand to act as a flexible organism.
- It encourages and inspires more original communication.

It facilitates the interlinking of marketing and trade marketing communication

In the context of communications planning, in-store communication has received very little attention. This is mainly because most of the noise about communications planning has come from agencies that focus on communication 'out-of-store', servicing the marketing side of client companies, as opposed to the trade marketing side.

So when we talk about communications planning, the traditional mindset is that it is about holistic planning that unites above-the-line and below-the-line communication options – things like TV, events, PR, sponsorship and CRM, all of which are fundamentally 'out-of-the-store', marketing budget options.

But the truth is, more budget is now spent in-store than out-of-store on communication, predominantly coming out of the trade market-ing budget. This means that the store environment is becoming an increasingly vital place in which to communicate, in both a brand-building sense as well as being a way to drive sales. It is a brand-owner business imperative now to 'win' in-store, because the alternative is to do lots of great work out-of-store and help drive cus-tomers in-store looking for your brand, only for the retailer to switch them to its own-label brand, at shelf.

The implication of this is that manufacturers or brand owners must fundamentally integrate out-of-store and in-store communication, to maintain the communication *momentum*, from the home, through in-life experiences, in-store and right up to the shelf. Let's look at all this in more detail and explore the dynamics.

Life is getting more complicated for the retailers. Consolidation has given the 'top 10' global retailers vast power, but it has also created ruthless competition between them. They are fighting it out on a daily basis over price. In the grocery retail area, the UK is now the most competitive and sophisticated market in the world. In the only market where Wal-Mart (Asda) and Tesco are present, Brits have a ringside seat watching them slug it out over 'everyday low pricing'. To walk down Tesco's aisles at the moment is to observe a 'bogof' (buy one get one free) on practically every gondola end.

They are also fighting it out for share of shopper trips and trying to maximise trip value to the shopper. This means managing a multi-format portfolio effectively and tailoring products/service to store catchments/shoppers, and trips for which format used. All the while, they are trying to build brand differentiation and loyalty.

Tesco in Europe has done a spectacular job in this area. It is seen as neutral and helpful by the consumer. It covers multiple, diverse categories, from telecoms, finance and legal to traditional grocery, web provision and nonfood (pharmacy will be added shortly). Consumers trust the brand and the 'quality at the best price' proposition – for example legal services, which launched in June 2004, is positioned as advice to help consumers cut through jargon and DIY solutions to basic legal issues such as making a will. In theory it could lead to a lawyer sitting in-store offering services:

The ability to buy a quickie divorce alongside the weekly shopping came a step closer to reality last week, when Tesco launched a range of legal self help products for customers to buy on-line. The Tesco.com 'legal store' offers products including a DIY separation and divorce kit for £7.49, a last will and testament kit for £9.99, and downloadable property packs, with tenancy agreements starting at £3.37, as well as an on-line legal jargon buster and a find-a-lawyer service. According to Tesco.com chief executive Laura Wade-Gery, the company's expansion into legal services follows in the Tesco tradition of moving into complex areas, such as telecoms and financial services, and offering customers products that are both easy to understand and represent value for money. (Marketing, 2004b)

But in responding to their challenges, retailers are also squeezing the blood out of the manufacturers or brand owners – so much so that the biggest challenge faced by brands is not from competitors, but from the retailers they sell through.

Reality 1: Everyday low pricing

Retailers' power is absolutely vast. Let's take Wal-Mart as an example. Its turnover was $256bn in 2004, which made it 250% larger than any FMCG manufacturer. It has grown at around 20% (CAGR; compound annual growth rate) over the last 20 years and is now the 15th largest economy in the world. It employs 1.5 million people. Its database is larger than the Pentagon's. Its own-label clothing brand, George, is now the no. 1 clothing brand in the world. Its share of the US toy market went from 10% in 1993 to 25% in 2005, challenging the existence of Toys 'R' Us.

So, faced with huge price competition between themselves and all of this power, it's not surprising that retailers are squeezing manufacturers on price. In other words, a manufacturer cannot put up the price of a product, in line with inflation or its internal costs, because the retailers control price. This obviously has serious implications for manufacturer profit. It wasn't surprising, then, when in September 2004, both Unilever and Colgate Palmolive were forced to deliver profit warnings. The *Financial Times* reported:

As well as competition from rival manufacturers, consumer goods multinationals have also had to cope with pricing pressure from powerful retail customers such as Wal-Mart.

Reality 2: Trade funding pressure

As retailers grow in strength, they are also forcing ever bigger sums out of manufacturers in the form of trade funding – the term used

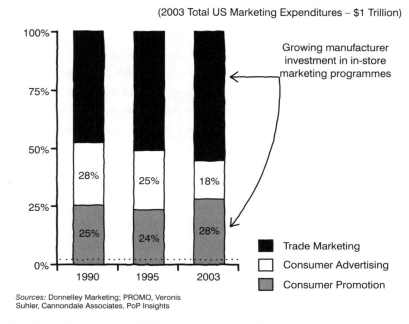

Fig. 2.2 Percentage of US marketing expenditures.

to describe a multitude of things like listing and delisting fees, price discounts, signage, co-op ads and so on. This is dramatically changing FMCG marketing budget splits.

So yes, there is a well-documented story about the movement of communication budget from above-the-line to below-the-line over the last 20-odd years – from things like TV and newspapers into things like CRM, sponsorship, events and so on. But the total 'out-of-store' monies have remained static in the face of inflation and the growing cost of media. And the real story of the last 20 years centres around the growth in 'in-store' monies. The amount extracted from FMCG manufacturers by retailers has gone through the roof.

Reality 3: Private label

Over the last decade, retailers have also built powerful private-label/own-label brands. Many are now rated more highly in quality terms than national brands at same price: two examples are Tesco's Finest and Carrefour Bio.

These private labels are a source of huge revenue and brand differentiation to the retailer. And as a result, retailers actively promote them. But from a manufacturer or brand owner point of view, this means that the retailer is constantly trying to switch your potential customer to its private-label brand at shelf. It also means that the retailer's private-label agenda in-store may limit the communication opportunities open to you, although this does vary by retailer. For example, Carrefour tends to limit manufacturers in terms of how and where they can communicate; whereas, say, Wal-Mart doesn't.

Reality 4: Knowledge is power

While in the past the manufacturers were the guys who knew everything about the consumer, nowadays it is the retailers who do. In the UK, Tesco has grown its share over the last two decades, to a point where it has nearly 30% of the UK grocery market, largely based on its consumer knowledge attained via its Clubcard loyalty scheme.

So, faced with this onslaught, how are manufacturers responding? Partly by wishing they were retailers too! P&G has said that, if it could have the last 20 years all over again, it would have set up as a retailer. But more pragmatically, they are doing three main things.

First, they are rethinking product, by focusing their efforts on fewer bigger brands, all of which are resilient in their own right and 'needed' by retailers. So we see Cadbury, Unilever and P&G all unifying their product portfolios around fewer brands. And when it comes to launching new brands, they only do so if that brand is designed to answer a specific consumer need or trend.

The second thing they are doing is rethinking their relationships with the retailers. They are trying to build collaborative relationships, which is already resulting in new initiatives. For example, Unilever in Holland has teamed up with Plus, a grocery retailer, to create a concept called Cook-It. This manifests itself in-store through a free-standing unit with recipe cards, which promotes Unilever foods.

And thirdly, they are rethinking in-store communication. They are using in-store communication in all its forms, in a more sophisticated way – trade marketing in particular is understanding better how to use and prioritise things like in-store activation, staff, the pack itself, free-standing units, displays, shelf units, signage and shelf talkers, to meet its communication tasks. All of this comes out of manufacturers' trade marketing budgets.

They are also spending more and more on what can be called 'retail media'. This includes elements such as plasma TV screens, baskets, trolleys, floor decals, even ads on own-label products like milk. These sorts of elements are relatively new and because a lot of them to date have been created and sold by third-party media owners, they are often funded by the marketing budgets as opposed to trade marketing.

Retail media is still fairly small compared to the other forms of in-store communication, but it is growing fast. The main reason for this is, I think, because retailers want it to. In other words, they want the money! In the UK, for example, they want to eat into the £4 billion TV budget. And besides the money they can extract in selling space, they also see better-quality in-store communication as something that can help them sell products and build categories and category value. But there are a couple of notable external factors as well. . . .

With the coverage and size of the big retailers, retail media are starting to offer the ability to reach relatively big audiences in one fell swoop. In-store TV, for example, offers an alternative to the fragmentation and PVR avoidance that is besetting TV in the home. Retail media can also be measured directly by sales data, and formats perfected and honed, maximising the impact and effect on sales, as well as enhancing the store environment and shopper experience. For these reasons, in the UK, retailers across the board are developing opportunities – Tesco and Wal-Mart (Asda) in grocery, but also the likes of Spar, Boots, Dixons, Homebase and McDonald's.

All in all, manufacturers or brand owners have realised the importance of in-store communication, and of transforming their in-store communication spend from something that is ineffective and extracted by retailers as almost 'key money' and a cost of doing business, into something that builds the brand and drives sales. As I mentioned earlier, this is maintaining the communication momentum, from the home, through in-life experiences, in-store and right up to the shelf.

This necessitates marketing and trade marketing working seamlessly in the in-store communication arena. And communications planning offers the natural way to do this, by putting both the marketing and

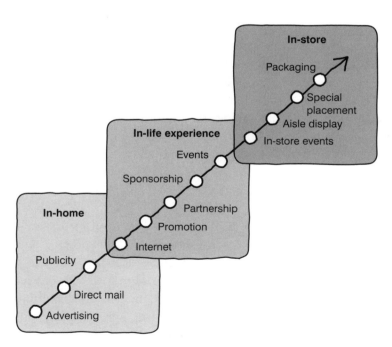

Fig. 2.3 Integrating out-of-store and in-store communication.

trade marketing budgets into one pot, and developing a strategy that will drive brand growth across out-of-store and in-store communication channels and disciplines.

Unilever deserves real credit here. In many markets, it pulls together both marketing and trade marketing to brief in the communication channel plan. In other words, it asks the channel planner to recommend a split between in-store and out-of-store communication budgets, and to recommend how to spend in-store monies. Given the need to integrate the two sides of marketing, this is a real breakthrough.

It allows the brand to act as a flexible organism

Over the last ten years, another consistent concept to come out from a number of sources is that of the brand as a flexible organism. Maybe the first to codify the 'flexible organism' thought into a new approach to marketing communication was Fusion5 in Connecticut, America. It is the brand consultancy company that developed episodic marketing – the idea that a brand goes to market in distinct, through-the-line episodes and that these are like chapters in a book or, indeed, episodes in an ongoing TV programme like *Friends*. Connecting these episodes is an overarching strategic brand idea that keeps the communication focused and ensures they build on each other and create momentum. This isn't just theory. Episodic marketing has been adopted and used beyond the realms of Fusion5. For example in the States, Miller beer uses this approach today.

Brand marketing consultant John Grant also wrote about the concept of a brand having a fluid identity in his first book, *New Marketing Manifesto*, and he called it 'authoring':

The very idea of the brand in classical old marketing was that of unchanging essences. Hence repetitive activity to reinforce these essences. Brands could be expressed in contemporary ways, but this was like painting a fence post to keep it white, so branding as a metaphor (livestock tattooing) was quite a good one. (Grant, 1999)

The alternative that John has put forward is the brand as an author – 'a constant presence behind new ideas, not a fixed image of itself'.

Now even McDonald's seems to have adopted the concept of brand as a flexible organism. Larry Light, executive vice-president and global chief marketing officer, talking about the 'I'm Lovin' It' idea, attributed it (and the sales growth that came with it) to a new way of looking at marketing communication in the company:

We think of our new marketing approach as 'Brand Journalism'. It means telling the many facets of our brand story every day in 119 countries. (AdAge, 2004)

As a client, it is very hard to embrace the notion of a fluid identity without also embracing communications planning. Because the traditional way of planning, which is predetermining discipline budget splits based on historical patterns, then just getting on and briefing the relevant executional agencies, tends to have the effect of painting the fence post white each year and means that the brand gets locked into a cycle of repetitive activity. On the other hand, communications planning tends to encourage more fluid holistic thinking. Again, this reiterates that the real need for communications planning is all about how channels and disciplines are used to best effect.

It encourages and inspires more original communication

Much communication is wallpaper and most brand owners insist on following category conventions and rules. This explains the following quote from Ravi Naidoo of Interactive Africa, taken from Neill Duffy's book *Passion Branding*:

Marketing is facing a huge challenge. It is a crisis of authenticity. The more you look at some of the campaigns leveraged by marketers, the more they look the same. We seem to live in an age of super parity – similar products being overlaid by similar marketing plans. Most marketers have access to like resources – consultants, PR companies, spin doctors, ad agencies et al. And this machinery is churning out vanilla. (Duffy, 2003)

From my experience of communications planning, seeing how I've used it in the past and seeing how my colleagues have used it, I can say this: more often than not, communications planning will genuinely liberate the brand and the communication and will give clients a fresh, inspiring and objective 'route to market'. It does so because it is a holistic, cohesive piece of thinking that is authored by one individual; because it forces the planner to think about how communication can be used to address brand issues and tasks in the widest sense; and because it focuses the creative delivery and makes it more effective.

This last point, about communications planning adding and not detracting to creativity, was something that Rob Hill, group planning director of Ogilvy South Africa, also felt to be the case when I spoke to him:

Norman Berry used to say, 'give me the freedom of a tight brief' . . . and in a way, the tightness that communications planning might introduce, might be a big bonus for creativity, rather than a restraint.

Dove, a global Unilever brand, is a particularly good example of this in action. At the beginning of 2005, it launched a worldwide project called 'Campaign for Real Beauty'. This featured women whose appearance differed from the stereotypical ideal, and asked viewers to judge them. So there was the question 'Oversized? Outstanding?' next to Tabatha Roman, 34, a plus-size woman, and 'Half empty? Half full?' next to Esther Poyer, 35, who has small breasts. These ads used above-the-line outdoor executions to drive consumers onto the web, to take part in a global debate and to vote on issues relating to beauty – body image and size, age, spots and freckles and so on. Dove then maintained the momentum using CRM, print, in-store and tabletops in cafés in an interconnected way to drive home the common message.

The campaign was brave and it worked well. Dove (using communications planning) managed to build a dialogue and relationship with consumers around the notion of Real Beauty. It used channels in innovative ways to connect meaningfully and began to play a role in

Fig. 2.4 Dove's Campaign for Real Beauty.

people's lives, above and beyond supplying them with a bar of soap or a bottle of shampoo. As a result, it became the fastest-growing beauty brand in western Europe. Could it have done this without the communications planning approach? It is doubtful. This was reiterated by MT Carney of Ogilvy New York when I spoke to her:

Dove is a really nice product . . . but it has been around for a long time, and so Dove could absolutely not have achieved the sales growth that they are experiencing at the moment, without communications planning.

The Dove brand has found a fantastic brand idea in Real Beauty, and have used communications planning to great effect to make this idea tangible and serve it up to consumers in interesting ways. Real Beauty is an incredibly solid brand idea, which is objective driven, as well as brand driven. It has created a space for Dove in a culture that had left it behind. It is making people reassess the way that they look at Dove . . . and allowing the brand to enter into a dialogue with consumers, which is not something that an FMCG product traditionally does. The idea is about driving a conversation. And you cannot drive a conversation just using broadcast media. To have millions of people entering into a debate with Dove about who's attractive and who isn't, has genuinely elevated the brand in people's eyes and has had a huge effect on sales.

So communications planning is, I believe, an antidote to the marketing and communication vanilla that surrounds us. It helps build brand salience and connects with consumers in new and interesting ways. Again, this reiterates that the real need for communications planning is all about how channels and disciplines are used to best effect.

First-mover competitive advantage

Until communications planning becomes commonplace, there's real competitive advantage to be had

Until now, communications planning hasn't been for the faint-hearted. Entrusting an entire communications budget to a single

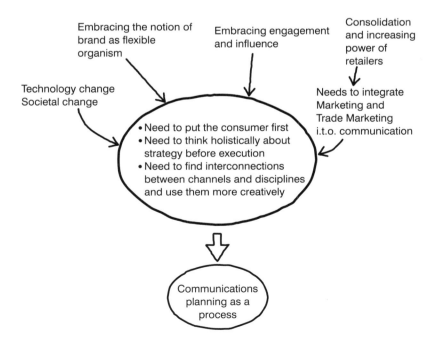

Fig. 2.5   Key factors driving communications planning forward.

agency or individual might seem like a scary prospect. And, as we'll see, there isn't an obvious place for clients to find people with the necessary skills. No one is really sure what a successful model looks like at this point. It's not as if Unilever is sitting there and saying General Motors has one. Or vice versa. At this point, everyone is learning rapidly as they go. But, as we've seen, if clients are brave enough to go for it, they have the chance of securing a genuine advantage over their competitors. Those who get their balloon up first will find they have the whole sky to themselves!

◆

Key points made in this chapter

- There are many good, sensible reasons for adopting communications planning, and in many ways it is common sense.
- The key reasons are:
  - ○ Being true to your annual objectives.
  - ○ Interlinking communication channels and encouraging better use of them.
  - ○ First-mover competitive advantage.
- But nevertheless, five years after it emerged, there is still very little genuine demand for communications planning from clients. There is no crisis.

3
Gravity

The issues that are holding communications planning back

There's been a lot written and said about why the communications planning balloon should be going up – but much of it seems to have been little more than hot air. Most clients remain unconvinced. Perhaps there's too much ballast in the basket, and throwing out the old ways of doing things seems like more trouble than it's worth. Perhaps there are too many vested interests keeping it tethered to the ground. Or perhaps people simply don't have the courage to put enough fuel on the burner.

Certainly, there hasn't been nearly enough written about the factors that are holding communications planning back. And in my view, the things that are holding it back are actually more interesting than those propelling it forward. They are certainly less written about. So here goes!

All too often in this debate, agencies scoff at their clients' inability to get on and adopt communications planning. But maybe that's because they sit in splendid isolation of many of the consequences of adopting it. Change is uncomfortable in all companies, but communications planning entails most change on the clients' side, particularly in their organisational structures and processes.

I did some consultancy work for SABMiller, the brewing giant, who was looking at ways of introducing communications planning to its organisation. And when you work alongside a client like this, you become acutely aware of how difficult it is to introduce the wholesale change that communications planning demands, within the marketing function and in terms of client–agency and agency–agency relationships.

We actually need to start seeing this whole thing from a broader perspective than our individual silos. Let's kick off this piece with more of a sense of collectivism. We – clients and agencies – are all in this together. Many of the reasons that are holding communications planning back are shared in terms of blame and ownership. And we are all, collectively, frustrated at this point in time. Clients – brand owners – are frustrated with the inability of agencies to integrate the different discipline 'pieces' and work together to deliver holistic thinking in the form of communications planning. They need the agencies to stop squabbling and fighting. And I think in the agencies themselves, there is also a frustration at how they are all working together.

So now let's look at the real issues that are holding communications planning back, with our new-found sense of collective responsibility and blame.

Inability to prove it's better in ROI terms

The first collective criticism that can be levelled at manufacturing clients and agencies is that on the whole, they cannot prove that communications planning is better – in other words, that holistic planning delivers more communication 'punch' than siloed discipline planning. At this point, based on experience and judgement, everyone genuinely believes that communications planning is better and delivers more ROI – because it ensures more focused, holistic, joined-up execution. But they've yet to prove it conclusively.

Obviously lots of agencies can show communications planning case studies inferring that the 'great achievement' was the result of this new discipline. But this is far from proof.

All of us need to step up to the table here and create single-source research that links communication consumption and influence from all channels and disciplines through to sales. Until this happens, we will never really prove that it's better.

Agencies are culturally and structurally hide-bound to execution

Another collective criticism that can be levelled at agencies is that they are culturally and structurally hide-bound to execution and implementation. This is absolutely true, they are. Culturally, this is because they are all fairly executional in their thinking. It's characteristic of human behaviour to be more interested and excited by execution than by strategy. Thinking about big issues all the time is hard. And this is particularly true in our industry.

What client is more interested in a strategy than in a creative storyboard? Not many. And this is a real problem in getting paid for strategy. What agency can come up with a strategic communication idea on its own, without rushing into executional concepts? Indeed, what agency can originate strategic communication ideas without them having first come out of executional ideas and concepts? 'Ah, so if that's the answer, let's work backwards to come up with the strategy' might be how many agencies choose to originate.

Structurally, agencies are tied to execution and implementation because that's what they generally get paid for – not for the thinking and ideas. Creative get paid for producing the creative work, media for buying the space. This is the way it has worked since agencies came into being, so most agency business models are based on it. The only real exceptions to this are the consultancies – the communication independents, and to a lesser extent the management consultancies – who are fee based only. But they have yet to get paid truly well for their thinking in this field.

So the main executional agency types are not structured or remunerated to give independent, solution-neutral advice. And, generally, they don't. Sir Martin Sorrell of WPP put it like this:

Visit a direct marketing agency with any business problem and their solution, however fine, will involve rather a lot of direct marketing. Take the same problem to an ad agency and the solution would involve a lot of 30s TV spots. And same again for PR, design, sales promotion, and so on. There's a whiff of self-interest here reminiscent of those recipes you find on the side of cereal packets, all of which seem to involve suspiciously large quantities of the manufacturer's own product. It's a case of people redefining every problem in terms of their proposed solution. Advertising people define the solution in terms of image, PR people in terms of reputation, media people in terms of ratings – and so on. To a man with a hammer, everything looks like a nail. (Sorrell, 2002)

Another way of putting this is, just as if you go into McDonald's you're going to come out with a hamburger, if you go into an ad agency, by and large you're going to come out with an ad. With the unbundling of the full-service agency, the resultant agency types have all become increasingly specialised and complex. This is both a good and a bad thing for communications planning.

Short term, it holds it up. It exacerbates the lack of mutual understanding, respect and trust that is now prevalent between agency types. And in the absence of any organisational structure that encourages channel and discipline neutrality, it helps maintain the status quo – clients' briefs to agencies assume that the solution will be advertising driven, and the budgets for different disciplines are set based on habit. Exactly the wrong conditions in which to drive communications planning forward.

But long term, it actually helps it. It is a prerequisite. To come of age, communications planning needs equality among the communication disciplines. And this can only come when the specialisms are true specialisms and are not subservient to advertising or creative agencies. Talented people need to work under their own steam.

So we mustn't beat ourselves up too much over the current state of play. And we can be sure that reintegration of the disciplines into one full-service offer, or the 'marriage' of media and creative back in the same building, is not necessarily in the best interests of

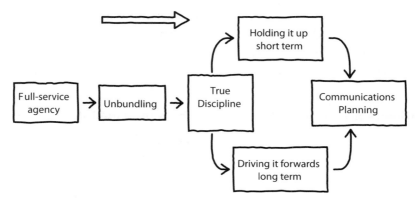

Fig. 3.1 Specialism as a prerequisite.

communications planning or clients, although it may make working together easier.

Maybe this helps explain the contradiction that Jeremy Bullmore refers to in the 40th anniversary issue of *Admap*:

Future historians of our trade will be baffled. Towards the end of the 20th century, more and more marketing companies were converted to a belief in seamless, 360°, harmonised, orchestrated, integrated communications. And at exactly the same time, the purveyors of those communications disintegrated completely.

Back in 1964 when *Admap* was born, clients who needed help with their marketing knew whom to turn to first; there was no hesitation. They would get in touch with an advertising agency. And if the agency was a full-service agency, it could provide the client with things like a market analysis, a business plan, a marketing plan, a communications plan, a media plan; as well as creative work in all media, including merchandising, packaging, point of sale and PR. Like the man who never realised that he spoke prose, clients got integrated communications without even realising it.

Forty years later, hesitation is rife. Today, as the first port of call, clients may choose between a brand consultancy, a media company, a corporate identity house, a management consultancy, a public relations counsellor – or, still, an advertising agency. (Bullmore, 2004)

Maybe this also helps explain the fact that many agencies who ten years ago were telling clients why they needed increased specialism are now going to the same clients trying to tell them that they now need to plan holistically and, of course, that they are the guys to do it!

Clients are not sure how to do it or who should do it

If a manufacturer or brand-owner client wants to adopt communications planning, the first question they ask is: What does this mean in terms of people? Who should be involved internally? Who should be involved externally? Which agency type should I give it to? Or do I give joint responsibility to a couple of them? It's far from clear.

And even when a client thinks they might have worked out the broader issues in terms of who should be involved, they then need to think about how to integrate the new process with the annual planning calendar.

There are few concrete answers to these issues, and each client who grasps the communications planning nettle has to work them out for themselves – which, in effect, puts many of them off in the first place.

Added to this is all the hyperbole about communications planning that is out there. Every agency under the sun is claiming they can do it 'in their sleep'. But given that the number of people who can really deliver communications planning, worldwide, is currently very, very limited, then clearly most agencies are bullshitting.

Politics

Hiding quietly down the list of factors that are holding communications planning back sits this little monster. For politics is absolutely one of the key factors, there is no doubt about it, as Dick Metzler, executive vice-president, marketing at DHL Express, knows only too well:

In terms of the relationship between many advertising and media planning agencies at the moment, it's a little like watching porcupines mate. In other words, who is in the lead is often not clear, it is painful for everyone and no one is really sure when the mission has been accomplished.

Looking initially at the agency world, there are genuine political problems and turf wars between agencies – everyone fighting to 'do it' and leapfrogging each other. Is this not inevitable? In my book it's unavoidable at this early stage in the game and until clients as a body either declare who they think should do communications planning, or manage it better.

The truth is that writing communication strategy fundamentally puts the author in a position of control and influence, and therefore unless you're doing it, as an implementer, it's threatening. All implementers see it as key to their future revenue models. And neither clients as a body, nor holding company bosses (like Sir Martin Sorrell), have said 'who should do it'. So of course it's going to be highly political.

But we need to recognise that clients really hate fighting between media and creative agencies in particular and that unless there is some sort of peaceful, respectful relationship on an ongoing basis, the whole communications planning project is threatened as being more trouble than it's worth.

How to deal with this? My personal view is 'have a big fight, then make friends'. We did this on Unilever when I was at Nota Bene. After winning the 'channel agency' account, we fought with the four creative agencies for a year – they made our lives difficult, because they were threatened by the role and had tried to persuade Unilever to give it to them previously. But after a year of fighting, we were tired of it. So we went to the four creative agencies and said, the area we can collaborate on is ideas. We'll take the brief, then we'll come to you and get together behind the scenes, and work out the ideas construct. We engineered two reverts to client. The first, a few weeks after the brief, was where we both presented something – where we let the creative agency present a 'communication strategy' and where we presented a 'communication channel strategy'.

Since this happened, all has been hunky-dory and the Unilever client has been happier. Mutual respect has been achieved. And because, as a process, communications planning is also a lot of work for the client, the last thing they want to deal with is agency battles. Had we gone to the creative ad agencies initially, just after we'd won the business, and collaborated, would we have arrived at the same outcome? Probably not. So it's not easy to achieve mutual respect. But you do need to. And what it comes down to is that as a media planner, or indeed communications planner, I think that fundamentally you have to get on well with the creative agency.

Politics around communications planning isn't just restricted to the different agencies. It is also a huge problem in client organisations, because one of the key factors holding back the growth of communications planning is the silos within client companies themselves.

Most client organisations are set up around certain implementational outcomes and lots of them are structured to reflect the shape of their suppliers. So all departments might have gatekeepers, who are judged individually by the size of their budgets and headcount. There may be a sponsorship department, for example, or an internal media coordinator. So what happens when the communication strategy comes back with no sponsorship on it – or no above-the-line media? Solution-neutral thinking can play havoc with their structures.

The Coca-Cola Company, in moving towards integrated marketing communication (IMC), concluded that the single most important barrier to creating more value in its communication spend was the lines inside its own organisation. The silos, lack of communication and different incentives between these groups often led to inefficiencies in the communication spend, so the simple solution was to do away with those lines, although it has proved complex to implement.

In most client organisations, marketing and trade marketing also work separately, as we've previously discussed, and fight over budget. The idea of them pooling budgets, or one side giving some to another, has to date been very alien to them.

All of this was voiced eloquently by MT Carney from Ogilvy New York, when I spoke to her:

Client silos are a huge, huge issue for communications planning. Our clients, from the '50s onwards, have structured themselves into silos – creating these multipronged beasts. This has worked efficiently, but is now proving dysfunctional in terms of creating communication that can work across the silos.

The communications industry has grown up to exactly mirror this 'siloing'. We agencies expanded around the world in just the same way, all the time mirroring our clients. So instead of producing a counterpoint to what could be perceived as client dysfunction, instead we created a mirror to it.

We all say there should be awards for the ads that don't run, well there should be awards for the communication plans that don't run as well, because I've seen so much fantastic work go through that dies on the altar of 'hands off, that's my direct mail budget'.

The whole mirroring, on client side and our side, makes communications planning extraordinarily difficult. It's very rare to find an individual that controls all that money. Also the guys who run client departments, their bonuses are governed by what they do with their money. We're talking personal money, not corporate money. The guy who runs events, his bonus is linked to what he does with his pot – to get him to give up any of his pot of money and you'll have to wrestle him to the ground. It's rare to find someone beneath the CEO who controls all the money. And what CEO is going to fight all those political battles for you? Because they're too busy fighting all the other political battles that are going to move money onto the bottom line, this year.

Client silos are particularly a big issue in the US, where the clients are much bigger, and the silos much more powerful and the marketing director probably doesn't control the whole thing. The budgets will be in different places run by different board-level members.

So I believe the way forwards is for agencies to create themselves in a counterpoint to clients. This will allow us to move back up that value chain, so we are genuine partners they go to for strategic advice, as opposed to vendors.

Conservatism

The marketing and communications industry is also inherently conservative. Not much has changed on either side of the fence, for the
last 50 years – at least, not compared to many other industries.

In the agency world in particular, you might think this surprising.
But for all its so-called creativity, it is inherently a conservative and
slightly parochial industry. It is one of its great paradoxes. We also have
a real service mentality. We jump when we're asked to. Various people
I spoke to put a different spin on this issue. George Michaelides, co-
founder of Michaelides & Bednash, put it this way:

The communication industry doesn't lend itself to change, like manufacturing business, where someone can come in from outside and transform things.
It's all to do with ideas and thinking as opposed to manufactured output. I
look at it differently. You have an industry that hasn't changed in about 50
years. Part of the reason it hasn't changed is because it's very fragmented,
like a village industry with lots of little businesses. This doesn't allow a
newcomer to come in and shake it all out. There isn't the imperative in our
business for change that there is in other businesses. When Japanese car
manufacturers went into America, it changed the industry overnight, because
they ate up market share very quickly, which caused a reaction from the
American manufacturers. The decline in the ad industry model is very
slow.

When I spoke to Will Collin of Naked, he also talked about the drag
in the industry:

There is a lot of friction and drag in the market. Things move in genera-
tions. It really needs a whole new generation of people to work their way
through to positions of seniority within clients and agency. Things in our
industry move at a very slow pace.

But are all agencies equally conservative? I don't think so. Of all the
types of agency, the media agencies are probably the most innovative,
entrepreneurial and ambitious, because they are young and freshly
coined and they've grown from small companies to very big companies, very quickly. They're on the up, on the offensive; they have an

appetite, and probably more money to invest than the other agency types.

On the client side there is a fair amount of conservatism as well. Speaking to MT Carney of Ogilvy New York, she said:

Clients know that communications planning is the way forward. Intuitively we all know that it is better. We all recognise a really good integrated communications planning campaign, and we all talk about it, far more than we do about a 30-second spot nowadays.

But nevertheless I think its like a bit like Blackberries . . . you really know you have to get one, but you really don't want to − or you'll end up being that guy on the Eurostar that never puts it down. With communications planning, clients know they are going to have to get their heads around it, and that it is the way forward, but the problem is conservatism. Even though they talk about and recognise other people's integrated communications planning campaigns, nothing is forcing them to do it today; because the model is not that broken, and the trains are still rolling.

Not a clear enough understanding of the consumer

Because communications planning involves putting 'channel' up front alongside (and sometimes before) 'content' in the decision-making process, one of the issues that is holding communications planning back is that we simply don't really understand consumers in enough depth to do this. This point was made eloquently by Paul Alexander of the Campbell Soup Company, when I spoke to him:

One of the factors that is holding up the spread or adoption of communication channel planning is that we (collectively) simply don't understand enough about our consumer to make really precise choices about when and how to reach him or her most effectively. So as a result, we tend to make some very crass assumptions about this, which leads to creative wagging the dog, because we really don't know. We come back to the lowest common denominator.

At Campbell's, I've seen a marked difference in our success and our willingness to employ channel planning, when we have a core, consistent understanding of the consumer.

It's impossible to quantify ideas

Remember those games of 'bullshit bingo' that people used to play in meetings in the 1990s? Well these days, if you had a game of 'effectiveness bingo' at the average media agency meeting, you'd have 'house' within seconds. The media industry has spent the last 25 to 30 years building towards the current focus on numbers, effectiveness models, reach and frequency, optimisation and so on. Media agencies can analyse components of campaigns with increasing effectiveness, from price elasticity to understanding how a competitor's campaign will affect a brand's sales. This helps planners to predict the outcome of campaigns with increasing accuracy.

In the ad agency creative arena, strategic planners increasingly research concepts several times prior to the start of a campaign, getting both qualitative and quantitative research on how a new creative strategy will make the consumer react. The cost of producing and airing a campaign is such that all parties try to cover themselves with research 'insurance' – 'It's not our fault the campaign didn't produce results, the research said it would.'

How does this relate to communications planning? When it comes to communications planning, we've seen that agencies as a group tend to accept and practise the 'ideas-first' approach. So to them, communications planning is about putting intangible ideas at the centre of the strategy and, to some extent, letting the numbers play second fiddle.

In a discipline that is about ideas, the inability of the industry to quantify and measure a good idea holds it back. Consumer research, one of the foundations of the creative industry, is flawed in this area. Therefore, as if finding a great idea wasn't hard enough, actually getting clients to implement it proves to be even harder. The traditional media plan, using proven techniques, is a known quantity and is sort of scientifically justifiable. Taking a flyer on an unresearched idea that informs every element of the communication mix is almost impossible.

The ideas proposed in the communications plan may well send it down a different route to the traditional numbers-led media plan. In the absence of research, it is much easier for a client or indeed an agency to recommend the traditional route.

Clients' mixed messages

Clients are currently sending us mixed signals. Do they really believe in communications planning? How many of them are that knowledgeable about it?

If they do believe in it, then in the case of media agencies, why are clients constantly pulling them back into buying? In theory, media buying has been commoditised – all the big media agency networks buy for roughly similar prices nowadays – and clients should be demanding great strategic thinking at every turn. But still, every media pitch seems inevitably to be buying and procurement driven. Even if a client asks for strategy in the pitch brief, at the end of the day it inevitably comes down to procurement-driven thinking – cost and media discounts.

Then there is the investment question. Agencies don't, collectively, have much money to invest: clients have cut back margins to a point at which it's very hard to invest in anything other than the research and technology that helps maintain core services. But if we assume that clients want us to go upstream and create a genuine capacity to deliver large-scale communications planning, is it worth investing significantly in? Will they pay for it? Or should we only really invest in implementational areas that we know will be profitable? Clients so far have also never shown any real willingness to pay for thinking or ideas. So how should agencies react? Should they rush on in, head first?

A last consideration is the fact that most agencies have very little room to breathe in terms of investment levels and options. The unrelenting pressure for double-digit growth to shareholders means that many agencies simply don't have the financial slack they need to get behind communications planning wholeheartedly. To quote John Partilla, president of Time Warner Global Marketing: 'The largest issue that's holding back communications planning is the relentless pursuit of double-digit margin for Wall Street.'

Conclusion

As the amount of communications planning being practised grows slowly but surely, many of the problems discussed in this chapter will fall away. However, I believe that the key to defying gravity lies in addressing the ROI question in particular. Unless we can prove that communications planning can deliver more in ROI terms than the traditional approach, the balloon will never rise too far off the ground.

◆

Key points made in this chapter

- The factors that are holding up the emergence of communications planning are:
  - inability to prove it's better in ROI terms;
  - agencies are culturally and structurally hide-bound to execution;
  - the specialisation in the industry might be holding up communications planning in the short term but is an absolute prerequisite in the longer term;
  - there is no obvious solution; clients are not sure how to do it or who should do it;
  - politics;
  - conservatism;
  - not a clear enough understanding of the consumer;
  - impossibility of quantifying 'ideas';
  - client mixed messages.
- In most cases, agencies and clients are equally to blame for these factors.

4
Reviewing
the Fleet

**A look at the different types of structural 'toe-dipping'
that are currently being used by different clients and
agency types**

It would be nice to picture the contenders in the space race as
gleaming new Apollo rockets or shiny new shuttles with flaming
afterburners or exotic matt-black delta wings bristling with futuristic
avionics. But the communications industry in the mid-2000s is
rather more like the fleet of a nineteenth-century navy sailing off to
war. There are vessels of all ages and of every size and shape, all
heading out to sea with more sense of hope than purpose. New-
fangled steam-powered ironsides jostle for position with traditional
wooden frigates and elegant three-masted sailing clippers. There are
huge hulks left over from long-forgotten campaigns top-heavy
with old-fashioned cannons and enormous crews. And if you look
closely enough, you can even spot a few gung-ho freelance buccaneers pulling hard on their oars as they weave in and out of the
throng.

All bets are off on who will return home with the laurels – or indeed
who will return home at all. It could be that the well-resourced high-
tech optimists will fall prey to a deadly ambush at the mouth of the
estuary before they even make it out to sea. Perhaps the ancient hulks
will prove their worth again once more, as they have so many times

in the past. Or maybe, against all odds, the gallant buccaneers will strike it lucky.

Certainly, the winds of change are blowing through the entire industry. But how did we end up like this? Forty years ago, when clients needed help with their marketing, their first port of call would be obvious: a full-service advertising agency. In those days these august institutions would provide clients with everything from market analysis and media planning to creative work in merchandising, packaging, point of sale and PR, to say nothing of the all-conquering prime-time, 30-second TV spot so beloved of ad men of yore! As everything was done under one roof, clients got integrated communications without even realising it. But these days, all that has changed.

The break-up of media and creative has turned out to be an initial step in the restructuring of the marketing communications industry, and certainly not an end in itself. When I spoke to Kees Kruythoff of Unilever, he felt that it was indeed just the start of a long line of change to come:

Looking at the face of the communications industry today, I think we're witnessing the first step in its evolution . . . there has been an increase in professionalism and sophistication as a result of the proliferation of communication channels and complexity of the marketplace. This in turn has resulted in the emergence of specialist, focused agencies . . . media agencies and communications planning agencies in particular. Specialists such as these are needed in an increasingly complex world.

So we can all feel more change coming. While I don't think we are yet at the pivotal moment, nevertheless we can all feel it coming.

So now let's review the communications fleet and assess its credentials for bringing home the spoils of victory in the communications planning race.

Some clients have committed to it and want to control it

Several very big clients are telling us all that the old model is broken and, rather than wait for the agencies to sort themselves out, they are getting on and working out how to introduce communications planning into their organisations themselves.

We've mentioned Unilever as the first big client to do this, about four or five years ago. It essentially defined centrally that there would be three key players in its 'communication channel planning' process: itself as client (ultimately responsible for managing the process), the creative agency (generally the ad agency) and the channel agency. Within this triumvirate, it was the channel agency that 'did' communications planning. And it made its two worldwide media agencies the new channel agencies.

Why did Unilever give communications planning to its media agencies? There were several reasons I know of. One key reason was that it saw channel understanding as a key driver in communications planning and therefore media had the best skill base. Secondly, it foresaw an evolution away from above-the-line dominance, as opposed to a wholesale move away from it overnight. And so it needed this evolution to be managed by those most capable of planning where the majority of money would still be going in the short term – advertising media. Another key reason was that in markets it worked with four or five ad agencies, and a couple of below-the-line agencies, whereas it only worked with one media agency. Rather than choose between the ad agencies in particular or have to split the function, it was much easier just to give it to media.

Alan Rutherford, Unilever's global media director, has been driving communications planning around the world, and due to his efforts the company has honed its process and is now getting good results from it. Since Unilever did this, General Motors and Philips have started introducing communications planning and, more recently, The Coca-Cola Company also started to do it in some markets.

But the client that has really caught the headlines lately is P&G. Last year it introduced communications planning in North America, as a trial. This is smart, because if it can work in North America it can work anywhere in the world. Again, like Unilever, P&G ended up giving it to media agencies, in this case splitting it between Starcom and Carat, although in the pitch there was also a CRM agency, which shows that P&G was thinking laterally about its options.

The interesting thing here was also that it went from doing media planning within the ad agencies (a very old model) to doing communications planning in media agencies, in one fell swoop. It leapfrogged, missing out on the 'media planning in media agencies' bit that is the norm in most of the world. So how will P&G 'do it' – what approach will it take to communications planning? My guess is that it'll have a stronger ROI flavour than Unilever's, because P&G is also innovating in another way. While it has now 'given' responsibility to the media agencies to drive and author communications planning, this doesn't mean that it will always be this way. At the moment P&G is developing its own through-the-line single-source measurement capability, using portable people meters to track exposure to communication, then linking this to scanners to measure product sales – in effect, it is future-proofing itself with its own ability to judge which communications channels best drive sales.

All of the clients above have committed to communications planning as a process, but are doing it with agency partners. However, there are other clients who are going it alone and doing it internally. As I mentioned in Chapter 1, some of the banks, telcos and energy companies are doing this, off a 'purely technical', data-driven platform. However, there are also one or two who are going it alone and doing it in a very creative manner. Nike is the one that springs to mind most readily. Its broad communication strategy appears to be outstanding from the outside. It does some great brand and product 'theme' ads. But then, it has also created a whole strand of activation around Street Sport, under which it has developed great activation ideas like 'Scorpion football' and 'Run London'. Nike is testament to the fact that you can indeed go it alone and create breakthrough strategies.

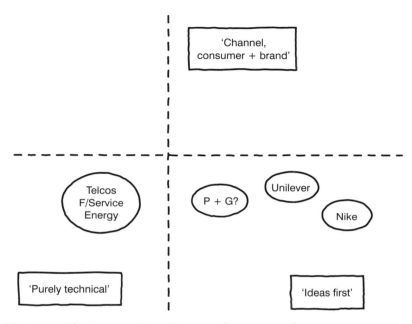

Fig. 4.1 The Strategy Map: Current client approaches.

But it seems to have done this by creating a very creative culture. And also by recruiting from agencies: it seems to be attracting some of the best advertising and media people around, and for agency folk Nike has become the acceptable stepping-stone towards becoming a client.

Many agencies have committed to communications planning, irrespective of current client demand

While some exceptionally big clients have committed to communications planning, the vast majority of clients are still not yet 'up for it' – not sure of exactly what it is, not really convinced of the benefits, unable to get around internal silos and so on. The overall lack of client 'pull', however, hasn't held back the agencies. Across the agency spectrum, and in most of the world, they are all steaming ahead, developing their offers and 'pushing' them at clients. They are doing this in the belief that there is a real client need for communications planning. But it's not all noble sentiment.

One of the main reasons that the agencies are all 'pushing' is because communications planning gives you power and control over how the communication budget is spent and so guarantees a 'seat at the high table'. Ad agencies in particular are at a tipping point in terms of their power base. If they lose communications planning it is likely that their importance will diminish rapidly.

Talking to Rod Wright of TEQUILA\, he commented:

Ad agencies are at this inflexion point in terms of control and power. A lot of them still see their future as just being great creatively rather than owning communications planning. This is naïve. As an ad agency, you absolutely have to own communication strategy. Because the future is not just about creative excellence. Creative can easily become a fragmented commodity. You might end up in a situation where there are multiple suppliers, with no barriers to entry and very little ability to really differentiate. So it's not a sustainable model unless the whole industry is going to implode and fragment. And I don't think that's going to happen.

Another major reason (which is slightly tangential) is that it is an excuse for an implementational land grab. The ad agencies, media agencies and integrated BTL agencies in particular have all been creating new implementational capabilities. A client could get promotional strategy and execution, for example, from a promotions agency, but also potentially from an ad agency, media agency or direct agency. There's a complete blurring of distinctions between them.

So if the agencies are all developing their offers, let's look in some detail at what they're doing, starting with the communication independents.

Communication independents

These are the new guys on the block, who have sprung up specifically to answer the client need for objective communication strategy, and they are certainly driving the whole rise to prominence of communications planning in the minds of clients. What makes communication independents different is that they are not tied to implementation. They don't do buying, they don't do production, so they are, plainly, very objective.

The rightful place to start discussing communication independents is with Michaelides & Bednash. It was, to my knowledge, the first of this type of agency, emerging out of HHCL London way back in the early to mid-1990s. It was then followed a few years later by Unity, again in London. But having kicked off in London, the model was quickly picked up abroad.

As I mentioned in the Preface, in 1998 I co-founded one of these type of agencies in South Africa, with Peter Vogel, called Nota Bene. What started as a media strategy agency has since evolved into an agency that purely does communication strategy, and it has become very good at it. When I came back to the UK in 2003, it had climbed from nothing (when we started) to working on around R500 million's worth of client billings. And since then it has gone even further − it now plans on some R700 million of business and works on some of the biggest advertising clients in the market, such as Unilever, Diageo, MTN and Sanlam. In other words, it is far from a niche player.

About the same time, communication independents emerged in Australia, with both The Media Palace and Bellamy Hayden. Around 2000, another couple emerged: The Media Kitchen in New York and Naked Communications in London. And then in 2002–5 there were more developments, with the launches of Rise Communications, The Ingram Partnership and Experience in London; Match Integration in Australia; and DaVinci in Dusseldorf. And then a string of new extensions: Naked in Amsterdam, Oslo, Sydney and Paris; Michaelides & Bednash in New York; and DaVinci in Sydney, Detroit, Los Angeles and London. All of these communication agencies are privately owned, I believe, with two exceptions − Nota Bene is owned by Mediaedge:cia and DaVinci is owned by Omnicom. But out of all these agencies, three in particular should be discussed more . . .

First, Michaelides & Bednash, perhaps the 'high priests' of communications planning. It is probably the most 'pure' about what it does. When I spoke to George Michaelides, the co-founder, he explained what it does as follows:

Clients don't really buy the current agency models on the market, but there's not a lot of large-scale alternatives. We are obviously an alternative. And the interesting thing about our company is we're small yet we work with lots of big multinational companies. I think part of our success is because we don't fit into the advertising box or the media box, we are brought in really around brand activation, when clients need to bring the brand alive and realise that television is not the only answer. It's taken eight years for us to develop what we now have. We know how to do it, we have the process and know how to quality control it. And we can articulate it better than anybody else in the marketplace.

Michaelides & Bednash is in London and New York. By the end of 2005 it may also have a Tokyo office.

Second, The Ingram Partnership. It was formed in 2003, when Chris Ingram left Tempus and bought Unity, as well as brand and marketing consultancies Butterfield 8 and The Gathering. So The Ingram Partnership is really interesting because it mixes communications planning with business, marketing and brand strategy. It houses these different abilities as one brand, one P&L, in one building.

Last, Naked. And of all of them, it is Naked that deserves the most respect and admiration. It really does. It is smart and feisty, yet its founders are also really nice guys. The three of them, John Harlow, Will Collin and Jon Wilkins, have grown Naked into a sizeable planning enterprise in the UK. It has spawned several joint ventures with ad agencies, and has launched now in half a dozen markets abroad, the Sydney launch in 2004 winning the Coca-Cola communications planning business after only a couple of months in operation.

So now there are communication independents in many countries. Which will be the next one? Where? Places like Hong Kong, Singapore or San Francisco look like 'white space' . . .

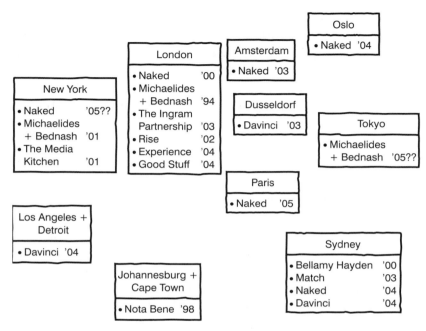

Fig. 4.2 Communication Independents★ around the world.
★Feb 2005 Excludes JVs.

Within the agency world, the communications planning agenda has clearly been set by the communication independents. So how are the bigger, traditional agency types responding? Let's start with the ad agency networks.

Ad agency networks

Now not all ad agency networks are totally committed to trying to develop a communications planning offer or indeed to 'owning it'. At this point it's probably 50:50, between those that see it as key to their futures and those that don't. Those that do are going about it in six main ways.

First, there are those agencies that see the communications planning function as an extension of the strategic planner role. In other words, they are growing and extending the remit of their strategic planners.

BBH and Ogilvy are a couple of ad agency groups with high-pedigree planning skills that are developing communications planning out of a strategic planning base at a worldwide level. DDB also seems to be adopting this stance – in London, it poached David Hackworthy from TBWA New York, with the brief to broaden the agency's legendary strategic planning skills into the communications planning area.

Secondly, there are those agencies that are tasking client service with communications planning. The logic here is that most ad agency groups nowadays have separate P&L units across a host of different disciples, not just advertising. They may have PR, direct, digital and even promotional units. And the heads of the units all sit on a holding board, and may have shares or incentives at this level, so theoretically they are discipline neutral. Now, client service people work on the clients' business, across these different discipline units. So if the client gives them authority across a range of disciplines, they are the ones who need to be able to advise the client on how to split the money up – it's the role of the conductor, which client service people have always played. It's about facilitation and collaboration with specialists, as opposed to one individual specialist doing it.

Which ad agency groups are doing this? Leo Burnett is one. It has developed what is called the 'loop team' concept. If called on to deliver an integrated solution, it uses this process of collaboration to sit and work together, aligning everyone so that they can cross-fertilise at key junctions. Bruce Haines, group chief executive of Leo Burnett London, explained it like this:

I think it is a mistake to rely on 'specialists' within companies to deliver through-the-line strategy. We need to create 'generalists' within agencies, who can understand how all the disciplines can work together. Within ad agencies, I think it's a mistake just to import a couple of media people – trying to create a bolt-on solution. Rather, I think account management is best suited to the function. In the past, account directors used to give clients genuine strategic advice, but account management has been downgraded versus its historical contribution. It is time to set this right.

Martin Thomas, a co-founder of Nylon, the communications planning JV between Y&R, Wunderman and Mediaedge:cia, also talking about the downgrading of account management, told me:

20 years ago there was no debate. Ad agencies had a 50-year-old suit on the business, who could talk business strategy . . . now it's totally fluid. Ad agencies are full of 24 year olds, and are run by 36 year olds. That's what agencies look like today. That's a radical departure from when I joined the business.

Thirdly, there are ad agencies that are bringing in new P&L units across a host of different disciples beyond advertising – PR, direct, promotions, events and so on. They are doing this because there are higher margins and new business opportunities outside pure advertising. But this in itself helps drive communications planning internally, by creating conditions for cross-fertilisation across disciplines.

Fourthly, there is the start of a move to create separate consultancies that work at a higher 'agency group' level in the realm of communications planning. TBWA, for example, has created the 'Disruption Consultancy' in South Africa as just such an upstream entity, and it looks set to roll this out around the world. Other ad agency groups might also do the same in future.

Fifthly, some ad agencies are trying to get 'media back inside'. This is essentially an attempt to go back to the old full-service model, by re-employing some media people. In this space, you have a mixture of big and small agencies. TBWA, for example, is a big ad agency network that has an internal unit in several countries, called TBWA Connections. This unit works as an integral part of the agency, in a full-service manner, delivering communications planning. In New York, FCB has created a media department (aligned to FCB main agency but also aligned to the Interpublic Media Agencies) and has given Rich Gagnon the title of worldwide media director of something called 'FCB Media'. In London there are also other, smaller agencies that have gone down this route: Miles Calcraft Briginshaw Duffy, and Soul.

Last, there are ad agencies that have 'borrowed' media people from media agencies within the same holding group, or have created jobs that sit halfway between ad agency and media agency. Ogilvy in London has also just gone down this route with MindShare in London by creating a joint appointment.

So if that's what the ad agency networks are generally up to, what about the media agency networks?

Media agency networks

I work for a media agency, so I know that they all see communications planning as their future. They all share a common vision and a common purpose and they are all developing skills in this area at a very fast rate, to reposition themselves as 'communications agencies'. They want to make communications planning an extension of media planning across the board, something that everyone does in five or ten years' time, not just the chosen few. So they are developing and building broad-based skills.

One expression of this is the development of robust communications planning processes or operating systems, which most media agencies now have. For example, Carat has Carat Sphere, OMD has Checkmate, while at Mediaedge:cia I helped to develop our own Navigator system.

Media agencies are also developing proprietary tools and modelling techniques that help evaluate and judge the best channels and disciplines to use. One good example is provided by MindShare, which has developed a PDA (personal digital assistant) approach called Mindset. It asks respondents to answer questions on channel exposure ('what can you see or hear?') across 70 channel types, including a raft of in-store options: channel impact ('would you normally notice this?'), frequency of activity ('how often do you do this?') and mood, from time pressured to relaxed. This means that it is quite an advanced study and it is the first time that PDAs have been used by a media agency as a way of capturing data. Another good example is Carat, which has developed a cognitive tracking approach now known as ICE (integrated communications evaluation). This identifies the effect of communication on a brand's 'associative networks', which are the relationships between the meanings and values associated with it.

Another important means by which media agencies are developing broader skills is by introducing and recruiting new talent (in particular strategic planners from ad agencies) and by extending their in-house implementational offer beyond media. So just as the ad agencies are bringing in new P&L units across a host of different disciplines beyond advertising, media agencies are doing likewise, beyond media. In other words, they are both 'filling in' towards each other. In both cases this is not really surprising, since they've been taking a hammering from clients over the profit margins in traditional areas of income.

So as well as bringing in both digital and sponsorship areas, which are relatively small extensions, media agencies are also going further afield, into direct/CRM, PR, entertainment and even retail. This new breadth of service is changing media agencies in terms of both structure and the type of people they employ. And many of them are now making between a third to a half of their income from non-media implementation, making a nonsense out of agencies being ranked solely on media billings, which simply don't indicate their size or scale any more.

Finally, some media agency networks have acknowledged the difficulty of skilling up the main agency in communications planning by opting for a dual strategy, in which as well as developing the main agency they also create an internal unit specifically for communications planning. For example, OMD has The Source, Mediaedge:cia has the Central Planning Group and MPG has Catalyst. One network in particular, Aegis, has taken a bold step and opted to create a second-string worldwide network called Vizeum, which stands alongside Carat but is positioned with a stronger communications planning focus than its sister agency.

What other agency types are also building communications planning capabilities? Next, let's look at the so-called integrated BTL agencies.

Integrated BTL agency networks

Below-the-line agencies have matured incredibly in the last 15 years, and now many of them offer implementation across the board, with a broad creative focus and remit. They do 'through-the-line' – and in a relatively neutral manner. In other words, of all the agencies that do strategy and implementation, these integrated below-the-line guys are the most culturally neutral in terms of discipline.

Agencies that fall into this classification would include those that started as through-the-line, like The Hive in Toronto and The Bank in the UK. But there are also those that have grown and broadened out of a particular discipline. Coming off a direct base, I'd include G2 Worldwide (part of Grey Global, known as Joshua in the UK), as well as Proximity, Wunderman, TBWA\GGT Direct and OgilvyOne. Coming off a promotional base, I'd include 141, TEQUILA\ and 23^{red} in the UK, while Chime Communications comes from a PR base and Circus comes from an event base. Many of these agencies have a grand overarching ambition in terms of communications planning and they now house many great planners.

Within the promotional-based agencies, there are many planners who are very capable of developing communication strategy, often in-store out. G2 Worldwide does this, for example, by fusing together direct, digital, econometric modelling and promotional executional abilities to create communication strategies that have a strong retail flavour, which is very interesting to many clients.

Within the direct-based agencies, over the last decade there has been a quiet revolution in the role of the planner and they are now extremely sophisticated, able to adapt 'upstream' brand or consumer thinking with the data inherent in their discipline. In this sense, they resemble the advertising strategic planners of the past. These below-the-line/through-the-line planners are increasingly driving communications planning on clients' business, so the other agencies should watch out!

JVs

All the players that we've looked at so far share one thing in common, which, not surprisingly, is the JV. But these JVs are principally being driven by the needs of ad agencies to skill up in the area of communications planning – a structural extension to activities like borrowing or embedding media agency planners. To date, they are all local and none has spread its wings abroad.

In the UK, several independent ad agencies have done JVs with Naked, who in their eyes seems 'creative friendly' and capable of adding communications planning rigour to their offer. Clemmow Hornby Inge (CHI) has 'Naked Inside', led by Tim Allnutt (and actually, CHI has also done a JV in the PR arena as well, with Freud Inside). Fallon has two – one a communications planning agency, another a digital agency. And then there is WCRS, the most recent Naked bedfellow, with its JV called Element Communications.

Again in the UK, Abbott Mead Vickers BBDO has done a JV with PHD Media, to create PHD Seed. This JV allows a number of communication planners to be 'embedded' in Abbott Mead Vickers BBDO's offices. Within WPP, there is a three-way JV called Nylon that I've already mentioned, the parents being Y&R, Mediaedge:cia and Wunderman. In Japan, Dentsu has done a JV with Asatsu-DK, to develop cross-media creative and content, as well as communications planning.

Nitro

The last type of agency that needs mentioning in the context of communications planning is Nitro. Nitro is an emerging agency group, led by Chris Clark from Asia and Paul Shearer from London. It differs from most ad agencies because it offers a strategy and creative, fat-free model. In other words, it offers clients both communication strategy and creative work, joined up, while stripping away as many account handlers as possible. It also puts 'swat teams' of Nitro planners and creatives in a client company for an extended period; so rather than say 'we will be back in four weeks', it maintains an ongoing dialogue with clients by sitting next to them. It is clearly picking up on what management consultancies have been doing for years.

Nitro as a group works with Mars globally. Recently it also won a pan-European Unilever assignment, on the back of which it opened its fourth office, in London. It'll be really interesting to see how it develops. What is clear to me is that it is developing what I see as the 'ad agency communication strategy approach of the future' – the linking of high-level communication strategy and creative thinking,

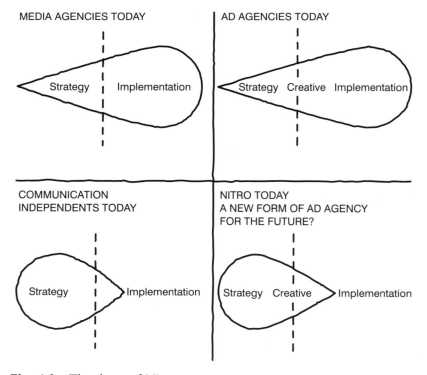

Fig. 4.3 The shape of Nitro.

fat free. It currently does production implementation. But who knows in future? Just as the communication independents largely broke away from media agencies and put strategy over implementation, maybe the same thing is poised to happen in future to the creative agencies.

As we've seen, there really are lots of different approaches being tried out at the moment – lots of 'toe-dipping' – and it's not clear yet if any of these are the right type of outfit. These are shown in summary in Figure 4.4.

And waiting in the harbour . . .

But it's not just the agencies who are starting to develop their offers. Management consultants and the research agencies are both waiting quietly in the harbour, eyeing up the potential.

Let's take the management consultancies first. They understand how to make communications planning a good business proposition for clients, how to give a sense of accountability to it and how to build in systems that give clients more control over it. They also position it to clients as part of a bigger picture, a 'value chain' where they can add effectiveness and efficiency all the way through.

James Walker, a Partner at Accenture's Marketing Sciences, explained it like this:

The first question for the client is, how much do I spend? Get that right and you might add around 10% in terms of cost-efficiency. In fact you might add around the same type of figure at every point in the chain: the allocation decision, communications planning itself and the implementation. All through this value chain you can add efficiency to a client's marketing process. And there's no doubt that if you can demonstrate that communications planning has a legitimate place in this value chain, you can get an appropriate fee for it.

The value chain that James describes, is shown in Figure 4.5. So the management consultants see the importance of communications planning to clients, and they feel they can do it – albeit in a

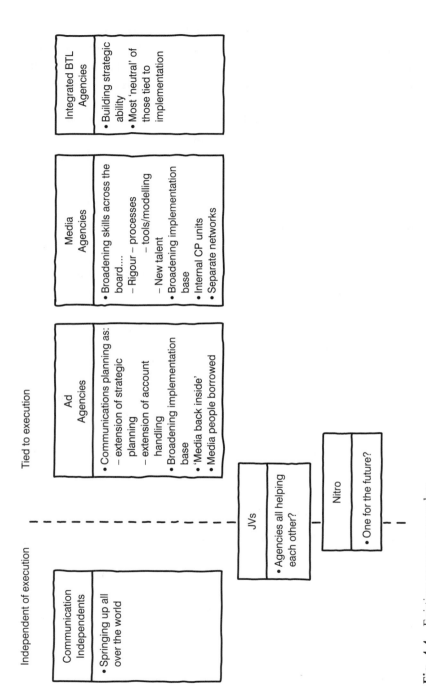

Fig. 4.4 Existing agency approaches.

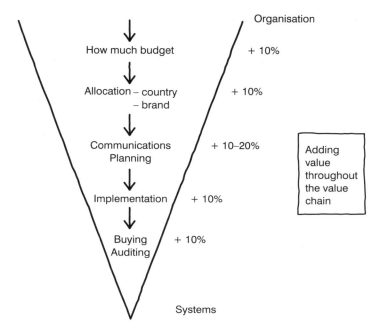

Fig. 4.5 Management consultants and the value chain.

data-driven way. They are simply waiting until client demand for it 'hots up'. And then, with their high-level contacts in most of the big client companies in the world, they'll no doubt be able to turn on the tap.

There is also no doubt in my mind that several research agencies or agency groups have a communications planning agenda and hope to compete actively in this area in the future. They can certainly fuel planning out of their core competencies in research, real consumer insight and their own tools. Many research agencies have also realised that within the communications planning piece, the retail environment is going to become a critical marketing medium. So they have already developed a lot of proprietary knowledge and insight into shopper behaviour by category. They are also objective and clients are used to seeing them as such; they are mentally viewed as 'outside' the agency fray, and sometimes as a little more grown up, too!

So where's the real action?

From all the fuss that's being made, you might think that communications planning was already widely practised by all manner of different agencies and consultants. Sadly, this isn't yet the case. In the UK, I'd estimate that only 4 to 5% of client business uses communications planning as opposed to the more traditional way of doing things. And it's probably true to say that the communication independents and media agencies are currently the most successful at getting this business, at least 'officially' – when big clients are making public decisions. But there is also a fair amount being done by the ad agencies and below-the-line agencies, unofficially.

Charles Courtier of Mediaedge:cia described the situation like this:

I think clients are throwing down the gauntlet to their media agencies today, and saying 'OK show me you can do it because you're all talking about it

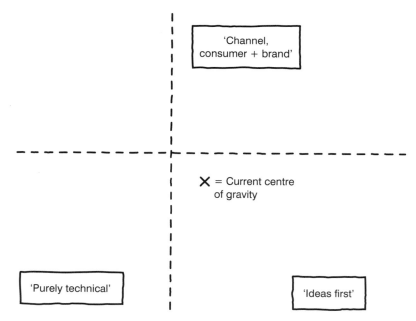

Fig. 4.6 The Strategy Map: Current centre of gravity.

as though you can do it', and to varying degrees we've been successful. But if the media agencies can't deliver on it, they won't keep throwing it down. They'll find it elsewhere. So I do think it requires the industry as a whole, and the holding companies, to really sit down and rethink this. I think that's where clients have got us at the moment, they think the most obvious skill set is in the media agency, but then media agencies have to deliver on that.

Which is an interesting perspective. So while most media agencies might grumble about their competitors winning big communications planning business – Carat and Starcom winning the North American P&G business, or MindShare winning the European Unilever business – maybe they shouldn't. Maybe they should wake up every day and all wish one another every success – because, collectively, they all need them to.

So far we've assumed that who gets to do communications planning is based on the client deciding the agency type. But in truth it often comes down to the individuals working on the business. My experience has been that it is the one who picks up the mantle, and who can deliver, that often gets this assignment.

So what makes a good communication planner? Here's brand marketing consultant John Grant's view:

In terms of a skill set for communications planning, the key is the ability to understand all areas or at least a bit of all areas: anything from Sunday newspaper consumer culture and the trends behind that, through to the way that business models are moving and the ways of markets, supply chains and economic models. The key issue is synthesising a very complex picture as opposed to differentiating a very simple one. One might draw an analogy with certain brands like Apple in i-music or the BBC, which both have a synthesising quality about them and are able to be a bigger envelope which can hold a lot of complexity.

Today, no one really matches up to these skill sets. But I guess the ideal would be a hybrid agency strategic planner, media planner, DM planner and even econometrician – with a broad understanding of different disciplines. Someone once said that the ideal communication planner is 'T-shaped': they have a deep understanding of one particular discipline, but also a broad understanding of all the other disciplines across the marketing spectrum. In other words, they're a combination of specialist and generalist.

However, as communications planning spreads around the world we will begin to see the influence of different business cultures on the way that it is practised. A stretchy cartograph of where communications planning is happening today might look like Figure 4.7.

The smaller markets like Singapore, Australia, South Africa and Scandinavia are well established and the UK is growing, but the most significant development is that the US has now entered the fray.

The US is traditionally a very conservative marketplace, with conservative clients, but with P&G's adoption of communications planning in the US, everyone has suddenly woken up and lots of clients have been going to agencies and asking for it! The media agencies are certainly getting in on the act in the US, but the ad agencies are close behind. And because the larger ad agencies are still closely

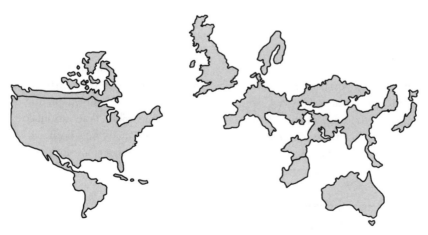

Fig. 4.7 Size of the country reflects the amount of communications planning it's currently doing.

aligned with their media counterparts, a lot of communications planning efforts in the US seem to be collaborative.

But the US will not necessarily adopt exactly the same approach to communications planning as the UK and the Commonwealth countries. Marketing in the US tends to be much more analytical and accountable. So already in the US we're seeing more emphasis on tools than in the UK; Integration's MCA©, in particular, is a big hit Stateside. This means that we're already seeing a degree of bifurcation between the US and UK.

American enthusiasm for communications planning is great news. While the UK (and Unilever) hasn't managed to create a worldwide demand for it, my guess is that the US (and P&G) just might. As we all recognise, the US does have the habit of driving world events!

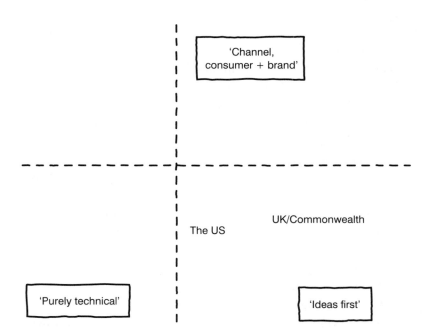

Fig. 4.8 The Strategy Map: Approaches – US vs. UK/Commonwealth.

So if those are the countries doing the most communications planning, who is doing the least? Apparently China is one market where it's just not relevant at the moment, as Guy Murphy of BBH explained:

The changes which tend to have forced the debate are very UK, Europe and US centric. It's not the case in, say, China. In China, people don't avoid ads; there's no clutter, no PVRs . . . what people want in China is to see as many ads as they possibly bloody can on television. Because it helps them understand brands and how to use them. You don't need 360 communications planning in China. You want to put it all on TV. You can get a billion people with a single spot.

◆

Key points made in this chapter

- The break-up of media and creative has turned out to be an initial step in the restructuring of the marketing communications industry, not an end in itself.
- Some clients have committed to communications planning and want to control it.
- Many agencies have also committed to it, irrespective of current demand. This is really because:
  - It's where things are obviously going.
  - It gets you control and power, a seat at the high table.
  - It's an excuse for an implementational land grab.
- Reviewing the agencies:
  - Communication independents are now springing up all over the world.
  - Ad agencies are not all pursuing communications planning. But those that are, are doing it in the following ways:
    - as an extension of strategic planning;
    - as an extension of account handling;
    - by broadening their implementation base outside ads;
    - by creating upstream consultancies;
    - by bringing media people back inside, or by 'borrowing' media people.

○ Media agencies are all pursuing communications planning, and this is one of their strengths. Their approaches are:
  ■ by broadening their implementation base outside media;
  ■ building up skills across the board, through processes and tools/modelling;
  ■ by bringing in new talent from ad agencies in particular;
  ■ by creating internal communications planning units, or indeed separate networks more focused on it.
○ Integrated BTL agencies are growing in creative and strategic ability. Of the executional agencies, they are also probably the most 'neutral' culturally, at this point.
○ JVs are springing up. Most of these JVs to date have been between ad agencies and communication independents.
○ Nitro is an ad agency with a difference. It offers both communication strategy and creative work, joined up, from senior individuals who are happy to spend extended periods in clients' offices to do this. It could represent the ad agency communications strategy approach of the future.

- The management consultants and research agencies are sitting quietly on the sidelines, biding their time.
- The skill base for communications planning does not reside in one place. It is a mix of account planner, media planner, DM planner and even econometrician; and often in reality who does communications planning is whoever is most 'up for it'.
- That said, in terms of who is doing most communications planning today, the centre of gravity lies with the media agencies.
- And in geographical terms, the US has now caught up with the UK and Commonwealth countries; although in doing it, it places more emphasis on data and tools.

5
Life Below Decks

An assessment of the pros and cons of the different agency types in terms of their suitability to do communications planning, and a look at alternatives beyond 'agency'

If you could look below the decks of any of the vessels currently jostling for position in the communication industry's space race, what exactly would you see? In some you might witness anxious board meetings devoted to painstaking analysis and debate, in others you might find nervous types furrowing their brows over strategists' reports, while in a few you'd probably still find a bunch of people casually shooting pool and playing table football just like in the bad old days.

In the space race, all types of agency are having problems adapting and evolving. No one has yet discovered the route map and everyone is nervous of taking their first few steps, for fear they may move in completely the wrong direction or offer a rival the opportunity to leapfrog straight over the top and scoop the prize. There's also always the chance that a complete outsider could steal in from the blind side, take on the established players and invest some serious money in it – which is something that most people in the industry have not even considered.

Of course, many of the industry's problems stem from the fact that so few people really know exactly where they're heading. But if we're to have any chance of grasping this, we need to have a clear understanding of the problems we're currently going through.

The most obvious problem is that of job denial. If your profits have always come from your expertise in a single discipline, then to start recommending other channels and disciplines in an entirely neutral way sounds to many like being plain foolhardy. Who deliberately sets out to do themselves out of a job?

Then there are the issues of focus and priority. Margins are tight and nobody wants to take their eye off the ball by overstretching and neglecting the sources of their current revenues. And for most agencies, trying to win communications planning business is just a plain hard slog, even when they are only trying to 'up-trade' their existing clients. Time and time again they are thwarted by client silos, client politics or client ambivalence.

There's also the difficulty of getting paid for communications planning. Because we cannot conclusively demonstrate the benefit, it's hard to convince clients to pay for it handsomely. And so we're in danger of giving it away virtually for free. In fact, this issue could jeopardise the whole future of communications planning. If it's done by agencies virtually for free, it will never be done well and will never 'fly' as a discipline within agencies. When I interviewed Chris Ingram, founder of The Ingram Partnership, this was his primary concern:

Communications planning should be separate and be funded separately. There's a real danger of us devaluing communications planning and of it being given away with the implementation, very much in the same way as account planning or strategic planning has been given away free by ad agencies. If this happens, it would be rather tragic.

So let's now look in more detail at the pros and cons of the main contenders for the communications planning prize.

Media agencies

Many of the insiders I spoke to took the view that media agencies had huge advantages over other agency types and might get the lion's share of communications planning. To kick off with, this is what Tony

Regan, a co-founder of Nylon (and a media man by trade), had to say:

Media planners have an absolute advantage because we understand what makes an idea come to life in the experience of a consumer in the real world. We can make recommendations which reflect commercial realities, so clients don't waste a lot of time on things which can't be executed in the marketplace. Our understanding of communication channels gives us the scope to create ideas with a time and place about them that makes them powerful.

Damian O'Malley, executive planning director UK and Ireland for McCann Erickson, puts a slightly different spin on it:

Media agencies have some huge opportunities. Yes, they have this connection to the 'real world' in a communication sense, but there are two things that are possibly more important. Firstly, they control the money – they already have one foot in communications planning, by virtue of their position as 'budget spenders'. They already have permission to tell the client how to spend their money and it's very easy for them in future to recommend that the client spends their budget using both above and below-the-line. And their second big advantage is the homogeneity of their culture – they all do the same thing. Part of the issue in ad agencies is that they house lots of different types of people and these people don't always get on. You have the account management/creative divide, the planning/creative divide, and so on – agencies are like a lot of puppies jumping around in the sack. But because of the homogeneity of media agencies, in a way you'd think it'd be easier for them to at least get consensus.

But one of the biggest issues for media agencies is that, by and large, they are culturally 'executional'. According to Will Collin of communication independent Naked, this is reflected in many ways:

You can see the importance that media agencies attach to execution from the kind of people they hire and how people feel they are expected to behave. If you fill an agency with numbers people you're simply not going to get enough creativity, freethinking and open-mindedness.

This cultural emphasis on execution can make it difficult for media agencies to compete effectively in certain areas. Damian O'Malley of McCann Erickson believes that they will struggle to keep up with other agency types when it comes to insight, for example:

Communications planning needs insight and this is a skill which is often lacking in media agencies because they are more numbers based.

But is it as simple as that? Will Collin's point of view is that it is not:

Someone from an ad agency once said that insights from a media agency often underwhelm. They are observations masquerading as insights. Maybe this is true, but the insight culture in media agencies is different to ad agencies. Insights that ad agencies cherish are those that lead to great creative leaps, so they are likely to be surprising. Whereas in media agencies, you're not looking for the surprising insight, but for the clear and present opportunity. The insight is just a clarity of vision and not necessarily an unexpected thing.

Lots of media agency people also suffer from what I call the 'strong desire to stay behind the computer'. In other words, they still spend most of their time doing cross-tab runs and using tools to help them understand consumers' relationships with media channels. But communications planning requires far more than that. It requires an understanding of consumers' relationships with categories and brands and how purchasing decisions are made, as well as trade dynamics. To get this level of understanding, planners need to get out there and start observing and thinking about communication. They need to examine the different forms that branding takes and the different things it says about a brand. And they also need to be able to talk to consumers, although if you ask most media planners to go out and interview a consumer they 'freeze' and really struggle with it.

This last point picks up on the broader issue of confidence. Phil Georgiadis, of Walker Media in the UK, made an interesting observation when he wrote in Campaign's Media Awards 2004:

Media agencies have spent the past few decades scaling the mountain of respectability and authority. The summit is now in sight, but we're wobbling.

It is almost as if media agencies lack the 'big match temperament', as John Grant explained:

Media agencies have a cap-doffing mentality when it comes to being at the high table, whereas ad agencies really relish the conversations with the managing director about their business. So media agencies don't feel quite so confident that they've got the right people to be in those types of conversation, and they tend to stick to their knitting.

As an agency type, they're also patchy when it comes to strategic delivery. Geographically this is certainly the case. There might be great communication strategy coming out of media agencies in Paris, London or Stockholm, but in many other markets this just isn't so. John Preston of communication independent Match Integration in Sydney told me that in Australia clients fundamentally just want good media thinking that encompasses all forms of communication, whereas media has been traded down to a commodity and in doing so the thinking side has been diminished. What clients want is for their agency to get the basics right first, with smart thinking applied to their business.

This is the case when it comes to dealing with individuals, too. As Guy Murphy of BBH put it:

Many media companies don't have a culture that informs and guides a certain style of thinking throughout the organisation. Instead you either get lucky or unlucky with individuals. It's all rather random.

So media agencies who are trying to compete in this area often find that they lack credibility. It can be hard for them to create an environment in which they can recruit and retain good communication planners. It can also be hard for them to pitch for and win this type of business.

An alternative to growing a communications planning capability organically within the organisation is to create separate structures, internal units: JVs with ad agencies or even separate networks. But this alternative is not all plain sailing either. The separate structures run the risk of becoming planning 'ivory towers' that question the abilities of the main agency or mothership. They also might not be fed business by the mothership and might not thrive. And if they do thrive, they might well go off into the sunset, giving no benefit back to the main agency or mothership at all!

So the jury is out on whether the media agencies can raise their game to meet the communications planning challenge. And some, like Guy Murphy of BBH, believe that the ad agencies are better placed to take on this work:

> I think ad agencies will find it easier to absorb media agency skills than the reverse. When you see most media planners, they have blind panic on their faces when asked to talk about brands or ideas. But I find the reverse much easier. Not least because a lot of it is just logic and information. And so if I was going to put a bet on it, I'd say ad agencies could absorb both, faster.

So next, let's find out whether that really is the case.

Ad agencies

Historically, the ad agencies have always had the most senior rela-tionships with manufacturing clients and this gives them a natural head start when it comes to communications planning. Their other key advantage is that what clients want most of all is strategy and cre-ativity joined up together – something that only ad agencies can offer. Rod Wright of TEQUILA\ summarised their advantages:

> I have to say that first of all, a lot of media agencies are playing a more central role in communication allocation and strategy than either side of the agency business (ATL/BTL), which is good for them; and the people I've met are good at commercial branding and more linked to the commercial side of how the money works etc. However, I don't think that media agen-cies will come out on top. In terms of planning's role, in the end it'll stay

with the creative execution rather than with the allocation of money. One of the weaknesses of media agencies is that the revenue still comes from where you execute and spend money, whereas there is the potential for ad agencies to be independent of executional revenues. The question at the end of the day is also who is able to get the best people. Clients start picking off where they get the best people and skill base. So the question is whether a media agency is able to recruit the people who are really good at the brand stuff, and whether these people will want to stay close to the creative execution. I suspect they'll want to stay close to the creative execution.

Although the ad agencies' ability to link strategy and creativity is a massive asset, many people think that they will never be able to accord strategy the same respect as they do creativity – or invest enough in it. Indeed from certain perspectives, the ad agencies look to be in a bit of a fix. Their core properties – ideas and production – are under threat as never before. James Walker of Accenture explained their predicament to me like this:

Creative agencies are under pressure because their job is to come up with a great idea and that can be sourced from all sorts of places. Coke famously went to Creative Artists, which caused quite a stir, even if it didn't quite work in the end. But there are all sorts of places that compete in the core value proposition that agencies have. Clients could even get ideas from film schools, for example!

So ad agencies need to work harder than ever to protect their existing revenues, at the same time as facing up to the realisation that they need to develop their skills in new areas – like communications planning – if they are to secure their long-term future. But this is something that the culture of ad agencies mitigates against, as they have always been more about 'art' than 'business'. Investing in creative talent and producing big-budget ad campaigns have always been more important to them than understanding communication channels through the line, or investigating return on investment. Will Collin of Naked told me:

Ad agencies still have a culture of celebrating ideas and creativity. They live and breathe great ads and they recruit people who love ads for their own sake. Now, there are two problems with this culture. Firstly, this work is in an increasingly narrow field. And secondly, when it comes to 360 degree communications planning, they are not really interested in any other way of building brands besides ads. It's just not what turns them on. So they often end up doing no more than trying to amplify an ad idea.

John Preston of Australian communication independent Match Integration echoed the sentiment:

On the creative side, one thing I found at TBWA was, as much as we talked about 360, there was still very much an above-the-line totem pole which existed and the best briefs still went to the guys who were best at TV. So who gets to work on which briefs is indicative of their above-the-line culture.

In John Grant's view, this is because ad agencies are somewhat out of touch with business:

There is a gestalt about business that agencies clearly don't get, which is obvious when you get into conversations with them about broader business issues. Agencies will assume problems and solutions are unitary, that there is one problem and there is one solution which will be an idea. But this is out of touch with business that is all about complexity and systems thinking. Business today needs acupuncture; it's like finding pressure points in a very complex system.

And as Martin Thomas of Nylon explains, if the culture of ad agencies is to move on, it will involve changes in both investment decisions and personnel, which seem unlikely:

Creative agencies won't get their act together on communication strategy. They're not prepared to put in the investment and they've let the strategy part of their business erode. And on the creative front, you'll find that 95% of the people in creative departments will be classically trained, so it's no wonder that it's hard to shift them to a multidisciplinary way of thinking. When you've got a tipping point where 30% of a creative department has a broader range of skills, then you can start bringing the others along with you. But in ad agencies, until you broaden the skills base in the main creative department, you won't get any traction. And that's not what they're prepared to do. For example, computer games are currently one of the big creative battlegrounds, but how many ad agencies are hiring computer games creatives? Retail is another big thing – and how many of them are hiring retail creatives?

It is tempting to accuse the ad agencies of simply being too conservative in their thinking and practice, but that's not the whole story. It seems that any attempt on their part to move forward is frequently hamstrung by clients' expectations. Rod Wright explained to me that this was certainly the case at TBWA:

We initially felt that the creative people were the block on the issue but actually, they said it's not that we don't want to come up with through-the-line ideas, its just that when we do, we're told it's not what clients have asked us for. To move things on, you have to start way back and say, how do you re-educate clients to want a different thing?

And, of course, there are also the problems of rivalries and turf wars within holding groups that James Walker identifies:

If the ad agencies did move in on communications planning, it would create an immediate point of tension with the media agencies within the same holding groups. And also clients might say, 'Hang on, I'm already paying for this somewhere else'. So they really are between a rock and a hard place.

So given all of these issues, how might you go about kick-starting communications planning in an ad agency? One thing's for certain, you need to do a hell of a lot more than just recruit a couple of media guys!

One idea might be to turn all of the ad agency strategic planners into communication planners overnight. They certainly have skills in understanding the consumer, which are transferable to communications planning. But the problem is that most strategic planners have always worked in an environment where the process of creating great advertising is cherished above all else. So what really motivates them is coming up with a great insight to act as a springboard for a creative idea. This means that the value in planning tends to follow the value in creative. Planners advance as a result of their ability to help creatives, to win plaudits from the creative department and to be associated with awards. And a lot of younger planners in particular are simply thinking, 'I need to get some good ads out, I need my brand to be famous.' Of course, some senior planners do get past all this and get interested in communications planning. But they're also the ones who tend to go off and start their own companies!

As Martin Thomas alluded to above, another way forward might be to change the type of person you employ in the main creative department and look to broaden the creative pool. This is practical and a good idea, but it would be a slow burn.

Another notion – and a faster burn – might be to take senior creatives and make them communication planners. The thinking here is that as creative people drive the culture of ad agencies, you have to change the culture at the root; otherwise you're always going to have a creative department that's led by TV. This could certainly work; after all, a lot of senior creatives are in fact very strategic thinkers as well. You would probably end up with three tiers: your strategic planner working with your senior creative director (as communication planner) working with the actual creatives. This might be possible at some point in the future if ad agencies felt they could remunerate senior creatives for strategy, and it would certainly change ad agencies. I also believe that if you could get senior creatives writing broad communication strategy, clients would fall over themselves for it.

Integrated BTL agencies

In the past, the problem for integrated BTL agencies in the area of communications planning was being taken as seriously in the strategy area as both the ad agencies and media agencies. And at the root of this is not being as in touch with communication and brand issues as the ad agency; and not being as in touch with the communication channels, and knowing what is or isn't possible, as the media agencies.

However, Jonathan Dodd, executive vice-president of integrated BTL agency G2 Worldwide, believes that this is no longer the case:

It's easier to plug creativity into a more complex, larger structure than it is the other way around, which will benefit the integrated BTL agencies and media agencies. When it comes to integrated BTL agencies, historically they didn't have the same creative culture as classic ad agencies, or the same understanding of the subtleties of creative brand building. But this has changed – nowadays they have very good creative skills. Furthermore, they are becoming far more strategic as well and, as a result, clients are increasingly putting them around the top table. Where they win is where clients see them really translating holistic communication ideas through the line.

Communication independents

The suitability of communication independents for communications planning is fairly self-evident. After all, these are the guys who are at the forefront of the discipline. They are independent of execution, they work well with creative agencies and they have a culture that celebrates strategy and creativity.

But their key disadvantage is that they represent another agency layer that has to be managed. In other words, more hassle for overstretched clients.

There is also the issue of rigour, which is something that clients are demanding more and more of. Martin Thomas of Nylon described the communication independents' potential shortcomings in this area:

Our view has always been, to do proper communications planning you need a massive back end which in theory we've got. You can't do it with just three blokes sitting around the table. On the media side the barriers are getting higher. Clients are asking, 'Where is your MCA©-type tool? These people over here have BAV & BrandZ, what can you offer me?' So the communication independents without a strong back end are struggling, they're being squeezed because the media agencies have upped their game.

Four internal factors for change

Any organisation that really wishes to succeed in communications planning needs to look closely at the four internal factors show in Figure 5.1 below.

As the diagram shows, the issue at the heart of things is the cultural sense of purpose of the organisation as a whole. To succeed at communications planning, an agency needs to create a cultural sense of purpose that is 'strategy before execution and implementation'. But as we have seen, with both ad agencies and media agencies this is certainly not the case. Most ad agencies' cultural sense of purpose is focused on great creative work and great production, while most large media agency networks still exist above all else to procure spots and space for clients. These are very different cultures from that of a communication independent, which puts strategy first and looks to solve

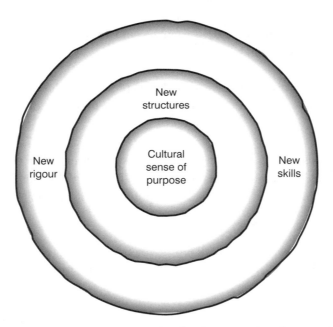

Fig. 5.1 Thinking about gearing for the future – what do agencies need to address?

broad communications problems for clients in new and exciting ways. This was certainly the case with Nota Bene, which I co-founded in 1998. There we started with a cultural sense of purpose that celebrated innovative strategy. This enabled us to attract interesting clients and some of the best thinkers in the marketplace. This created a self-fulfilling prophecy – it all flowed from how we set up the company and our cultural sense of purpose.

So for all agencies, this cultural sense of purpose is the key determining factor that needs to be addressed. But how can they do this? It really needs to come from the organisation's top five individuals: what they believe, what they think and feel, and what they say both publicly and privately. And this needs to be backed up by action. There are many levers that the top tier of a company can pull that can either contribute to or detract from creating a 'strategy-friendly' cultural sense of purpose. The investment decisions that are made, for example, send out very clear signals to the company's employees and the marketplace as a whole. How salaries are scaled and bonuses awarded has the same power. Even if a company is paid by execution – by creative production or media implementation and buying – this does not mean that individuals cannot be given bonuses for strategic thinking or, indeed, for facilitating this. In short: strategy needs to be made into the 'internal hero'.

The culture of an agency was an issue that Rob Hill from Ogilvy South Africa put his finger on when I spoke to him:

I think part of the problem with the ad industry is its legacy is so strong, that it is really struggling to escape its history. And here, the impediment to change is not so much structure but mindset, or culture. But the agencies that'll overcome the challenges facing them are those that will be able to adapt culturally. It'll come from creative people who are able to operate within the nuances of this new world.

But it's not just about culture – although this must come first. Structural changes are also needed to align an organisation with its cultural sense of purpose. Some might be tempted to do this simply by siloing a few strategists into separate internal units; or, indeed, siloing them into separate P&Ls or external company entities. But to my mind, this would be tokenism. It still says that what this company deems organisationally important is execution. In my view, far more significant structural changes are required. For example, it might mean ensuring that at least 25% of the employees are communication strategists. They could perhaps be integrated across the business, as 'strategy leaders' alongside the current client service business directors.

Another way of deploying these communication strategists might be to split the agency in two. As you come in the agency's doors, you go left for strategy, right for execution – quite a radical proposal for most agencies today! This would allow strategy and execution to build their own distinct cultures, without compromising either. It would also allow each to attract and retain the best people in their own fields. But because this idea would also mean that strategy and execution were both housed within the same building, it would still be easy for the two sides of the agency to communicate with each other. They'd still share the same café or bar, after all!

There is certainly a big debate to be had about the relative merits of splitting strategy from execution – and it's one that we will return to later in the book – but for now perhaps it's best to say very simply that if you are running an agency, 'new structures' is an important potential lever.

Let's now come on to the third factor, which is 'new skills'. This must be seen as something that can 'help', but not something that can create wholesale change in its own right. In other words, it can complement changes that might be based around structure or the cultural sense of purpose of an organisation.

This point was made by George Michaelides when I spoke to him:

The idea that a football team can ship in some foreign star players and instantly succeed, is a nonsense. . . . If you look carefully at any successful team, you will almost certainly find that it has a culture nurtured over many years that is strong enough to withstand the loss of any individual player, however talented. But often what happens when people want to transform themselves is they try to ship in the talent rather than changing their internal culture from the core. Culturally you just can't change that quickly and it's instructive that in the US, when the Japanese car manufacturers came into the marketplace, General Motors set up a whole new division called Saturn – based in Tennessee, not Detroit – and it had a different culture and set of work practices that it created in order to reinvent.

In other words, importing skill is the 'cream on the cake'. It's something that helps change, but doesn't drive change. But if an organisation has been successful in aligning its structures with a new cultural sense of purpose, what sort of new skills might be needed? At strategy level, if we assume that the ideal communications planner might be a cross between an ad agency strategic planner, a media planner and a DM planner, then it means ensuring that you have this type of planner mix internally – whatever type of agency you are. And within the executional base, the same broad mix of skills is required. If you're an ad agency or indeed an integrated below-the-line agency, you should certainly make sure that your creative department can work effectively through many types of communication channel.

The last of the four factors is 'new rigour'. In terms of importance, it is equal to 'new skills' and so is shown alongside it as the third ring in Figure 5.1. From a client's point of view, there is no doubt that communications planning needs more rigour. At the moment some agencies have a bit of it – media agencies and research agencies have some tools, media agencies have some small econometric units, and all agencies have some brand, consumer and channel understanding. But as we move forward, agencies as a whole are going to have to bring a lot more rigour to bear on communications planning.

So those are the four internal factors that organisations need to address if they are to meet the challenges of communications planning. Leading on from this, what might the perfect agency structure look like (from today's perspective)?

A perfect agency structure

You need to be at the centre of the three approaches

I would suggest that at this point in time, the perfect agency structure needs to strike a balance between the three main schools of communications planning that were discussed in Chapter 1: the 'purely
technical' school, the 'channel, consumer and brand' school and the
'ideas-first' school. This is no easy feat, because these approaches have
always been culturally at odds with each other.

But the importance of creating this balance was underlined by Paul
Alexander of the Campbell Soup Company when I spoke to him:

I think that the companies that'll win in the area of communication channel
planning will be those that are able to blend data analysis with a real insight
into consumers that comes from anthropological research. At the end of the
day I firmly believe in the AG Lafley 'consumer is boss' philosophy. Because
even with the best data and channel planning, if we don't fundamentally
understand the consumer, we're still going to be inefficient; even if we'll be
good at measuring this inefficiency!

Part of this is also understanding and insight across race and gender. In the
States in particular, with the growth of African-American, Latino and Asian
populations . . . those agencies and organisations that go beyond the political correctness of reflecting their consumer base, and actually incorporate
that into their channel planning, are going to thrive.

Within my Strategy Map, if we take the two extremes of 'ideas' and
'ROI', historically, clients have perceived ad agencies as being the
leaders of 'ideas' thinking and management consultants as the leaders
in 'ROI' thinking. Damian O'Malley told me about the implications
of this:

There is a really fundamental gulf between management consultancies and
communication people, to do with our thinking styles. Management consultancies are fundamentally analytic, and we are fundamentally synthetic.
They believe that you can analyse your way to solutions and insist that you

need to put in the hundreds of hours of analysis before you can get to a solution. The idea that you could walk in and tell a client quickly within 90% certainty what the solution is undermines their whole business model, and that's why they'd find it very hard to work with companies like us.

So how do you, as an agency manager, breed best practice in both 'ideas' and 'ROI' areas, and manage to fuse them into a single strategy? It might sound hard, but there are other professions that manage to do it. Take architects for example. They work at both levels: they develop the 'big picture', but then they've also got to be unbelievably cute about bringing things in on budget and getting the ROI right for the client.

So the 'perfect structure' for communications planning means integrating left-brain ROI and right-brain ideas thinking – the left side of the Strategy Map and the right. At the moment, however, within agency organisations you have those that are good at 'ideas', those that are good at 'ROI' and those that fall between both stools. These are shown in Figure 5.2.

There are a couple of things to take from this. First, the people who currently fall between the two stools are the ones to watch in future, because they are probably the only ones that have the potential to be good at both. Secondly, for any agency to align itself with either position is to shoot itself in the foot. So for ad agencies to position themselves around 'ideas' is potentially foolish. And for an agency to position itself around ROI is maybe likewise. Now, if as an agency you can become genuinely good at both left-brain and right-brain thinking, and reconcile the inherent differences in culture, your suitability for communications planning in the future should take a big step forward.

You need to understand both 'in-store' and 'out-of-store' communication

As we've seen, communications planning is all about the integration of in-store and out-of-store communication opportunities, but very

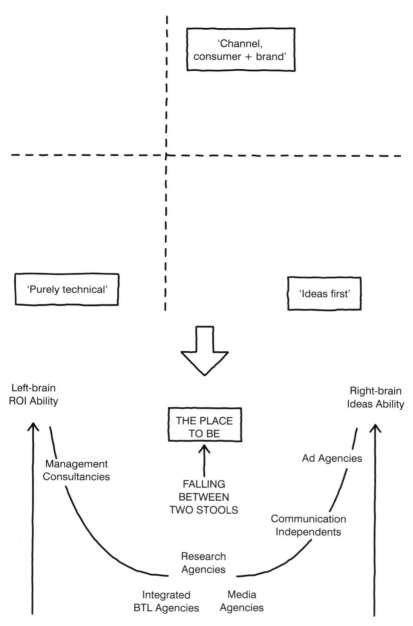

Fig. 5.2 Falling between two stools today . . .

few agencies actually understand both of these. Ad agencies, communication independents, media agencies and most integrated below-the-line agencies really only understand out-of-store communication opportunities, because their clients have always been marketing individuals. Sales promotions agencies or field marketing agencies really only understand in-store communications opportunities because their clients have always come from trade marketing. So marketing and trade marketing have had their own dedicated agencies.

There are a few agencies that understand both – so-called through-the-line agencies, like G2 Worldwide out of WPP, and even some research agencies like RI/Kantar. However, for all other agencies, being prepared for communications planning in the future means investing in new skills and new research to understand in-store communication. Here are a few examples of typical issues that need to be addressed:

- How to classify retail vehicles. These go beyond the obvious 'retail media' (plasma TV or trolleys) to include things like the gondola end or communication on the pack itself.
- How to attach metrics to in-store communication vehicles. What is the value of a gondola end in a Wal-Mart store in Miami? (Remember it won't have a ratecard!!) How many GRPs does it represent?
- What proportion of the total budget should go in-store, dependent on your objectives?
- What to say to shoppers, when, where in-store, according to both category and shopper mission. This is really complex and I think requires sustained, in-depth, single-source qualitative and quantitative research. It is one of the holy grails of research in many senses – which means big bucks!

Ignore in-store communication, as an agency, and you'll always have a big communications planning weakness. But get it right, and your inherent suitability for communications planning in the future will take another significant jump up.

It's not essential, but it helps to be independent of execution

Theoretically it would seem that communications planning demands independence of execution. How else can you be genuinely 360 degree, discipline- or solution-neutral in your perspective? This is certainly the view of the communication independents. John Harlow from Naked made this point at the 2004 AAAI conference in Shanghai. In answer to the question 'What's wrong at the moment with existing agencies?' he said:

Quite simply, the way they are structured is a major issue; they seek to offer both solutions (strategy) and then implement them (execution) – a conflict when the sheer range of strategic solutions far outweighs the expertise most agencies have in a limited number of channels. For example, most can comfortably produce advertising, but not necessarily content, PR, retail marketing and so on.

Of course, structural independence is an advantage, but it's not quite as simple as that. There is also the point of view that strategy needs to be linked to execution to keep in touch with what's happening at the 'coal face'. Communication planners need to be able to live in a 'grey zone' between objectivity and subjectivity. Certainly, their objectivity shouldn't be compromised even when it threatens the interests of their institution's executional income. But they must also be sympathetic to executional interests as well as to pure strategy and know when to bend. They also need to know what's possible and to be able to make things happen after the strategy is approved. Sharp-end interface is critical.

They need to know when the nature of a piece of creative content should override academic communication channel considerations: for example, when to 'bend' when outdoor or DM is technically better but creative have come up with a 'killer' ad idea for TV. They also need to know when the nature of media implementation should override academic communication channel considerations: for example, when magazines might be most appropriate but media implementation has managed to achieve a breakthrough deal with lots of value-add on radio. And they need to be in touch with people like media owners, who are at the sharp end of things. So sometimes implementational ideas can and should drive strategy, not vice versa. It all comes down to judgement and, at the end of the day, implementation drives success, not strategy, which at times can be somewhat abstract.

John Grant has this to add:

The idea of separating strategy and execution is against the interests of both, because as a strategist I'm never comfortable unless I'm dealing with executions and executional disciplines. You don't know if it's a good strategy until you start to see it being executed.

At the end of the day, I think too much can be made of 'being objective' in a structural sense. Now I do think that this might change in future, but at the moment '80% objectivity' is more than enough from most clients' points of view. So as an agency, being independent of execution offers an advantage – but it's not the be-all and end-all.

To summarise

I've said that from today's perspective, to improve your communications planning chances in the future, you need to be at the centre of the three approaches, and you need to understand both 'in-store' and 'out-of-store' communication. It also helps a bit to be independent of execution.

The relative importance of these is shown in Figure 5.3.

Is 'agency' the only structure we should be thinking about?

A lot of the discussion so far has assumed that an 'agency' (singular) is the only answer. But down the line, 'agency' might not turn out to be the right model at all. John Grant echoed this view when I interviewed him:

I wonder if an agency is the right model? There have been lots of attempts at this, none greatly successful. Naked have done well and are trying to go

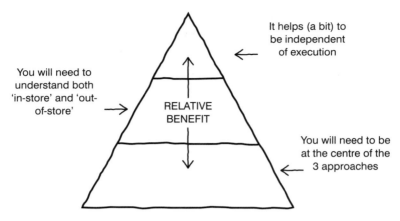

Fig. 5.3   Agencies – improving their chances.

worldwide but they are predicated upon something specific and local, a bit like hiring a production company. In any case, don't people always want tailors rather than off-the-peg? So that whatever system you've got has to be capable of reformulating or changing itself to serve P&G, in the same building as Innocent Smoothies or Yahoo or whoever.

With this sentiment as a springboard, let's look at some alternative ideas, to stir the pot and help us break out of the immediate tendency to default to 'agency'.

Clients

Clients themselves offer an obvious alternative to the agency model and there are many reasons why they might want to take on communications planning. But it's fair to say that very, very few clients could manage to pull it off alone at the moment. Either they don't have the data to understand communication channel effectiveness or they don't have the right internal culture and skills. The last point is particularly important. In general, most clients are not intuitive enough about communication and they have too many things on their plate, like setting objectives, briefing and managing others.

But all this could change. Clients could do communications planning themselves and the predominant skill set within marketing in particular could change and evolve. But this could only truly happen by creating an internal culture that could attract and retain the right people and could compete with the agency environment. This is the real challenge for clients, because the internal culture in many of these organisations is very corporate. And the people that they generally attract are those who enjoy and are good at the process of career building within a corporate environment.

The only person I spoke to who talked about the possibility of clients dominating the communications planning field was James Walker from Accenture. This is what he had to say:

I think if you look at the different agencies, then really you could bundle communications planning in various different ways. You could bundle it with the ad agencies [shown as A in Figure 5.4]. Or indeed you could bundle it with media planning and buying [shown as C in Figure 5.4]. And indeed, as and when media buying gets jettisoned in a holding company-owned entity with its own building, then it's even easier to envisage communications planning being bundled with media planning [shown as B in Figure 5.4].

However, I don't necessarily think it'll get bundled with the agencies' functions. My somewhat contrarian point of view is that it'll be the clients who lead this, not agencies. Clients will tool themselves up and empower themselves, because there's so much organisational change going on within clients at the moment, and there's so much demand within clients for financial accountability. And then there are systems. Everyone is demanding leaner organisations where there are more systems, so clients want really good systems which allow them to have visibility in terms of what's going on across different business units and across the different communication disciplines and channels.

However, I think you'll see some strong differences by category in terms of communications planning uptake and style. The businesses that are very customer centric – financial services, telcos, energy companies – obviously own their own data, tend to have strong analytics groups, and are pretty sophis-

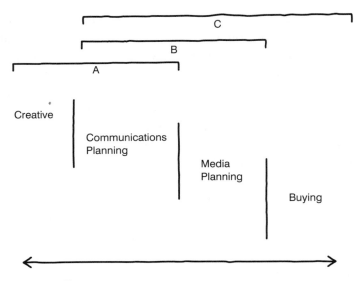

Fig. 5.4   Bundling.

ticated already in terms of how to do communications planning, whereas more classic categories like retailers or consumer goods will probably rely on their agencies a bit more, and for longer. After all, if you are trying to sell more baked beans, you can afford to have a more traditional approach.

Holding groups

Agency holding groups – the likes of Interpublic, Omnicom, WPP and Publicis – are another obvious alternative. Within a holding group, most operating companies are executional – all the ad agencies, design agencies, media agencies, below-the-line agencies and so on. Given that this is the case, it is logical to consider the creation of strategy companies that are a level up, at holding group level, independent of execution and therefore very objective.

It's also logical, given that more and more business is global and clients increasingly look for not just global coordination of their business, but also global strategy that cuts across geography and local management.

Furthermore, while a lot of the debate is very focused on today, the holding groups are the people who, arguably, have the ability to see beyond today. They have all the pieces in play, and are the ones who have potentially got the ability to anticipate the change that's coming and drive forward what needs to be done commercially. As opposed to the agencies, who are going to be more myopic and protectionist.

So one of the holding groups might choose to create something new and establish a new model. And I'm sure many of us have long wondered why these sorts of strategy entities haven't already been created by the holding groups.

Would this idea work? Well maybe, but there are a couple of fundamental flaws in this idea. The first flaw is client conflict – a strategy unit could only accept one client per category, which it could never do. It could not be seen to choose and arbitrate. The only way around this would be to create several 'holding group' strategy units. But in effect this would just create another string of executional agencies.

Related to this is the fact that clients have traditionally viewed the holding group model as being relatively toothless. This is being challenged at the moment by the increasing number of holding group pitches – 2004 witnessed these pitches for HSBC and Samsung. But this type of pitch makes other clients in the same categories nervous, and any venture by a holding group directly into communication strategy would make them even more nervous.

Some global clients obviously do want global thinking. The way around this for holding groups like WPP has been to create client managers who have a global remit, but come out of an executional agency. However, these individuals manage, they don't really write communication strategy.

The second flaw is the complexity of managing P&Ls. If a holding group created a communication strategy company, it would probably have to create client P&Ls to layer on top of operational agency

P&Ls. This would mean that the strategy company would be responsible for dividing the budget among types of executional agency within the group – cutting up the cake. And to compensate agencies for the inherent risk to their incomes, agency managers would need to be compensated based on both their own agency P&L as well as the broader holding group client P&L. All fine in theory, but in reality this would be an absolute nightmare, bogged down in horrendous politics.

When I spoke to Chris Ingram, he thought that the model of public companies mitigated against the holding group strategy company idea:

It's very tough to really coordinate strategy at a holding group level. How do you change this when agencies are judged by quarterly profit cycles? When there are constant earn-outs? Global agency networks are like vast distribution warehouses, all publicly owned. It's very difficult to make strategy important in this context, in a structural sense.

But there are ways around some of these issues. To start with, we could consider that a holding group solution might not directly involve the holding group. It would just be designed by a holding group. They could take pieces of existing agencies and massage them together. They might involve existing brand consultancies or research agencies, for example. And if such a solution was to be global, which clients would want, potentially you'd need, say, 25 offices around the world. You'd need scale. If you had 25 offices around the world, couldn't you get around conflict issues?

So I feel that a holding group solution could possibly emerge. It's certainly not impossible. But it would be tricky, politically. And I think each holding group would have a different philosophical view of whether communications planning should ultimately sit with the executional agencies or not.

Media owners/vendors

What about media owners? There's been a lot of talk lately in the UK about media owners or vendors effectively doing media planning. So for large conglomerate media owners or vendors, which have multiple content outlets, why not do their own form of communications planning directly with a client? Well, according to John Partilla from Time Warner, this is absolutely unrealistic.

There's an inherent conflict of interest. We can provide ideas that leverage our properties. But not more than that; because it'd be transparently self-serving.

Some lateral thinking

Apart from clients or holding groups, what are the other alternatives? Here are three thoughts.

The first idea is what could be referred to as 'distributed communications planning'. It is based on a more diffuse model, with communications planning sitting across different organisations. It still gets done, but just in different places. No one 'owns' it; rather, there's a shared responsibility to do it and deliver it together, in one document, which might be produced across two or three agencies.

Traditional agency thinking would generally say 'there must be a separate company that is responsible for it'. This is pragmatic, and it accepts the limitations of our business, which is not very grown up about these things. But it could also be seen as somewhat old-fashioned. The best strategies might well come out of inter-agency collaboration. If you can get highly talented, complementary people to work together – by creating the right conditions – they can create real magic. There's also an interesting book that points to the benefit of groups of individuals making decisions. It's called *The Wisdom of Crowds* by James Surowiecki (2004). Through some great examples, it shows how groups of experts are better at decision making than individuals; and that groups of experts plus laypeople are even better still.

So teams can have real benefits. But in the case of communications planning, I don't think we're talking about large teams working together; or indeed those horrendous workshops with 20 people in

them. Rather, I think the optimal 'distributed communication planning' model consists of two or three strategists from different agencies and disciplines – a small team of senior people, with roughly the
same headspace. But to achieve this takes good management from the
client. It takes individuals who are prepared to put the invisible agency
hierarchy to one side, and get on with each other as equals. And it
also means the client and agency individuals getting together frequently. So this lateral idea is about 'agencies' (plural). It's about coher-
ent teaming. And it is an absolutely plausible alternative to 'agency'
(singular), with some real potential benefits.

The second idea can be thought of as the 'strategy team for hire'.
This is based on the notion of a specific agency creating a team of
brand consultants and communication strategists, which could be
called into marketing departments to help with launches, repositions
or marketing problems. It would almost work as a 'Red Adair'-style
team that would act as a fulcrum, and do the '100 days to change the
world' type of thing. And indeed, if Richard Branson came into our
industry, this would be what he might do. He'd create a team of brand
consultants and communication strategists, and he'd call them Virgin
Consultants. Well, maybe!

The third idea I'll put on the table is outsourcing. In this scenario,
an agency would act more as a recruitment company, supplying personnel, rather than offering the traditional strategy, creative or implementation services. As an outsourcing agency, you'd get to understand
your clients' needs and you'd be able to supply them with the right
individuals to solve their communication issues. You'd specialise in the
coordination of teamwork and talent. This type of agency model
could be much more profitable than traditional agency models, by
taking perhaps as much as 25% of the fees. But is this idea realistic
in our industry? Again, no, I don't think so, although in other types
of industry it might work.

So now we've looked at a few alternatives to 'agency', in terms of
who does communications planning, and there are probably several
other alternatives I haven't put my finger on. But of the ones I've

looked at, there really are some realistic alternatives: certainly the 'distributed communications planning' model could work really well and, indeed, clients are a blindingly obvious alternative, in the near future, once they've put their minds to it.

How many winners will there be?

Thinking about this question across a broad range of industries, brand consultant John Grant thought there might be two types of winners:

Generally speaking there are two sorts of winners. There are those that specialise in low aspiration, high complexity, high volume of transactions; for example, a telco market. Here you end up with very big companies like UPS that manage complexity. The other winning segment tends to be based around high-value advice ideas. These types of company tend to be small and unique. So in the communications industry, you might end up with enormous media agencies or enormous 'integrated' agencies – like Ogilvy – and then tiny creative agencies. And these might include lots of creative specialisms we don't know much about now.

Charles Courtier of Mediaedge : cia thinks there won't necessarily be a 'fight' with one winner:

I don't think there will be a fight and someone will win. Rather, I think the whole industry will start to function in a different way over time, and in a bizarre way we will go back to being much closer to full service than we are now. But it won't be full service in the old format or structure. I think all the marketing services suppliers will be more integrated around these global clients rather than the very cherry-picking format which exists right now. So I hesitate to call it full service because that suggests it's going back to the full-service agency – I don't think it's that – but I don't think there'll be one obvious winner or loser, I think it'll end up being driven by global business and global clients, and the way marketing services are organised around a global client will be more at a holding group level and much more integrated, more client focused and organised – as opposed to from a discipline point of view.

I think that communications planning is going to be very dependent on both the left- and right-hand sides of the brain, and I think that the ROI issue, channel by channel, will be absolutely key. All the empirical research that exists, into consumption habits, across all channels, will play a very key role as well. All these areas – ROI, econometric modelling and consumption research – are areas where media agencies have already made an investment, because they've had to for traditional media, and it's an extremely expensive game to get into. There's no way you could justify from client fees or from an investment point of view at a WPP level that an ad agency goes and rebuys all of that investment, the research, the ROI stuff, the modelling; and I don't think you can do it without that.

So I think if you take what's happening now, or what appears to be starting now, and if you take it to the nth degree, I think structurally what will change is that media agencies by and large will morph into communications agencies, by some way, shape or form they'll have that channel-neutral capability, and it may be on the inside or through a Naked/Nylon type operation, but it'll belong to a media communications agency, and they will be the companies that will be required to be big and global.

I think the ad agency account planning function will evolve; but in the end I think it has to be linked heavily with the media communications agency. They are the obvious bridge. But I don't know if their future is going to be in ad agencies. It could be in a number of places by the way, not just in a media agency. But I don't know if it'll be in an ad agency.

I think in the future there'll be much less need for big global ad agencies. There'll be less need for them to be big and global, because with content, you don't need that in 83 countries around the world, you need one set of content which is adapted around the world, plugged into a distribution machine which will be the media communications agency. So in a way, ad agencies will have gone from being creative hotshops to global monolithic organisations; and I think they will move back towards being creative hotshops again. They'll be competing from a content point of view, with a whole load of other areas as well, content providers in general, including some media owners, people like Time Warner, or entertainment companies out of Hollywood. Content will be so much broader than ads, it could come from anywhere. But I think there will be less reason for McDonald's to need a creative agency in every market in the world.

That said, I think ad agencies will come out on top in terms of suppliers of content. You know at the moment they're on top in terms of the suppliers of advertising to clients, and that makes them. . . . just as I said a natural place to have channel planning is in a media agency, for all the reasons we talked about, equally the natural place for the supplier of content, the message and the visual nature of that message, the natural place to win on that is the ad agency. They have a head start on the competition in that area, because they are the arbiters of the advertising right now, which in most cases right now is the biggest chunk of the content.

◆

Key points made in this chapter

All agency types are having problems adapting and evolving. To look in more detail at their pros and cons:

- Media agencies:
  - Have several advantages: they understand what is and isn't possible, in the real world; they control the budget; and they are relatively homogeneous in their internal culture.
  - But on the other hand:
    - They are culturally quite executional; their understanding of insights is different to ad agencies. And they experience a 'strong desire to stay behind the computer'.
    - They have some confidence issues.
    - They're patchy in strategic delivery.
- Ad agencies:
  - Also have several real advantages, namely their relationships with clients; and the fact that only they can really provide strategy and creativity, joined up.
  - But on the other hand, it is claimed:
    - They are experts in an increasingly narrow field.
    - They have let the strategy piece erode irrevocably.
    - They have creative departments without a broad enough perspective.
- Integrated BTL agencies:
  - Their advantages are that they are the most genuinely 'through-the-line' in their outlook, and they also combine creativity, strategy and a respect for ROI.

- ○ On the downside, they are playing catch-up strategically with media agencies and ad agencies.
- Communication independents:
  - ○ Their strengths are their independence from execution, but also their culture, which celebrates strategy and creativity.
  - ○ On the other hand, they represent 'yet another agency to work with' for overstretched clients; and it is claimed that they don't have a strong enough back end.
- All of these agency problems can be framed by four internal factors:
  - ○ cultural sense of purpose, which is really driven from the top;
  - ○ new structures;
  - ○ new skills;
  - ○ new rigour.
- At the end of the day, looking at things from today's perspective, to succeed as an agency you need to be in the centre of the Strategy Map – in the centre of the three approaches, at the centre of the Silk Road. You need to be able to embrace both left brain and right brain; ideas and ROI.
- You need to understand both 'in-store' and 'out-of-store' communication.
- And it helps (but it is not essential) to be independent of execution.
- Looking beyond 'an agency' as the solution to communications planning, there are some other important alternatives to consider going forward:
  - ○ clients themselves;
  - ○ holding groups;
  - ○ media owners/vendors;
  - ○ more lateral ideas, such as 'distributed communications planning', 'strategy team for hire' or outsourcing.
- There won't necessarily be 'one winner'.

Part II
Learning to Fly

2005–2010

A period of great pressure to be accountable
A period of realism, knuckling down to it
A period of 'conscious incompetence'

6

A Slow Wind on the Water

Developments 2005–2010

The whole marketing and communications industry is in an extremely pragmatic and reactive phase of its development. It trades on the here and now and the day to day. Talking to Grant Millar, head of media for British Telecom, and a Marketing Society and ISBA member, he felt that this was indeed the case:

We're currently in a difficult environment. Technology's capability to deliver data far outstrips the ability of the average marketer to draw upon it in a cohesive way. This applies to channel performance or customer-level data, or any of the mountains in between. Basically we are awash with data that is open to endlessly varying specificity and interpretation. But there is nothing available that meaningfully draws the basic components together to provide objective and expert planning (in the widest definition of a means to reach customers). This means marketing lacks the ability to build a solid enough business case for communication that has a long-term perspective; and as a consequence, business in general is chasing short-term results.

Understandably, people working in this environment find it hard to make long-term predictions, by focusing on the pieces in play today. So to get some kind of grip on where communications planning is heading, it is important to pull back from the detail and debate in the agency world itself and take a helicopter view of the situation and the macro drivers that are shaping it. In the rest of this book, I'm going to put forward my view of what will happen over the next 15 years or so. The purpose of making such predictions is not to be able to say 'I told you so' but to stoke constructive discussion and pick the debate out of the rut that I think it's in. This is certainly how I see this book. So, here goes!

I believe that during the second half of the decade, there will be a slow but steady movement in the direction of communications planning. In part this will be propelled by the agencies themselves as they build up their skills base and start to push it more aggressively at clients. The amount of communications planning being done around the world will rise slowly. The small gains will come from countries like the US and Canada, as well as places like Germany and France. It'll be driven mainly by agencies up-trading some of their existing clients.

It will also evolve very much to the same pattern as you can see today – with a whole bunch of organisations doing it, namely the ad agencies, media agencies, integrated BTL agencies, communication independents, management consultants, research agencies and indeed manufacturing clients.

As the pressure for communications planning slowly builds between now and 2010, I believe that we will see three significant developments in the communications industry:

1. A new rigour in demonstrating ROI for marketing spend.
2. More emphasis on digital, direct and in-store communication.
3. A fundamental change in the nature of media buying.

Let's examine them one at a time.

Putting ROI at the heart of things

On the client side, there will be more demands for marketing to become more accountable than ever before. To quote Grant Millar again:

The average decision-making marketing person has so much more complexity in terms of the marketplace, but also intense pressure within their organisations to demonstrate a genuine return on every pound spent.

Ten years ago, agencies – research agencies, econometrics agencies and media agencies – identified ROI as a big issue in marketing communication. Since then marketing directors and chief executives have really got this message and are actively preaching its gospel; in fact, nowadays there is hardly an annual report that doesn't talk about media and marketing effectiveness. But for all the talk, marketing still finds it difficult to put ROI at the heart of things.

Rob Malcolm, president of global marketing sales and innovation, Diageo, has made some really good points in several speeches about looking to continually improve and build on ROI learning. This quote comes from one he gave in 2002 to The British Brands Group:

The great brand-building companies are rigorous in their analysis and in the measurement of results over time. They improve their track record of delivery by constantly learning, sharing this learning and embedding it in the organisation. This rigour takes many forms – quality business reviews, pre-market testing, concept and advertising research, the right kind of tracking and ROI analyses. If we could improve the effectiveness of our marketing spend by just 5% per year, the value we would create for the commercial enterprise would be tremendous. The supply-chain people in most organisations are struggling to find 1% or 2% cost savings to cover the cost of inflation. They constantly radically restructure organisations to get 2% to 3% out of overheads. When you think about the amount of money that is spent on building brands, the 5% improvement in that efficiency may be the best return a company can get. Why is it, then, that so many marketers shy away from the cost and efficiency challenge? Partly, it is because this has not been part of marketing culture. Marketers invent and create, while accountants measure. This is faulty thinking, and the sooner we recognize it as such and address it the better. (Malcolm, 2002)

Over the next few years, marketing, and indeed trade marketing, will no longer be able to pay mere lip service to ROI. Now that the easy cost cuts have been made in brand-owner companies, marketing and trade marketing will increasingly be on the rack, as managers and executives search for ways to get more out of their marketing communication efforts. This will be passed on to agencies in the form of demands for much more rigour in demonstrating effectiveness than we have ever seen before.

In response, the media agencies, integrated BTL agencies and research agencies will all develop 'second-generation' channel and discipline tools. In other words, the first-generation channel and discipline 'selectors' – agencies' proprietary ones, and industry ones like MCA© or TGI's Compose – will be superseded by tools that are more complex and can take into account a whole range of factors that influence choice of communication channel or discipline. Ad agencies will also import more and more media people and will be trying to fuse these new resources with their existing strategic planning base.

Clients will increasingly be looking for communications planning to help them change consumer behaviour directly (as opposed to changing attitudes first). This will demand more in-depth research and insight into how consumers relate to communication channels and categories. It will also mean changes in the communications budget split.

More emphasis on digital, direct and in-store communication

Direct and digital thrive

In many agency types, these two disciplines will get bigger, fuse and have their own networks of people around the world. More and more communication will follow the sort of model quoted below from an article by John Wood of Beechwood, in *Admap*:

Imagine we have a hypothetical new drinks launch in the spirit sector. Once distribution has been achieved, the process diverges. We select a list of category drinkers in the UK: we overlay it with demographic data and refine it down to geographical location tied into our distribution. We offer a free miniature of our brand to sample – simply by logging onto a website or calling a number. We collect and profile the data on those individuals and use this information to create a whole series of relevant benefits, all accessible via a website. We encourage opt-in to a programme of regular communications, offers and events.

Soon we have a database of over 20 000 regular drinkers. We know them individually and we communicate with them regularly via email at a very low cost and with very little time required. The database allows us to go out using matched lists for direct marketing and the online environment to recruit new drinkers, but we can now be more targeted and we start to generate the sort of volumes that drive the brand further into the mass market. This provides the justification for the use of more mass media to recruit new drinkers, many of whom join our club. The brand breaks the target of 50 000 cases, with 100 000 individuals on the database.

Three years from launch the client sits back content in the knowledge that over 50% of sales volume comes from a dedicated, loyal group of drinkers. The cost to recruit each new drinker through advertising, DM and online advertising has been calculated at £7 and the five-year value of new drinkers has been proved to be £50 . . . the cost is a fraction of the money that would have been spent on mass communication.

Database drives internet, drives direct communication, drives advertising, drives database. (Wood, 2005)

Growing importance of in-store communication

In the next five years, in-store communications planning will become more important to both brand owners and retailers. Brand owners in particular will start trying to spend more and more of their communication budget in-store, in more strategic, brand-centric ways. And retailers will be scrambling to work out how to react. Should they restrict the amount of communication so that it doesn't clutter up the aisles? Or should they encourage it, given that this is likely to mean new revenues that they haven't got their hands on before?

I believe that retailers will start to think a lot more about in-store communication options from a shopper's point of view. At the moment much in-store communication is far from optimal in terms of usefulness or friendliness to shoppers and does little to change shopper behaviour or build sales. Much of it is unsophisticated, low level, messy and confusing – and boils down to little more than in-store wallpaper and noise. In fact, a lot of the communication vehicles exist only because they have always been there, and not because they serve a meaningful purpose.

Of course, this situation differs by both retailer and category, as Casey Pronk, who heads up confectionery trade marketing globally for Nestlé, explained to me:

The health and beauty category is the highest margin earner in dry grocery for retailers; and it looks sensational in general. But confectionery in general is the second highest margin earner and it looks like it's got leprosy.

Certainly, some of the new technologies like plasma TV that have been going up rapidly in the US and Europe don't seem to help the point-of-purchase situation much. In most retailer stores, plasma TV screens have been positioned to reach the most 'eyeballs' while not obstructing the shelves, which means that they are stuck high above the aisles. But as a result, their potential to engage consumers is severely compromised. Who is going to strain their neck to watch something above them while dodging shopping trolleys? It's not that in-store plasma TV doesn't work; it's just that it doesn't work nearly as well as it could. In the rush to get plasma TV screen networks up and running and so compete with mainstream TV, I think some of the big retailers have created what will be looked back on in five years' time as a white elephant.

Because over the next five years, retailers will learn an awful lot about in-store communication. Communication vehicles will increasingly be based on fulfilling a clear and useful role that is relevant to certain in-store zones, targeting the right shoppers, and using the right type of communication content and tone.

This is borne out by shopper insight gained by Danielle Pinnington of research agency Shoppercentric. In her opinion, shoppers have learnt to read and work with traditional point of purchase based on 'roles' that have become accepted over time. So, for example, colour-coded tickets suggest retailer promotions to shoppers and dump bins suggest bundled offers. The lack of a clearly defined role for new media such as in-store plasma TV can confuse shoppers. She points out that this is exacerbated by the mixed content of in-store plasma TV, using loops that contain shopping information plus retailer advertising plus supplier advertising plus news and weather.

So in the near future, I think retailers will start to use in-store communication more strategically and they will strip out a lot of the communication vehicles you see today. Gone will be the clutter, the shelf-wobblers and 'noise' in the aisles, and in its place retailers will have installed a series of interactive technology devices – replacing the existing TV-like plasma screens with shelf-level interactive devices. And while these devices might block up some shelf space, their ability to engage shoppers and create change in their behaviour and sales will be much higher than existing paraphernalia, because the messages they contain will be linked to products immediately around them and the messages will be embedded in content that is useful. This sort of interactive shelf-level technology is already being tested by retailers such as Sainsbury's in the UK, as Figure 6.1 shows.

In the coming years, retailers will increasingly control in-store communication with a vice-like grip. To manufacturers, communication 'space' in-store will become much more limited and more highly sought after. Retailers will increasingly 'divide and conquer' by getting manufacturers to bid against each other for this communication space, much in the same way as they do today for promotional space like gondola ends or end caps.

Agencies will have two main roles to play in these new developments. First, they will help retailers themselves to identify and create new communication formats, possibly by setting up communication concept stores where new ideas, new layouts and new forms of communication furniture are developed and tested through live in-store qualitative research and via sales effect. Secondly, they can help brand

Fig. 6.1   In-store interactive plasma screen – Sainsbury's (UK). Reproduced by permission

owners navigate this rapidly evolving in-store communications arena and develop fruitful partnerships with the retailers.

The most obvious agency types to be able to rise to these challenges will be the integrated BTL agencies, research agencies and, increasingly, the media agencies, many of whom are getting their heads around retail.

Changes in media buying

For the last 10–15 years or so, in Europe and the US in particular, media buying has been a compelling source of competitive advantage between brand owners, in the form of media price or discounts. Clients could get a better media price or a bigger discount, either by virtue of their budget size or, indeed, who they appointed to buy for them. In Europe, for example, Carat has rocketed up the ladder in billings, because it was perceived to be cheaper and better at buying than any other media agency in the marketplace.

To clients, media planning was never really as important, because it wasn't as tangible as price or discount. As a marketing director, it wasn't something you could take back to your board as a demonstration of how well you were managing media, unlike good old discounts. Basically, what you bought wasn't as important as what you paid.

And historically, within a lot of media agencies, buyers have been the heroes. So in the early 1990s in the UK, you had some really big buying names, people like Tony Kenyon or Christine Walker. The culture of media agencies has reflected this reverence of buying, internally and externally. But this is now changing. It's not that media buying or media price is becoming less important. It's just that the competitive advantage to be gained between different buying points has diminished. Media price has become fairly even among all of the top buying points.

This was starting to become the case even before the creation of a group buying function. But in the last few years, the agency holding groups – the Omnicoms, Interpublics and WPPs of the world – have formed sub-holding groups for media. So Interpublic now has Magna, incorporating Universal McCann and Initiative Media. WPP now has GroupM, which incorporates Mediaedge:cia, MindShare and MediaCom. And Omnicom now has OPera in the UK, which incorporates OMD and PHD. Add Aegis in there as another, and there are currently four big group buying points. The only group outside the fold at the moment is Publicis Groupe, but it is actively considering the creation of a group entity, merging the negotiation units of Starcom Mediavest Group and ZenithOptimedia.

These sub-holding groups for media, or media holding groups as we could call them, have been set up to help foster media growth at a group level, as well as to combat the consolidation of media owner selling that has been happening globally. So they have been set up not to control the individual operating companies, but to provide services and resources that benefit from economies of scale and add benefit to clients. This includes things like IT and finance as well as some research projects that need group resource and can complement research at an operating company level to help to build competitive advantage. It also includes media negotiation, so that media holding group negotiations with media owners are fast becoming the norm in the US and in many markets in Europe. They have gone from passive back-room entities, to active front-room.

And it is rapidly becoming the case that, if your media is in one of the media holding group operating companies, then your negotiations and corresponding media price will be part of big holding group negotiations. You'll be in one of the big four. As a marketing director, as long as you have your buying done in one of the media holding group operating companies, you can effectively tick the buying box.

Now with media buying at a negotiation level starting to operate in more and more countries, at a media holding group level, it's only a stone's throw away from media buying itself operating separately from the individual media operating companies; in other words, for the buyers to get up and move their desks to a separate building that houses group media.

If this happens, it will be no great revelation. Many observers are already speculating that media buying will leave the media operating companies at some point. It is a logical outcome of the need to consolidate buying muscle, as well as a reflection of the increasing difficulty and specialisation in the buying arena, in terms of reaching audiences through the line. We are already seeing signs of this, with Magna's reported plan to add programming expertise and market intelligence to its offer.

But it is not a fait accompli, by any means. There are potential problems with this. First, there are client and market sensitivities in the area of holding group power and visibility. Historically, the essence of holding groups was they were relatively toothless and this 'mental model' includes their media component.

So there are sensitivities. Take WPP's recent purchase of Grey Global. Before sanctioning the deal, the European Commission waded into the fray, looking to scrutinise the deal under anti-trust rules.

Secondly, one can question the impact of removing buying from planning and implementation. Planner–buyer interaction is still important, after all. Isn't this the mistake (in their view) that creative agencies made when they let media go?

And thirdly, it might be stifled by politics. If buying relocates out of the operating companies, it will make the media holding groups stronger and the operating companies weaker. There will be some devolution in power. Nevertheless, I personally do believe that buying will relocate. This will come to pass at some point in the near future.

The question then is: Where are these new buying entities to be based? Do they need to be in central Manhattan or downtown Sydney? If the buyers do not necessarily need ongoing client interface in future, should we not be prepared to move these entities away from the more expensive rental property districts? There's been quite a lot of conjecture in this area. I personally believe that buying will remain close to planning and implementation, and indeed close to the offices of media owner sales representatives. In other words, they will stay in central Manhattan or downtown Sydney.

But the key point in all of this is that media buying is likely to relocate, isn't it? In the next five years, this will be a significant 'blip' in the relative sameness of the marketplace. This is indeed a key development, because it is likely to accelerate media agencies on their voyage towards communications planning, as it will remove a lot of their housekeeping issues and free them up culturally and in terms of investment focus. It will make the communications planning 'push' that is coming clients' way even stronger.

What are the implications for agencies?

In these very pragmatic times, clients that decide to go down the communications planning road will end up giving their business to whomever is easiest to give it to. They'll want it as pain free as possible, with the least political disruption. This will favour the main big agencies that they're already working with.

Furthermore, the integrated BTL agencies will benefit disproportionately from the changing channel mix, as will the media agencies who will also thrive because of the demand for more rigour and the relocation of media buying. In other words, the zeitgeist will be in their collective favour.

Clients will not necessarily hold out for the objectivity promised by the communication independents. They'll say, 80% objectivity will suffice for me, if I don't have to go through all the disruption of appointing another agency supplier.

So communication independents will get squeezed; and the older, more established among them will inevitably sell up to the holding groups. However, they will seek to continue with their independent positioning rather than be folded into the group media agencies. They will want to continue to run their own ships. But what they will be looking for is access to the back-office rigour that they've lacked until then − the research and the tools.

In the next five years how I see the communications planning market developing, in terms of size and share, is detailed in Figures 6.2–6.5.

The centre of gravity moves up and slightly to the left of the Strategy Map

The drive for more rigour and more data will start to tell in terms of how different agencies approach communications planning. This will mean that my Strategy Map changes slightly. Between 2005 and 2010 the centre of gravity will move up and slightly to the left (Figures 6.6 and 6.7).

Watching the wrong thing!

During this period, there will be no sudden escalation in the amount of communications planning in the marketplace. Within agencies, everyone will be holding out for PVRs to be the change agent, hoping that finally they create the impetus for communications planning to 'take off'.

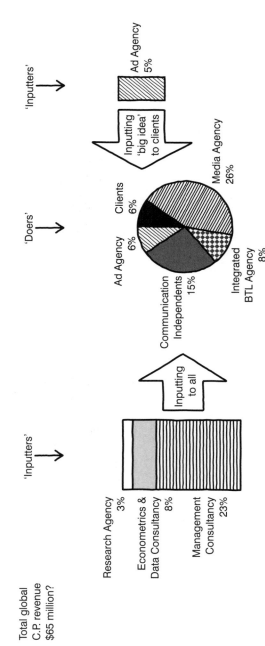

Fig. 6.2 Communications planning estimated size and share – 2005

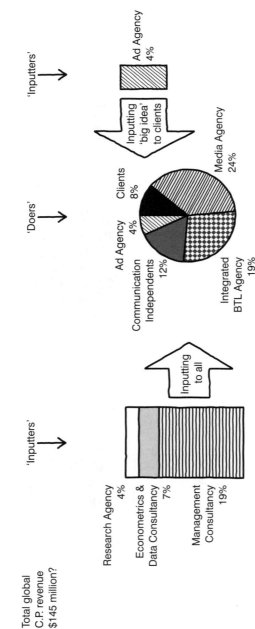

Fig. 6.3 Communications planning estimated size and share – 2010

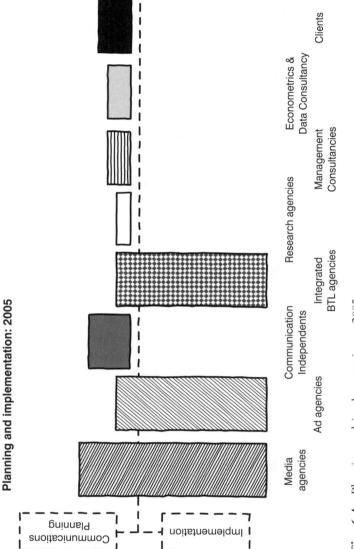

Fig. 6.4 Planning and implementation – 2005

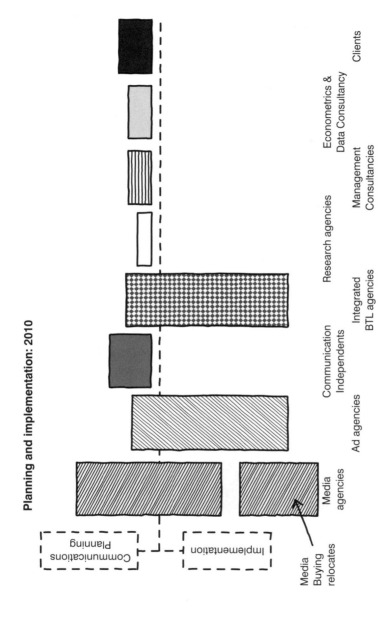

Fig. 6.5 Planning and implementation – 2010.

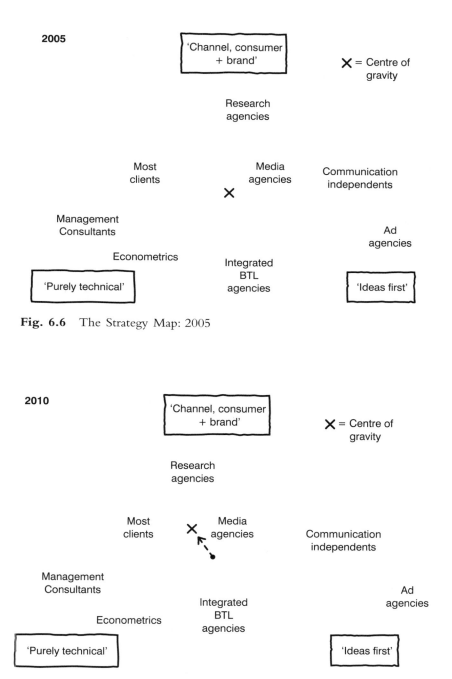

Fig. 6.6   The Strategy Map: 2005

Fig. 6.7   The Strategy Map: 2010

As I described earlier, the PVR is a high-profile new technology that allows consumers to avoid ads easily. Current research in multiple markets puts ad avoidance when viewing recorded programmes on a PVR at around 75%. And research has also shown that the longer a household has a PVR, the more it uses it and the more it screens out ads.

PVRs are likely to grow quickly in penetration terms over the next few years, in the US and Europe, and then in the rest of the world. They'll become the de facto norm. And these TV content storage devices are also likely to be emulated in other media forms, like digital radio.

All in all, consumers will be using TV and radio differently down the line; they'll increasingly be 'pulling' content from storage banks, rather than accepting those pushed at them on the networks. This technology will gradually start to liberate communications planning and break the back of the old model, founded on people's historical relationships with their TV sets.

But while the PVR will be important to the progress of communications planning, it won't be the technology that causes the 'pivotal moment'. And if we're holding out for PVRs to be the change agent, we'll be watching the wrong thing.

◆

Key points made in this chapter

2005–2010

- In the next five years, the amount of communications planning being done around the world will rise slowly. The small gains will come from countries like the US and Canada, as well as places like Germany and France. It will be driven mainly by agencies up-trading some of their existing clients.

- Within the system, there will be an increased pressure for account-ability. So while there won't necessarily be an overwhelming demand from clients for communications planning, there will be an overwhelming demand for ROI.
- Clients will be looking for communication to change behaviour directly. Within the media mix, there will be a rise in the amount of money spent on digital, direct and in-store communication.
- There will be a strong level of pragmatism among clients.
- On the agency side, media buying will relocate, freeing up the media planning function to move further upstream.
- These developments will mean that in the next five years, the media agencies and integrated BTL agencies will do better than the other players.
- Everyone will be waiting for a tipping point. Everyone will be preoccupied with PVRs as the technology that might bring this about. But they'll be watching the wrong thing.

7
The Soul Meter

Technology as the change agent that allows communications planning to 'take off'

I believe that communications planning will really start to take off some time around 2010. But the step change in its development won't come as a result of the factors discussed in Chapter 2 – changes in consumers' behaviour, the development of new communication channels or the need to integrate marketing and trade marketing. It won't even come as a result of the spread of PVRs, although all these factors will still be helping to build its momentum. The factor that will lift communications planning out of low-level orbit and into space will be a little piece of technology that nobody has really seen coming – a technology that allows us to forge a real link between marketing communication and its effect, using single-source data. It will be what I call the Soul Meter.

Over the past 60 years marketers and advertisers have spent billions in the attempt to understand human motivations and desires. What makes a person save for years to buy a certain make of car? What subconscious prompt makes you reach for a certain chocolate bar when you had only intended to buy a newspaper? Why work all year in a job you hate for the chance to spend a week in a resort that promises paradise? Despite the best efforts of armies of researchers, our answers to questions such as these are shaky at best. All too often we fall back on hunches and intuitions, gut feelings and instincts. And so when the chairman of the board demands of the brand manager

'How do we know our advertising really works?', the brand manager can only blush and bluff it. Because the truth is that deep down, if we're honest, nobody really knows for sure.

Forging a link between marketing spend and return on investment has long been the holy grail of the communications industry. But how do you measure the human heart? How do you put a meter on someone's soul? Surely any attempts to do so can at best deliver only very limited success? That may have been true in the past, but it is my belief that in the near future we are going to see technology emerge that has the ability to make a clear, measurable connection between a consumer's exposure to communication and their pur-chasing decisions: in short, a Soul Meter.

The type of technology I'm talking about is already being pioneered and used at the moment, with Arbitron and VNU's Project Apollo (aptly named, given the title of this book!). Here, respondents wear pager-like portable people meters (PPMs) that collect communication exposure data (at a brand level) that is then linked to sales data (at an SKU level). PPMs are already being used for ratings systems in Canada and Belgium. In the US, Procter & Gamble is one of the first brand owners to have signed up. But it's clear that over the next few years such devices will become far more sophisticated and far more commonplace. The measurement technology train is coming at a rapid rate, and much faster than we think.

In a few years' time we should be able to measure brand communi-cation exposure from all sorts of sources − from a logo on a T-shirt, to an ad on the back of a bus, to a gondola-end promotion in a supermarket, even to a branded lounge tent at a music festival. That's because all these things will be equipped with short-range transpon-ders that will register on receivers worn by volunteers on watches or spectacles or even embedded in their mobile phones or cars. Comparing this data with sales at, for example, a supermarket till can then be achieved with just a couple of clicks of the mouse. All of this will be single-source data. In other words, it will come from the same respondents. It will not rely on fusion or other integration techniques, which are much more suspect in terms of the conclusions they draw.

We will also be able to take single-source data research beyond 'communication exposure' and sales. From the same respondents we will be able to get a lot of information on things like frame of mind and shopper missions and how they influence shopping mode, as well as communication effectiveness. In fact as we've already mentioned, MindShare, with its Mindset research, is already using PDA technology to interact with consumers and ask them what mood or frame of mind they are in when they are exposed to communication.

The type of emergent technology I've described could deliver a true step change in our understanding of the marketing spend–ROI link, but even a slight improvement in our knowledge in this field will have a revolutionary effect on the communications industry. There's such a desire within client systems for marketing to be accountable somehow that if you can link communication to sales in any shape or form, clients will grab it and they won't look back. They won't necessarily even look at the finer detail in the short term.

Certainly, if things are to change over the next 20 years – and who genuinely believes that they won't? – the change will have to come from technology. Because in the puzzle, if we're honest, the only thing that *can* move quickly is the technology piece. It's the only thing that can force a big change. Clients and agencies won't do it, not if left to their own devices anyway. And there isn't a Richard Branson on the horizon to create the new communications planning agency of the future. But before we look in more detail at the technology that will drive the shift to communications, let's think about the nature of disruptive technologies in general.

Disruptive technology

In 2000, Clayton M. Christensen wrote a book called *The Innovator's Dilemma* in which he contrasts what he calls 'disruptive' technologies with 'sustaining' technologies. Most technologies are sustaining – they create gradual change and are targeted at known markets in which there are clear consumer needs. However, in the case of disruptive technology, the resultant change is rapid and the market applications are unknowable at the time and cannot be planned for. One is a deductive technology if you like (build it and they will come), and one is an inductive technology (meeting a consumer need).

Christensen's central thesis is that even the best companies, which have their antennae up and listen acutely to their customers, often stumble and fail to defend themselves against disruptive technologies, precisely because they are listening so intently. They study market trends carefully and they invest aggressively in new technologies that consumers claim to want. Yet they still lose out.

What happens in many markets is that technologies emerge that are not, at first, what the consumers think they want, or claim in research to want. They are usually cheaper and often have a functionality that is at a tangent to the direction the market has historically taken. But once their benefits become apparent, consumer opinion switches quickly in their favour. And for the established companies – good, successful companies – it is then usually too late to try to catch up with these runaway successes.

Christensen adopts a broad definition of 'technologies'. He means both technology in engineering terms and technology as a concept incorporating marketing, investment and managerial processes. One example of disruptive technology that he cites is Honda's invasion of the US motorcycle market. In the early 1960s, Honda was trying to compete with Harley Davidson in particular, in a market that was dominated by fast, powerful motorbikes. To do this, it dispatched three executives from Japan to sell Honda's equivalent, but to no avail. Most dealers refused even to take in the Honda product with its unproven heritage. What changed Honda's fortunes was the fact that these three individuals had brought with them their own Honda 'Supercub' delivery bikes from Japan – no-nonsense, cheap little bikes that Honda had designed for distributors and retailers to make deliveries in urban areas like Tokyo. And these three used to take their Supercub bikes off-road at the weekend, going up into the hills, where they proved to be a lot of fun. People soon started asking them to import the Supercub for them too. Consumer demand started to switch and the off-road bike phenomenon was born. Honda's fortunes changed overnight.

Of course, there are also many more up-to-date examples. In the mobile telephony market, SMS or texting was one of the most disruptive technologies of recent years. Although this relatively basic technology has provided excellent revenues to the mobile telephony industry, it has also caused all sorts of problems. After all, weren't consumers meant to adopt MMS and 3G services instead? SMS was something that beforehand I am sure was not 'what consumers wanted', whereas MMS and 3G no doubt were. In Europe, the German discount retailers Lidl and Aldi are disrupting the retail marketplace by severely undercutting the prices of the mainstream supermarkets in every country they enter. And what about digital photography for the consumer electronics market? Or downloading music for the music industry?

If one thinks of technology in terms of types of organisation, Christensen's thesis can also be applied to the communications industry. Here the disruptive technologies can be seen as both the media agency and the communication independent. From a global, last-10-year perspective, the media agency is definitely *the* disruptive technology. It is relatively cheap, in terms of the percentage commission it takes. And it has been really disruptive to all other agencies and to the market in general. Overlain on the disruption that the media agencies have caused are communication independents. In the markets where these exist, in the last five years, they have added greatly to the disruption already caused by the media agencies.

But what about the piece of technology that will trigger the next wave of discontinuity and disruption in the industry? Next, let's take a closer look at the Soul Meter itself.

The Soul Meter

It's clear to me that, taking the engineering view of technology, our measurement device, or Soul Meter, will be a very disruptive piece of technology indeed. By comparison, new communication channels, the PVRs and new in-store plasma technologies will all prove to be sustaining technologies.

But how realistic is a Soul Meter? My contention is that, since the advent of the barcode, such a measurement device has been inevitable. When barcodes came along, they had a catalytic effect on in-store marketing. They allowed retailers to be more innovative with promotions, by creating a lot of sales data that the retailer could capture. This data then allowed econometric modelling as a profession to develop. It also allowed businesses like Wal-Mart and Tesco to develop their whole business models around an understanding of their customer needs, by linking sales data with information about the individual through loyalty cards.

So now that sales data has become of considerable use and value, all that remains to make it even more valuable is to link it to communication. This will certainly be possible, and I've already floated some notions of the type of technology we might be talking about. But it will not be easy. The challenges are as follows.

Measuring exposure data through the line

Let's start here by going into a little more detail about VNU and Arbitron's Project Apollo. VNU and Arbitron are both global media and market research firms. VNU is most famous as the owner of ACNielsen sales data, while Arbitron has recently developed the portable people meter (PPM), which is a device, the size of a mobile phone, that is worn on the belt or wrist and 'hears' an inaudible code in the audio stream coming from a TV or radio ad (both at home and in-store) as well as from the internet. It actually detects what ads (at brand level) the respondent is exposed to. Some of the additional benefits are that it also detects how long they spend watching the TV, or indeed how long they spend in a store. It is even equipped with a motion sensor to know when the PPM is being carried.

The key to the technology is Arbitron's audio encoding system, which it has been developing since 1992. It is based on the science of 'psychoacoustic masking', which makes it possible to hide tiny bits of sound energy in normal audio output, which creates a distinctive 'fingerprint'.

Project Apollo combines Arbitron's PPM technology with VNU's ACNielsen Homescan consumer panel. As the name suggests, Home-scan respondents self-scan their shopping when they get home. So this project means that the PPM data and the self-scanning sales data are known for the same respondent.

Arbitron and VNU are now approaching brand owners, hoping to get them on board and signed up to the resultant data. P&G has already signed up and is helping to round up other like-minded brand owners to create a significant consortium. If all goes according to plan, this data will supplement existing marketing-mix modelling data sources in the short term – and in the long term, it will replace them.

There are a few drawbacks to this project. First, PPMs only measure electronic communication channels such as TV, radio and the inter-net at the moment. Secondly, this research is very expensive. And thirdly, the PPM uses a very narrow panel of people. In other words, the number of people on the Homescan panel who will be willing to accept the further burden of wearing a PPM device might repre-sent only 0.2% of the shopping population.

This raises a broader point. This is an area in which we'll need to ask for a lot of detail from the numbers. And that will be impossible if we are not dealing with large aggregate sales-volume figures and respondent numbers. Talking to the econometrician Paul Baker, who is MD of Ohal (the largest econometric modelling company in Europe) on this point, he took cars as a category example:

Go back to cars. When you talk about value sales, they're enormous numbers; whereas if you talk about volume, they're quite small. And volumes represent the decisions that are actually made. So if you think about the number of people exposed to a review of a car in a TV programme like *Top Gear*, it'd imply you'd need really big sample sizes to pick this kind of thing up accurately. (Baker, 2004)

Regardless of how Project Apollo does in the US (and no doubt with P&G's sponsorship it has a good chance of getting off the ground), the important point in a broader context is where this is all going. In the future, measuring exposure through the line will require developments in the 'meter' or receiver technology itself. But, as importantly, it will also require the 'embedding' of short-range transponders in virtually each and every potential communication channel. This could well be a big issue. After all, how would you feel if every billboard had such a device in it? Would we get freaked out by the thought of all the radio waves floating around us? The spectre of legislation raises its ugly head.

Going beyond exposure

Communication exposure data on its own may well be enough for some. Linked with sales, it will demonstrate communication effectiveness, if looked at for long enough through an ongoing panel of respondents. But I think we will also need to use the same technology that collects communication exposure and sales data to collect other information.

To get a full, holistic picture in terms of quantitative data, we will want to know 'what's on offer' – what is the communication message being pushed out there? And what is the retail product/price/ promotion combination? We can then match this with 'what is consumed' by the consumer – what products are bought? What products are actually used? And what communication is consumed or is the consumer exposed to?

The 'what products are actually used' element will be interesting. Perhaps with the emergence of RFID (Radio Frequency IDentification) tags on products, in households we will have a device that can scan the products we have in the home at any one time and know when a product has been used; a form of in-home stocktake. The so-called intelligent fridges are the first sign of this. But imagine you had a device on your PDA that could do the stocktake for you, and transform it instantly into a shopping list.

For respondents on single-source panels in future, you can imagine PDAs potentially being a key piece of technology. They could collect a lot of the quantitative data using embedded receiver technology that picks up communication exposure, and register products bought at store and those products used and consumed at home.

However, potentially the same device could also collect qualitative data. It could register consumers' attitudes to communication, to products and to shopping. It could help us build a dialogue with a respondent and understand their use of different communication channels in the context of their lifestyle. It could help us understand their receptivity and attitudes to different types of communication, as well as which communication channels are best suited to which communication task. It could also help us to get to grips with how they shop and choose within categories.

Will such a technology platform really be able to deliver good qualitative information? Will respondents interact with it and be prepared to treat it almost as a personal diary? Given younger consumers' willingness to interact with technology, I don't see why not. So while things like in-depth interviews will always be a good way to understand consumer attitudes and motivations, nevertheless a device like a PDA could in future also fulfil a qualitative function.

It's clear that getting ongoing single-source data sets in future – in particular if they go beyond 'sales and communication exposure' data – will require a lot of collaboration between parties: technologists, manufacturers, retailers, cable operators, mobile phone networks and media owners or vendors. No one today owns all the pieces of the puzzle. No one will be able to go it alone.

Disentangling the data

Disentangling data really means working out which factors explain sales movements and their relative strengths; and within this, which communication channels have had short-term and long-term effects.

To me, it seems very difficult to work out which communication channels and disciplines have had the most effect on sales. In an integrated campaign where you are using a range of through-the-line programmes, how do you work out whether a sales effect was caused by the creative, by the nature of the product being communicated or by different channels or disciplines?

By around 2010, we can expect there to be yet more communication channels and more complexity. So won't this make the process of disentanglement rather complex? Yes, absolutely it will. Modelling will become very complex. It certainly won't be a case of sticking all the data into the 'black box' and looking for the best fit. As Paul Baker of Ohal mentioned to me, it will be more like 'detective work'. But assuming that marketers can get high-quality data from single-source respondents, which applies across multiple retailers and multiple product categories, the quality of the data will be fantastic. As Paul states, 'the quality of the data will overcome the difficulties'.

Going beyond supermarket retailing

Will we also be creating single-source data pools for categories beyond supermarket retailing? What about in the car category? Will we also track sales of products against communication exposure? How do we do this effectively when consumers only buy a car every five years or so? What about in the financial services category? What about business-to-business categories?

I don't have the answers to these questions. But no doubt, in all categories technology will empower measurement and the same type of device we are talking about in grocery will be applied in different ways, across different categories.

Who might create a Soul Meter?

The value of such a piece of technology is immense. Think about the billions spent around the world every year on communication. So who apart from Arbitron and VNU might actually create a Soul Meter? There are actually quite a few people who would have a vested interest in doing this. For starters, there are the existing technology and media companies. In the UK at the moment, RAJAR (Radio Joint Audience Research) is looking to upgrade its audience measurement from 2007 onwards, and is considering its ratings technology options, which consist of Arbitron's PPMs, Italy-based Eurisko Media Monitor and a wristwatch system from Switzerland-based Gfk/Telecontroll. Of these, Arbitron's PPMs seem to be the most advanced, with their audio encoding system.

The point is that there are a few technology and media companies busy working on new technology as we speak. However, none of them seems to be truly connecting the audience measurement piece with the sales data piece. So in my view, the piece of technology that really gives us the quantum leap may indeed come out more from the sales data side. Here, I've a couple of thoughts about the kinds of companies that could do this.

Light

Marc Lewis, founder and CEO of Light, is a fascinating individual. He used to be an ad agency copywriter (and still dresses like one), but in his own words he was 'crap at it', so he started to learn about technology and became a genuine technology entrepreneur instead. His first venture took him into developing and patenting pop-up video technology for the internet. On selling this venture, he could probably have retired (while still in his 30s), but as any entrepreneur would, Marc ploughed back his profits into creating a new company, called Light.

Light is what is called a mobile marketing company. What this really means is that it uses mobile or cell phones as a medium for communicating; in this case, Light offers promotional couponing. This service is being used in the UK by the supermarket convenience store retailer Sainsbury's@Jacksons. A consumer can sign up in a supermarket to receive promotional offers and receive an immediate free gift. They are then sent (via text or SMS to their phone) a membership ID barcode. After this, on a weekly basis, they are sent promotional offers to their mobile phone – for example money-off products, which they can redeem at the till by showing the till assistant their membership barcode stored on their mobile phone.

Marc designed the business model with Unilever's CRM team and it is a robust, scalable solution with banking-level security standards developed in house by industry technical authorities. At the back end of it all is something called the Campaign Manager. When an enrolled customer is at the till, busy redeeming their offers, the items are scanned as normal by EPoS. EPoS communicates with the Campaign Manager and looks up the offers available to the member. If any of the items being promoted to the member are in the shopping basket, the discount is automatically given and the coupon is then cancelled.

But the Campaign Manager is also a very sophisticated data box, which captures information about coupon redemption for a member on an ongoing basis. Marc explains the benefit with this illustration:

Allow us to introduce you to Mr X. We don't know his name. In fact we are guessing it's a man, not a woman. All we knew about him when he joined our service was his mobile phone number, the make and model of his phone, his postcode and his date of birth. He asked for a free bottle of Grolsch beer when he registered. Since then, he has redeemed offers for beer, Lynx deodorant, fish fingers, pizza, more beer, Kellogg's multipack, McCain oven chips and cider. When we saw that he redeemed the Lynx deal, we sent him an offer for Sure. He didn't redeem it, so we sent him a more generous offer for Sure, but he didn't redeem that either. We then sent him a stingy deal for Lynx, but he didn't redeem that, although he did redeem another offer for beer that week, as well as a Philadelphia offer. Mr X always shops on a Wednesday between 11.10 a.m. and 12.25 p.m. and always pays cash. Ten of the nineteen offers that he has redeemed were multi-buys, six offers were money off and only three were percentage off. Mr X redeemed offers for Grolsch (free gift) and then bought Tetley beer and Strongbow cider when we sent him an offer. He likes a good deal on alcohol – he's never turned down an offer in that category.

So the Campaign Manager is actually a great way of collecting and using customer sales data on an ongoing basis. But over and above offering customers or members targeted promotional offers sent to their phones, Light and Sainsbury's@Jacksons have also done this by using general offers that are offered in-store at individual aisles. So if you are a member, and you see an offer for a Coca-Cola SKU at 25% off, you can text a number immediately and put the Coca-Cola in your basket. By the time you've reached the till to pay, the promotional offer will have been entered under your membership number on the Campaign Manager, and you'll automatically get the offer.

Sainsbury's@Jacksons is currently the only retailer running this service, but it certainly seems to be working. It has increased its revenue by 4.7%, by increasing the frequency of member visits to the stores and by ensuring that the offers are only redeemable there. It has not slowed down the speed at the till and it has given Sainsbury's@Jacksons, as well as the partnering FMCG companies, free customer loyalty data. Customers also seem to like it, because the offers are targeted at them, so Sainsbury's, Sainsbury's@Jacksons' much bigger parent and the third or fourth biggest UK retailer, is now rolling out Light's mobile couponing. In the UK, Light has interest from two mobile network operators that are keen to help develop and distribute this service. It is also looking at JVs in Europe, the Americas and Australasia.

Why do I think that this company and its technology has anything to do with the type of technology we're interested in – the type of technology that can link communication exposure to sales data? As I mentioned, I think that the right type of technology might come from the sales data side. In Light, we have good-quality sales data being captured, which is bubbling out of a promotional tool. But how might we link this to communication exposure? Light is certainly not blind to the importance of linking the two. To this end, it has developed an interactive TV campaign that it is running at the moment in Hull, UK. Here, it is using the Belmont ITV transmitter, which is a transmitter that is localised to Hull. I believe that it is transmitting promotional messages of two types: first, general messages asking customers to sign up; secondly, offers to existing members for specific offers (like the aisle offers, in which a member texts a number to accept the offer). In this way, it can directly gauge the responsiveness of TV promotional messages to sales for individuals and can cross-reference this with what it already knows about that person. It can then start slicing and dicing the data!

dunnhumby

In the context of communications planning, dunnhumby is one of the most interesting companies on the planet. Let me explain: dunnhumby is a company that collects retailer sales data and turns it into meaningful knowledge. It was set up in the UK in 1989 by husband and wife team Clive Humby and Edwina Dunn, and it got its big break in 1995 when it teamed up with the UK retailer Tesco to launch its Clubcard.

This little company has become a very big company, although you still don't see much about it, certainly not in the advertising-focused trade press. But it has revenues of around £30 million per annum and has grown outside the UK, opening offices in Ireland, the US and Australia. It has also started to work with clients other than Tesco, including Kroger in the US and Coles in Australia.

But it is Tesco that has really put dunnhumby on the map – and vice versa I guess. Back on 13 February 1995, Tesco made a decision that would catapult it to growth, from number 2 to number 1 in the UK, and worldwide. It decided to put the customer at the heart of the organisation and it decided to use data as a means of staying in touch with customers.

Tesco – through dunnhumby – did this with its Clubcard scheme. Since 1995, this loyalty scheme has become probably the most successful in the world. The programme boasts around 10 million active UK households and it captures 85% of weekly sales. Clubcard members get mailings four times a year, individualised according to the segment they fall under, geography, products bought in the past and interests. In fact, Tesco prints four million unique mailings – with roughly only two people ever getting the same exact mailing – a great example of what is known as 'mass customisation'. And the system certainly seems to work: coupon-redemption rates are in the 20–40% range on average, an extremely impressive figure.

Through the Clubcard data, Tesco has been able to tailor products and price points according to local store. This has consistently helped drive its growth and has helped improve the targeting of the direct mailings, so that they contribute to cost-effective sales uplifts. Tesco has also been able to run promotions in-store more effectively, by evaluating their effectiveness and tailoring them to those people who are most responsive to them, thereby reducing their overall cost. It even sells its Clubcard data to brand owners, media companies and research companies, which means that, at the end of the day, the Clubcard programme actually makes a slight profit.

This is all well and good, but why is dunnhumby so interesting in the context of communications planning? It is because the company has the potential to be a significant 'communications planning consultancy' in the future. And it is well aware of this possibility.

Think about it. It has access to sales data from a range of retailers – two of which are global top-10 players – particularly through loyalty cards, to an unheard of level of understanding. It understands which consumers buy what products – from food, to clothes, to electrical products, to financial services. It understands these same consumers' tastes in books and music and their sensitivity to price. It even understands their responsiveness to promotions in-store, and their responsiveness to couponing out-of-store. In fact, there is little it doesn't know, through data, about customers. And here, if you take Tesco for an example, we're talking about 11 million consumers. An 11 million sample base that Tesco gets in its stores every week.

What dunnhumby doesn't understand, through data, it seems keen to find out in other ways. For some of its clients, it also maps attitudinal insight onto the behavioural data it has. For example, for one global FMCG client (it also works with clients beyond retailers) it created a customer segmentation for a category, by modelling the loyalty data it had and identifying those individuals who were most responsive to the category. Then it also ran 1000 telephone interviews to improve its understanding of specific purchase barriers for these segments. As a result, it helped the client create mailings that were highly relevant to potential customers' attitudes and behaviours, addressed specific barriers and really helped drive up sales for the brand.

So really all dunnhumby now needs is the ability to fuse its customer knowledge and sales data with consumers' exposure to communication, and potentially their attitudes to communication. In theory, it then knows pretty much the lot. It has 'magical' data on its hands.

dunnhumby understands this only too well. In the recent past it has partnered with media owners to try to get a handle on a 'communication' database. In the UK in 2004, it created a strategic alliance with Thomson Intermedia, a media intelligence company that has advertising intelligence and together they have been cross-referencing data sets. One set is the Clubcard sales data from Tesco, across FMCG, electrical goods, clothing, health and beauty categories; the other set is consumer intelligence on TV, print, the internet and direct mail.

In the UK, dunnhumby is also working with BSkyB, a digital pay television operator. Here, dunnhumby helped BSkyB develop a segmentation to identify non-subscribers. But it is feasible that BSkyB has a quid pro quo going on here with data, passing back viewing information to dunnhumby. In the UK, dunnhumby has also been keen to show how its knowledge about Tesco's 11 million customers is representative of the population as a whole. And this allows it to tell you, as a client, who you should target nationally and even what your next piece of copy should say!

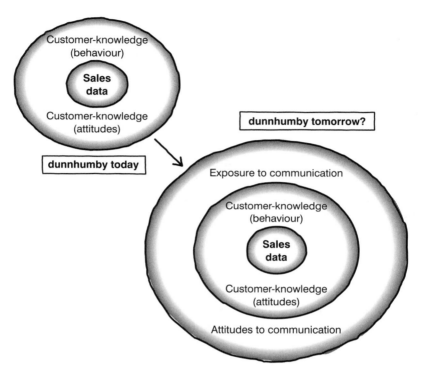

Fig. 7.1 Magical data.

This also points up an interesting opportunity for broadband and cable suppliers to emerge as important partners for retailers in future. With the convergence of TV, telephone and the internet, they will be in a position to track a consumer's exposure to brand communication through TV and web advertising as well as monitoring internet and telephone use. Without even setting out to do so, these broadband and cable suppliers have access to a goldmine of information about consumers.

dunnhumby underlined its ambitions recently by appointing Martin Hayward as its director of consumer strategy and futures. Martin came to dunnhumby from The Henley Centre, the WPP consultancy, where he was executive chairman. And before that, he was the founding managing director of BBH's Futures division. On joining, Martin commented:

dunnhumby represents the next generation of marketing consultancy, reinventing the whole process of how we track, understand and implement consumer trends to enhance long-term brand value. The research and consultancy worlds will look very different in the future as clients reap the benefits of truly actionable, integrated consumer insight.

So it seems to me that dunnhumby has the vision and is gearing up for the future. And why wouldn't it get on and create the piece of technology that will enable it to be 'master of the universe'? Or if it chooses not to do that itself, it could partner a technology company that could do it. And it could certainly obtain financial backing from its global retail clients. Stay tuned very closely on this one: dunnhumby is going to have a big say in things in the future!

Conclusion

The real space race of the 1960s was a time of great ambition and hope around the world. In 1960 Russia built Space City, amid the birch trees outside Moscow – a community that was secret for the first three years of its existence and housed the beginnings of Russia's cosmonaut training programme. At the time, Russia was winning the space race hands down and John F. Kennedy would have done anything for the knowledge and expertise inside Space City. But this was also far more than just a training centre. It was, in fact, a home for Russia's ideological fervour and self-belief. At a drunken gala dinner on the night of Yuri Gargarin's return from space, Nikita Krushchev shouted, 'Universal communism is just around the corner'. At the time, Russia and Space City were at the limits of human achievement and anything seemed possible.

While the Russians got into space first, as we all know the Americans got the first man on the moon. And although it was a spin-off from the Cold War, in many respects the space race was nevertheless humanity at its best, and we haven't come close to repeating the spirit and imagineering that characterised the decade since then. So yes, it was all about the US engineers versus the Russian engineers, and who could get the technology pieces working together most quickly. But there was also a lot of imagination and ambition involved in the design of the technology – and who would deny that the Apollo capsule that landed on the moon was indeed a beautiful object?

In the communication industry's space race, it seems that again imagineering will be vital. Technology will play just as important a role, but those who get there first will also need the same spirit and imagination, drive and ambition.

◆

Key points made in this chapter

2010

- The change has to come from technology. There's nowhere else it can really come from.
- So in maybe five years from now, a piece of technology will emerge that we haven't seen coming: a measurement device that will allow us to measure exposure to all sorts of communication, through the line, and link this to sales. This will mark a pivotal point.
- In hindsight it will be obvious, and we should have seen it coming. But our fixation with PVR technology will make us overlook this one.
- This technology will be disruptive, rather than sustaining, in its effect, rather like media agencies and communication independents are disruptive technologies in their own way.
- The challenges to building this technology device will be fourfold:
  - ○ measuring exposure data through the line;
  - ○ going beyond exposure;
  - ○ disentangling the data;
  - ○ going beyond supermarket retailing.
- There are nevertheless many parties who might be interested in developing such a device.
- There are existing players but also companies like Light or dunnhumby.

Part III
Cutting Through the Earth's Atmosphere

2010–2020

The marketing machine phase

A period where data will become the dominant driver of communications planning

A period of 'conscious competence'

8

The Dark Days of Data

Developments 2010–2015: data driving communications planning

Measure what is measurable, and make measurable what is not so. (Galileo Galilei)

By now you might be thinking that I like data – that I'm a numbers kind of person and a fan of tools and efficiency. But the truth is, I'm absolutely not. In fact, I've tried to ignore the numbers side of things for most of my life as a media planner. I've always felt that media long ago taught clients to judge it by numbers – just because the numbers were there to use – and that this was a big mistake. Instead, it should have taught clients that media was subjective and about judgement – which it truly is – and it should have spent more effort demonstrating its real contribution as *the pilots of a brand's behaviour* in a media or communication sense.

Nowadays, you rarely hear a 'trends' presentation that doesn't talk about media fragmentation or ad avoidance. But we seem to hide from the implication of this, which is that there is a growing chasm between 'potentially saw' ad figures, and 'actually saw and paid it a blind bit of notice' figures. We quote figures like '80% had the opportunity to see our ad three times', which might translate into '10%

actually saw it twice and 5% actually read it'. The deception of data is all too present in the media industry.

I believe that from around 2010 onwards, numbers will become the dominant driver of communications planning and I fear that the deception of data may get a lot worse. Benjamin Disraeli said that there were lies, damn lies and statistics. He was very right. But this hasn't held back the statisticians, has it? Of course, this doesn't mean that ideas won't still be important, but data will be the new toy in the marketing department. And here, the danger will be that there will be 'data for data's sake' and that the human voice will be lost. It's a bit like the frustration of dealing with a computer messaging system at the other of the phone instead of the human voice. Measurability may mean a quantum leap forward for marketing, but there is no doubt that creativity will suffer.

There is a clear parallel in the way that media agencies work. Media planning tells clients what to buy and media buying tells them what to pay for it. Logically, planning should drive a brand's growth more than buying, but because buying has always had a more easily graspable output – that is, a discount figure – it has often been seen as more important.

And the same thing will happen with data. Rightly or wrongly, once there is a graspable, direct ROI metric for communication, clients will hang on to it for all they are worth and marketing communication will become more accountable than ever before. Certainly, some time after 2010, we should start to see things changing radically.

Data storage and ownership

So let's assume that post 2010, we have the ability to link sales data to communication data. How and where will we store all of this data?

Let's look at the situation first with sales data. At the moment, most big retailers collect and store their own transactional data in data warehouses. This is in itself a massive undertaking and it requires real skill not to be overcome by the sheer volume available. When the UK retailer Safeway abandoned its ABC card several years ago, it complained that trying to generate insights was 'like drinking from a fire hose'; the data was simply overwhelming.

And indeed in 1997, KPMG stated that the largest organisations were losing share to the smaller companies, because of the amount of resources that they were soaking up in trying to build and use data warehouses. But by 2005, retailers have learnt a lot from their experience in the area of data storage and they have become masters of managing data and extracting knowledge (and even the occasional insight) from it.

Post 2010, we will be adding 'communication' to the transactional sales/loyalty data that exists with retailers, but this won't mean that the amount of data doubles. That's because we won't be looking at all consumers all the time in terms of communication. Rather, we will be looking at a few consumers, all of the time. And here, clients and indeed retailers will have a couple of choices.

A large manufacturing client could team up with a large retailer to look at a set of consumers for which they have sales and communication information. In other words, the manufacturer could add to the sales data that the retailer already has. Or a large client might want to try to control the data itself. It might have the communication data for a set of individuals, and it might want to buy in the sales data from, say, the top five retailers in a market – in effect, creating a wider link in terms of sales, rather than restricting it to one retailer.

However, it may well struggle to buy in sales data that it can tie together with communication data, for two reasons: the retailers might not give up the data; and also, because it would have to do this on the basis of known individuals. In other words, because it would have to set up a pool of respondents for communication data, on a known name/address/date of birth basis, linking this through to sales would mean asking the retailers for sales data against the same known individuals. Here, there could well be issues of customer privacy. Certainly in the UK, retailers are prohibited under the Data Protection Act from providing data on named individual customers to third parties; as in many other countries, their personal information has to remain confidential.

But this does not mean that these same big clients couldn't get their own sales data for these same individuals in other ways. For example, they could use a home-scan panel, in which individuals scan their own groceries. It's just that the quality of data would not be so good, because it would miss out on all the richness that can be obtained by retailers from their loyalty card data.

Whatever happens in this area of data ownership and control, there will be real political difficulties between manufacturer and retailer. The retailer owns the transactional data, but what about the communication data? Who will own that?

Post 2010, my belief is that it will be the retailers that will own the best-quality data sets, combining all they know about customers from their loyalty cards with communication information. Retailers will probably create their own 'datamarts' for these combined data sources, smaller silos of data that become, in effect, laboratories of customer attitudes and behaviour. These could be anywhere in the world and may well go to countries with low labour costs such as China or India. Indeed, retailers are already busy building the systems.

You can also envisage a situation whereby retailers in future will start pooling and combining sales and loyalty card data, creating alliances of sorts – a little like the airline alliances. Given that people shop in multiple retailers, combining data makes sense and this would make the value of the data exponentially higher to manufacturers. Nectar in the UK is starting to work this way already: it's a loyalty card amongst multiple retailers – Sainsbury's, Debenhams, BP, Barclays and many others. Maybe in future its members will include Wal-Mart and Carrefour.

However, this doesn't mean that retailers will end up doing communications planning for manufacturing clients themselves (what a thought for the FMCG clients that are already under the thumbs of the retailers!). Yes, the retailers could go out and hire communications planners, and just ask clients to specify a budget, from which they would then create a communication strategy for that client. But I don't think that retailers would see this as an area where they could compete effectively – and it would also mean one communications plan per retailer. How would clients combine these together seamlessly? It would seem to defeat the object of developing a communications plan in the first place, namely that it is one piece of holistic thinking.

So I think we are looking at a future in which retailers (and others) will choose to sell their combined data to clients at a high price, very much as they do now when they sell their transactional loyalty data to help suppliers (at a hefty price too!). So if you're an FMCG client in South Africa, for example, you can use Click's Clubcard data; in the UK, you can use Tesco's Clubcard data. You might target 'brand switchers' in a particular category, with a coupon in the retailer's mailings. Or you might, if you are the Dove deodorant brand manager for example, target consumers who have bought Dove body wash or cream bar in the past six months and include an offer in the retailer's mailings.

Retailers in the future are therefore likely to have two big businesses: selling products on shelf; and selling data to manufacturers.

Data use

Data usage is another key issue. Unless it is used wisely and transformed into knowledge that has a real-time effect, there will be very little point in having all this 'magical' data.

Big manufacturers like P&G have often been the pioneers in this area of capturing and exploring data. Often just a step behind the big manufacturers, the specialist companies that have historically understood how to extract real value from data are marketing econometric consultancies (like Ninah, Hudson River Group, Marketing Management Analytics, Pointlogic or Ohal), data/CRM agencies (like dunnhumby) and, indeed, management consultants (like IBM, Cap Gemini and Accenture). These companies will be important in the future, and they will be paid handsomely.

The IBMs and Accentures are the companies that are currently helping to put into manufacturer organisations, the automation, systems and dashboards to cope with all the data. In future, the whole econometrics thing will move more towards automation. Speaking to Stephan Bruneau, managing partner from Mediaedge:cia, he put it like this:

Today how we look at data is quite mechanical. Imagine data is like water. Today you have a well. And you go with your bucket to the well. It takes weeks to get the water, and take it to the farm. Tomorrow it'll be like huge hosepipes of data on demand. And someone will have to cope with this data, so you'll need the systems, automation, dashboards.

Regardless of who owns the data and where it is stored, these are the types of companies that will be telling clients what it all means. They will be the key 'inputters' in communications planning, inputting the following.

The 'who'

Segmentation in the future will measurably drive brand growth. Building strong brands will be even harder than it is today and segmentation will prove a very useful tool in identifying the consumer or customer segment with most growth and long-term profit potential, relative to the brand's situation and category. It will also be critical in understanding their needs and in how to get them to respond.

This segmentation will not be based on things like consumers' age, income or ethnicity; nor will it be based on geo-demographics. Using postcodes to target might have worked well in the past, but in future we will be able to do a lot better than this. We will be able to segment according to product sales and usage patterns, linked to responsiveness to different types of communication. We will understand how many and which consumers are most profitable short term and long term and what the role of communication is for them. Segmentation will be very 'real': no pseudo-measures needed!

The 'what'

Here, we will need to understand what consumers or customers care about, to be able to develop the best proposition. This can mean a client working with a research agency to develop insights. But increasingly, management consultants are advising clients in this area. For example, McKinsey has developed a simple grid, looking at relevance of attributes on the vertical, with differentiation on the horizontal. At the top left you have 'Antes', features that are important to consumers but are provided by all competitors at a similar level. At the top right you have 'Drivers', features that are both important to consumers and highly differentiated from those of the competition. At the bottom left you have 'Neutrals', features that are irrelevant to the consumers. And at the bottom right you have 'Fool's Gold', features that are distinctive but do not drive consumers' loyalty to a brand.

To populate this type of grid, and to work out the Antes and Drivers, management consultants use social science techniques to identify the underlying brand attributes driving loyalty within a specific segment of consumers. This is known as pathway modelling.

The 'where'

The same data, manipulated by the chief 'inputters' – econometrics agencies, data/CRM agencies and management consultants – will also be able to guide decisions on channel and discipline choice and share of budget.

By slicing and dicing the combined sales and communication data for a segment, we will understand how consumers on that segment respond to brand advertising and how this influences short-term and long-term sales of certain categories and, indeed, brands of products. We will also understand the same for events, promotions – you name it!

The current set of 'tools' that are used by the industry – those developed by individual media agencies, and indeed the industry-wide ones like MCA© and TGI's Compose – measure consumers' exposure to communication, or their attitudes to communication channels in a category, or how communication channels relate to a communication task. They do not link smoothly to sales on an ongoing basis.

But in future, we will be using econometric modelling to understand, for a consumer or customer segment, the key roles for communication channels and which will deliver short-term and (hopefully) long-term sales. We will certainly have much better and more integrated data, which will mean that the current 'tools' and the second-generation tools that follow them will go out the window.

The 'when'

The same data will also be able to guide us in understanding when to talk to our most promising segment(s), not just in terms of overall deployment strategies and whether we phase communication in episodes, bursts or continuous dialogue, but also in terms of mood and frame of mind to decide when certain brands, categories and communication channels are most effective.

Supporting the doers

These same chief 'inputters' will also be looking to help the 'doers' (such as the integrated BTL and media agencies) use the data, in a few ways.

First, they will ensure that there are feedback loops, to see what has worked and what hasn't, so that it can be acted on extremely quickly. This should ensure continual learning and adjustment of the communication spend. Is the communication working? If not, what should be done about it? Normally today this means monitoring key performance indicators (KPIs) that are only obtainable periodically or annually. But in future, we should be able to achieve feedback loops of just a few weeks' duration.

Secondly, they will help the 'doers' set the right KPIs in the first place. Post 2010, sales as a KPI will obviously become more important for communication; however, all KPIs that relate to behaviour will be important. And while we will need to understand how communication affects sales, we will only really understand it by looking at how the communication ladders up to sales, through a series of behavioural KPIs (such as trial rates or click-through rates on the web) or, indeed, through customer acquisition, cross-purchase and attrition rates.

Thirdly, they will supply and install systems and software that help see across geography, category and brand, both in terms of communication data as well as sales and other KPIs. This will be a form of new marketing resource management software, like Veridiem, Unica or Aprimo.

General implications

In general, improved data will prove a godsend to marketing, as Grant Millar of British Telecom admitted to me:

The way through all of this uncertainty and complexity, as you've correctly identified, is through the data. Data is what you can always present back, into the business, provided you've got a good grasp of it and can correlate it with performance. It's the only thing that people are going to stake their survival on, and it's the only way that marketing is going to flourish in this business environment.

And when we focus back specifically on communication measurability and its new-found link to sales, this will mean that we can finally start to prove that communications planning, as an approach, is far superior to the 'old way'. Those clients that do adopt communications planning will see immediate jumps in ROI and will tell other clients. In turn, this will mean that the number of clients taking up communications planning will accelerate quickly. And because clients will start to value it, practitioners of communications planning will finally be able to ask for good fees for it.

This will mark a watershed for the whole industry, as it will be the first time that strategy has been paid for properly. This might be the single biggest benefit of our Soul Meter. It will transform communications planning from a niched, unprofitable business model to a lucrative one. And the rest of this book is based on the premise that this does indeed happen.

Kees Kruythoff from Unilever, discussing this notion, commented:

I fully endorse your view that new technology will drive how we judge and we measure communication impact, and we will all start to be paid on that: agencies, marketing directors, everybody. It'll be a great jump forward . . . the intent has always been there, and now at last we'll be able to do it.

The management consultants will probably set the pricing benchmarks for all players and their revenue model will be adopted across the board. This means charging partly based on day rates and partly based on risk sharing (with the philosophy that if you can demonstrate success, you share the apple). Agencies in the past have been very poor at risk sharing and their deals have tended to be only fixed-fee. But at this point they will start to get more confident about what they can ask for.

So with these developments, it is likely that between the years 2010 and 2012 we will see a sharp leap in the revenue earned from communications planning. My thumb-suck estimate is that it might jump from £140 million to around £540 million, globally.

Post 2010, a brand's market valuation will also start to become an interesting area. A brand's market valuation is what a brand is worth; Interbrand and others publish these figures for the world's top brands, annually. They are a lot, lot higher than the book value of a brand – roughly 70% of the market value of McDonald's is in its brand, for example, and only 30% in its book value.

We will also start on a voyage of understanding into how much of a brand's market value is made up from the effect of communication, short term and long term. So we will start to be able to see the brand or market value being comprised of 'book value', 'communication value' and other.

This is logical enough. In many categories such as telcos, communication already has a direct effect on brand value. For example, British Telecom (which uses a data-driven approach to communications planning) sees its stock price go up when it records increases in broadband acquisition; when there are increases in broadband churn, its stock price goes down. And the acquisition and churn rates are responsive to communications planning.

Within the communications mix, digital, direct and interactive channels will become dominant.

As you would expect in the years after 2010, there will be a significant move to the left on my Strategy Map. All the players that have a handle on research, ROI and data will grow quickly in revenues.

When I spoke to Grant Millar, he underlined the real importance that the left-hand side of the map would play:

Most agencies, even looked at from today's perspective, are increasingly being worked out of the territory that you indicate on the left-hand side of your Strategy Map; whereas management consultants like Accenture's marketing science department are really performing here. They are taking a classic consultancy approach and outstripping all agencies in this area of rigour.

Management consultants

Management consultants bring out a variety of reactions in agency folk. On the whole agency people don't like management consult-

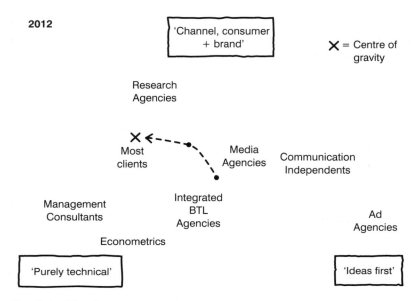

Fig. 8.1   The Strategy Map: 2012.

ants, but they are intrigued and slightly in awe of them. I suspect that the sense of awe comes from the 'grown-up' language they speak. It probably also comes from their power over clients at a very senior level, because they have great relationships with CEOs the world over.

Once communications planning starts to boom and there is real client demand, with significant revenues to be had, the management consultants will start to get very actively involved in this area. Here, as I've already suggested, they will be 'inputters' in the process. In other words, they will give strategic input of the type I've discussed earlier, but will not actually write the communication strategy or plan. However, at this juncture, I think they will have a decision to make. Do they stay just as 'inputters' or do they become 'doers' as well?

The relationship between 'inputters' and 'doers' will be interesting. The doers will be the general strategists, who can understand the ideas and insight piece *and* the data piece. They will be the ones who can take the input, which will largely be data-driven knowledge, and use it wisely to take brands forward. This will obviously mean having huge respect for what the data-driven knowledge is pointing towards, because let's not forget that the ROI of communication will be in the balance. However, it might be that the doers sometimes need to go beyond the data-driven knowledge and use a bit of intuition.

But to flip things around, it might also be important to remove any doer temptation from the inputters. Data is easy to twist to suit a purpose, so clients in particular will want input into the 'who', the 'what', the 'where' and the 'when', from objective sources, and they will also want the ROI from communication to be judged and monitored independently. This last point would suggest that should management consultants enter the doer space, they might end up being asked to 'mark their own homework'. I guess how this works out will depend on clients' views at the time.

For all of these reasons I believe that it will be to the benefit of everyone if the doers and inputters remain mutually exclusive in most cases. Regardless of whether management consultancies take the plunge into becoming doers (and I am going to assume they don't), they will need some new skills within their organisations. Here, they might poach a few people or, potentially, even buy a communication independent or two! If they did go the latter route, for example if an Accenture were to buy a Naked or a Bellamy Hayden, this would not necessarily mean that the communication independent would be subsumed within the management consultancy. It would probably be left to run itself independently, but there would be an exchange of skills going on behind the scenes.

Research agencies

Post 2010, research agencies will still be doing the quantitative and qualitative research that they currently do. And the insights that they gain from this, on things like consumer attitudes and shopper studies, will be more important than ever, so research agencies will grow naturally.

But at this point, the focus from the research agencies will be in the area of econometrics and data. Already they are getting into this game. Recently, for example, Millward Brown launched a 'brand investment unit' called Millward Brown Optimor. Headed up by Joanna Seddon, Nikhil Gharekhan and Marco Forato, it is designed to provide port-folio strategy, analytics and ROI measurement.

Research agencies will also be facing the same dilemma as manage-ment consultants about whether they should get into 'doing'. They already seem to want to and they could easily import the skills. But again, the central question will come down to clients' attitudes to objectivity in this area, particularly around econometrics and data, and whether as doers they would end up marking their own homework.

In Figures 8.2 and 8.3 you can see how I think things will look in 2012. The size of the blocks represents their value. You can see the value that I think will be attached to the inputters on the left-hand side. You can also see the fusing of research agencies and marketing econometrics consultancies.

Media agencies and integrated BTL agencies

In the mainstream agency world, the media agencies and integrated BTL agencies that are already at the centre of things should certainly do well. After years of 'pushing' communications planning at clients, they should find that clients will be starting to 'pull' themselves. These agency types will be making good incomes out of communications planning and, as a result of the increasing revenue in the strategy area, there will be far more emphasis placed on strategy within their organ-isations, at cultural and structural levels, and in terms of recruiting, developing and retaining communications planning skills.

The three concentric circles I drew on page 94 will now become key to these agencies, as they seek to win communications planning assignments. The media agencies will be competing with the inte-grated BTL agencies and these agency types will be competing within themselves. Luckily, there will be plenty of business to go round.

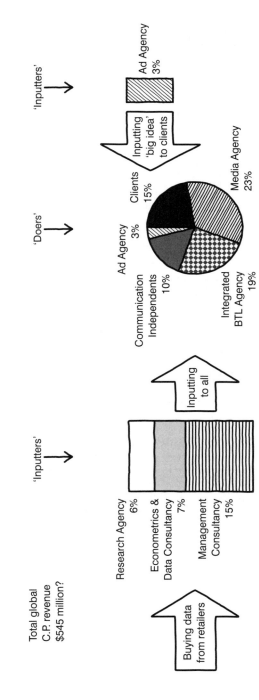

Fig. 8.2 Communications planning estimated size and share – 2012.

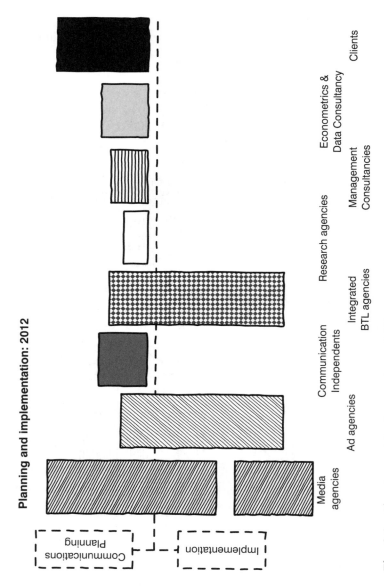

Fig. 8.3 Planning and implementation – 2012.

Between these two agency types, there will also probably be an exchange of skills. Media agencies will hire planners from integrated BTL agencies and vice versa.

Many media agencies already own econometric consultancies, or have econometric units within their walls. From 2010 onwards, these consultancies and units will flourish and the media agencies will gain substantially from them. However, these econometrics units and consultancies will have to be careful to remain separately positioned from their media agency parents, so that they can be seen as objective. As I've mentioned, objectivity in terms of communication ROI will become important, and the econometrics consultancies will be some of the strongest client advisers, so they definitely can't be seen to be marking their own homework!

Independence of execution?

In Chapter 5 I discussed the 'being independent of execution makes you more objective' card that is played by the communication independents. I surmised that though this is an advantage, it is not critical to most clients in 2005. So how important will it be post 2010? This is a tricky question.

At one level, being objective will be more important than ever. But objectivity will be easier to see. The implications of the data will be clear for all, so for a planner post 2010 – although life won't be as simple as 'following the data' or simply using a black-box tool of some kind – to ignore it, or to be obviously subjective, will simply not cut the mustard.

Furthermore, the agencies that will be doing most communications planning – the integrated BTL and media agencies – will still derive most of their income from through-the-line execution, maybe as much as 70%. So the degree to which they struggle with real objectivity and a 360-degree perspective will depend on how broadly they've managed to spread their implementational wings between now and then – because the more widely spread they are, the more neutral they will be. For media agencies, it will depend on how far they've covered non-media implementation, while for integrated BTL agencies, the issue will be how far they've gone outside core competencies like DM and promotions.

So I believe that 'objectivity' will be more important than ever; but it will also be something of a given – a 'passport factor'.

Communication independents

Far from being subsumed by the media agencies, in these times of healthy communications planning income, this agency type will thrive and more and more communication independents will start up. The reason for this will simply be that there is enough income and business around to sustain them.

Because of their fresh thinking and entrepreneurial spirit, communication independents will continue to attract senior individuals from other agencies, keen to start their own businesses. They in turn will bring new clients with them. As a result, even more so than today, clients will see communication independents as places where huge amounts of the right talent reside.

However, there is a big 'but' to all this. To do well in these times, the communication independents will need to be connected to a 'back end' that gives them access to the right sorts of rigour. Granted, we can expect the inputters to be feeding good knowledge and insight from the data. But the communication independents that do best will still be those that can show their own rigour credentials.

As a result, existing players that are privately owned will probably sell up, while staying separate and running themselves separately. Who might they sell to? Well, they might sell to media agencies. But in this case there would always be a temptation for the media agency in question to pull the independent in and absorb it for the benefit of the media agency brand. So instead, they will probably sell up to those slightly removed from doing and execution – namely, holding groups or management consultancies.

Although there are no barriers to entry for communication independent start-ups today, in the future the need for rigour will impose significant financial obstacles. So start-ups in this area will either be funded by venture capitalists, or indeed will be established as JVs with organisations that can offer research and tools.

All in all, communication independents will be more 'business' focused and more 'upstream' than many of them are today.

What about the ad agencies?

At this time, with data as the driving influence in communications planning, 'classic' ad agencies may struggle; while they might seriously want to get into the data modelling side, the costs will be prohibitive.

That said, the more integrated types of ad agencies, those that have already made moves into this broader strategy area – the likes of TBWA and Ogilvy – will probably be fine, and by this stage they may have merged their ad agency strategic planning people with their DM planning people. So they might be creating planners who have genuine expertise across above-the-line and DM. Where these people – effectively now communications planners – sit will be interesting. My guess is that they might start sitting on the DM side. So an Ogilvy/Ogilvy One 'super-planner' might sit in Ogilvy One, or a TBWA and TEQUILA\ 'super-planner' might sit in TEQUILA\.

However, I believe that those agencies that see themselves as positioned purely around creativity and content production – ad creation, but also increasingly content of all forms, including things like music and films – will find it increasingly hard to keep in the strategy game.

This will mark the very start of a bifurcation of the ad agencies that I see happening in future, into those that are more oriented towards 'strategy + creative', and those that are more inclined to 'creative + production'.

Conclusion

My best guess is that in the years immediately following 2010, as data and the ROI–communications link move centre stage, we will see a boom in communications planning. The overwhelming importance of data will favour those agency types that can demonstrate a more rigorous data-driven approach, over those that find it difficult to tear themselves away from their creative and intuitive heritage. For the same reason, the management consultancies will be licking their lips at the chance to muscle into the communications arena with their armies of analysts and number crunchers. Clients desperate to justify their communication spend will no doubt be happy, as they should find that life gets easier – at least for a while. But their feeling of enlightenment may well be an illusion, because I fear that true clarity of thought and genuinely penetrating ideas may well get lost in the haze of facts and figures thrown up by the new metrics and technologies. Indeed, we may one day look back on this period as the dark days of data.

◆

Key points made in this chapter

2012

- Once there is a direct ROI metric for communication, clients will grasp it with all their might; and post 2010, data will become the dominant driver of communications planning.
- It is probable that the retailers will own the combined sales/loyalty and communication data sets in future.
- Although this could put them in a position of doing a client's communications planning for them, the chances are that they will not see this as an area where they could compete effectively.
- So they will prefer to just sell the data sets to clients.

- The companies that have historically understood how to extract real value from data on behalf of clients – marketing econometrics consultancies, data/CRM agencies and management consultancies – will be very important in future.
- They will be the key 'inputters' to communications planning. And they will input:
  - ○ the 'who' – segmentation based on product sales/usage and responsiveness to different types of communication;
  - ○ the 'what' – best propositions;
  - ○ the 'where' – optimal combinations of communication channels and disciplines;
  - ○ the 'when' – deployment.
- The number of clients that take up communications planning will accelerate quickly.
- Clients will now be valuing strategy and paying well for it, marking a huge turning point in the industry.
- The management consultants' revenue model (payment by results; portion at risk) will be widely adopted.
- Post 2010, clients will start to better understand their brands' market valuation.
- Post 2010, agencies in general will be doing well; but there will be a move to the left on the Strategy Map and those players on the left will do disproportionately well.

9
Antarctica

Clients starting to want to own and do communications planning

No one owns Antarctica. It is governed by the Antarctic Treaty, which was signed in 1959 by 45 member nations who declared that the continent should be used peacefully for the mutual benefit of all humankind. But this hasn't stopped Argentina, Chile, Australia, Norway, the United Kingdom or France from – somewhat preposterously – making territorial claims on it. There has even been a claim from the unrecognised state of Westarctica, whatever that might be. None of the existing claims is recognised by other nations, by the Antarctic Treaty or by international law. So the nations of the world have been engaged in a form of 'space race' for Antarctica – a race for the territory. They have all assumed that by sticking up their flags and building infrastructure, they will inevitably be at an advantage down the line. It's all rather like a Klondike land grab.

And some might say that this is rather similar to the situation with agencies and communications planning. Agencies seem to be engaged in a tussle over territory that isn't really theirs to own. They assume that by acting proprietorially and building infrastructure, they will be able to convince others that they are the rightful inheritors of the communications planning mantle. But the truth is, agencies have no more natural right to it than, say, the British do to the mineral wealth under the polar plateau.

If anybody can be said to 'own' communications planning, it is probably the brand owners. And it is my belief that somewhere down the line, perhaps around 2015, they will start to take it back from agencies and do it themselves. Not all clients will try to do it. But those who do will do so because they believe that it is a core competency of marketing and that they can do it better than, or at least as well as, the agencies. Let me explain my thinking.

Bringing it all back home

Let's start off with the situation today. There are four main reasons why most clients are not really trying to do communications planning (en masse) at the moment themselves.

First, there are headcount issues. There are not enough people within marketing departments to do it; and therefore existing marketers are far too stretched and busy. This is because, for chief financial officers, having people on the books is potentially a financial risk. When you want to get rid of them, you have to pay them large sums of money. When you look at assets and liabilities, lots of people mean lots of liabilities in terms of redundancy pay. So client companies have slimmed down the marketing function and outsourced a lot of the responsibility to agencies. After all, as a client if you don't like what an agency comes back with, it's much easier to get rid of it cheaply. But as a result of all of this slimming down and outsourcing, clients have painted themselves or been painted into a smaller and smaller corner.

Secondly, most clients just don't have the right skill set. They are generally good managers — they are good at managing other people and briefing agencies. And they are good at managing spreadsheets. But they are not necessarily good at intuitive communications planning thinking or producing creative 'leaps'.

Thirdly, most clients aren't really thinking like this yet. They're just trying to make today work. But when clients feel they understand the skill sets, and the process and capabilities — which they don't at the moment – then they might say, 'we can do this'. At the moment, however, it's all too dynamic and unclear.

Fourthly, there is a perceived 'in-house' problem, as Dick Metzler at DHL Express explained to me:

One potential problem with clients doing communications planning them-selves in the future . . . it's potentially the same limitation you have with in-house creative. It becomes a bit incestuous. Whereas one of the reasons you deal with an agency is to have best-in-class talent, on an ongoing basis. And if you have a team that is not performing, as a client you always have the ability to change the situation. That said, there will be clients who inevitably insource nonetheless, because creating your own communications planning unit internally can cost a lot less for mark-up reasons alone. Even if you had to turn them over every year or so, it might still make financial sense.

Nevertheless I believe that none of these current issues will stop clients who want to, from regaining the communications planning role in future.

They always used to do it

In the past, clients – particularly brand and marketing managers – always used to decide how to carve up the budget. It was a core com-petency. So why wouldn't they want to do the same again in future? When I put this point of view to Nick Emery of MindShare, he felt that there was a certain obvious logic to it:

It certainly makes sense in some respects. Part of the reason that agencies are trying to reinvent themselves is because there is a skills gap within a lot of client marketing departments. So what they are asking us to do in terms of communications planning or managing the account is what they should be doing really. So yes, that would make sense.

The 4 Ps

If you look at the 4 Ps – Product, Price, Promotion and Place – over the last 20 years, a lot of marketing's influence has been stripped away.

This point was made eloquently by Stephan Bruneau of Mediaedge: cia when I spoke to him:

If we look at Product first of all, here R&D has given marketing a hammering. With all the innovation going on within manufacturing organisations, R&D departments have grown so much in importance. L'Oréal, for example, often states that they spend 3% turnover on R&D. So marketing's influence on Product has diminished. If we look at Price, here the growing power of retailers and EDLP (Every Day Low Pricing) has meant that marketing has less and less influence on it. Retailers have the dominant say in the price of a product on shelf. Turning now to Promotion. Here, globalisation of communication has really debilitated local marketing individuals. If you're a local marketing manager, you often can't decide the main creative work because it's global; you can't influence launches because they're global. And when it comes to in-store communication, you're in the hands of retailers. You're completely paralysed. So at the moment it's very frustrating for marketing. And now with communications planning, here's an opportunity to put marketing at the heart of the organisation again. It makes perfect sense for marketing to want to do it.

Functional reasons – data

As we saw in the last chapter, the ability to link communications to sales will have a huge effect on communications planning. It will become more widely adopted and highly valued, and those who benefit most will initially be 'doer' agencies such as the integrated BTL and media agencies and the communication independents, as well as 'inputter' consultancies that can manipulate and make sense of the data. These agencies and consultancies will have started to make big strides up the ladder to the so-called top table.

But in client organisations, as a result of these changes, marketing will have become much more accountable and, indeed, important. Finance directors and marketing directors will have become friends. As a result, marketing will also have started to climb up its own ladder, in terms of importance and respectability. It will be elevated internally and many more marketers will start to get places on client company boards.

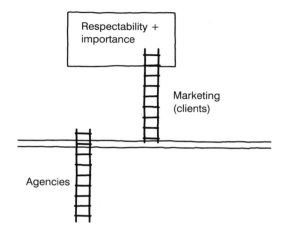

Fig. 9.1 Marketing and agencies both climbing their own 'ladders'.

All of this will be based on marketing's ability to prove that communication actually works. There might even be a situation in which
not only are agency and consultancy fees dependent on the ROI of
communication, but the marketing director's salary and bonus are as
well. As a consequence, many of these marketing individuals will
increasingly feel that if they are going to be so much more responsible for the effectiveness of communication, they will need to control
it much more tightly. As a price for the added responsibility, they will
demand (of the CEO) that communications planning comes back in
house.

Functional reasons − brand governance

Since the Enron scandal, good corporate governance is something that
has featured on the agenda of many senior managers. To protect
society and investors, company directors are required to act with fair-
ness, accountability, responsibility and transparency in all of their decision making. It is also something that can pay for itself, as it gives
stakeholders and shareholders confidence. According to McKinsey,
84% of global institutional investors would pay a premium for shares
in a well-governed company.

Now, if brands are generally a company's most important assets, shouldn't corporate governance also cascade down to brand governance? This is a notion that Rob Hill of Ogilvy South Africa believes will come into the spotlight soon, and he has written several articles on the subject:

If brands are the most significant assets owned and operated by many companies, the way that they are managed should be assessed for risk and evaluated in terms of governance principles . . . But brands are not conventional assets, and managing brands is not a science: it is more often a complex and highly subjective endeavour. It involves people and can be 'opinion intensive' . . . in the worst scenarios, brand management can become politicised where personal power plays and 'factional fighting' determine direction and strategy. (Hill, 2005)

There is no doubt that brand governance is coming into the spotlight. Think of how many times in the past big, long-term sponsorships were signed up for, based on hugely subjective decision making. In the future, things like this are likely to happen less and less often. Consumers nowadays also watch brands like hawks and increasingly criticise them on ethical grounds. Corporate social responsibility, or CSR as it's called, is big news.

Alan Brew of EnterpriseIG talked about this issue at an Economist conference in March 2005. He believes that organisations need to do more than just pay lip service to CSR. They need to join up reputation management and brand, under something he called a 'compelling truth'. They need to find something within themselves that is compelling and true, and then ensure that this filters through, via their staff behaviour, to what they say and do in terms of brand communication. So EnterpriseIG sees corporate governance and brand governance fusing together in future as well.

Brand governance points to marketing being more accountable and more disciplined in terms of decision making. It points to more transparency of information and more use of 'forensic evidence' layered on top of intuition. It also points to more attention paid to how marketers work with agency suppliers and clarity in terms of who signs off what.

In this climate where brand governance is in the spotlight, clients may also feel that communications planning – effectively deciding a brand's communication 'route to market' – is too important to be left to outside suppliers. It carries too much risk. And this is another functional reason why some marketers in future may see communications planning as a core competency of marketing.

Emotional reasons – control

Fundamentally, I believe that clients want more control over their brands. In the last 20 or 30 years we've seen the rise to prominence of the guru creative director – the likes of Dan Wieden and Trevor Beattie. These guys have wielded enormous power and have done enormous good for brands. But at an emotional, subconscious level, I believe that the strength of these creative directors has also hurt clients. They have been the kings of the brand and not the marketers. So I believe that emotionally, clients 'want their brands back'. They've given a lot of the say in things away to agencies, and they feel a bit out of control.

There's also the issue of control in the sense of avoiding politics. Faced with competition among agencies to 'do it' for clients, clients may see a more peaceful life if they do it for themselves.

When I spoke to James Walker at Accenture, he pointed out that globalisation was also part of this need for more control and that big global companies were increasingly demanding more central control and ways of staying in touch with what was happening in their markets:

The dreaded globalisation of our clients . . . a P&G, Unilever or a Samsung wants a very consistent solution globally and in Samsung's case, the guy in Korea we're working with has a 'marketing Bloomberg terminal' and he can look at sales of mobile phones in Russia or how much is being spent on media advertising for microwaves in Argentina . . . he has it all at his fingertips. Samsung is a good example of a 'command and control' organisation. They have really brilliant systems, and they are taking a single-minded view on global systems and a global approach to marketing and control of marketing. The part deal they've done with WPP is another example of that desire for control. On the one hand you could say they're giving a lot away to WPP and the agencies, but on the other hand they're taking a lot back, in terms of cutting down on the number of disparate agencies in disparate countries . . . so it actually brings more control back into Samsung. And in future, 360-degree communications planning will sit more in companies like Samsung than it will in the agencies.

Emotional reasons – a more interesting job

I think a lot of marketing people yearn to get their hands dirty again. For them, marketing has become too much about managing agencies, judging their output and spending time forecasting objectives and juggling budget spreadsheets. They want to get back into the real business of brand building again; they want to create a tangible output of their own. And for these people – who I think are the majority of clients – communications planning may well be the mechanism to do so.

Client environment more appealing to agency people

More and more agency people around the world seem ready to make the transition to the client environment. Often agency people make great clients, because as poacher-turned-gamekeeper they understand what makes an agency tick. They can cut through the spin and bullshit. And they can also understand how to maintain the relationship with an agency more effectively.

Campaign magazine's John Tylee writes:

The expectation is that the number of senior agency managers joining client companies will grow from a trickle to a flood. Improved financial rewards are helping to fuel the trend. The time has gone when agency managers earned significantly higher salaries than their client counterparts. But the prospect of fatter pay cheques isn't the only reason. As supergroups such as WPP have grown, so the ad industry has become more corporate.

It's not just ad agency people crossing over. We've also seen many media people move from the agency to the client side, spearheading client in-house media departments. Numerous big international clients now have these – examples are Unilever, P&G, GlaxoSmithKline, Reckitt Benckiser and Anheuser Busch.

The key to all of this developing further in future is the 'informalisation' of the client environment. Tim Delaney, chairman of Leagas Delaney in the UK, writes:

Should ad people become clients? Why not? But I suspect that it's quite a culture shock for most of them. Agencies are, rightly, informal, while client companies are a lot less so. Agencies also have a roster of clients, which can make every day and every hour different.

In the future, when we witness a real growth in communications planning revenue, we'll also witness a corresponding growth in the number of people who can genuinely 'do it'. In other words, there will not be a skill shortage. So clients' ability to do communications planning in the future will very much depend on their ability to attract the right individuals from agencies and then retain them.

Those clients that decide to go down the route of communications planning will find this the most demanding and challenging aspect. How do you create a culture within marketing that is far more informal and creative? Although some of the biggest clients might most want to do communications planning themselves, these very same companies might also find it hardest to create the right internal environment, because of their size, which is usually accompanied by a corresponding amount of bureaucracy and politics.

Dick Metzler of DHL throws some light on this issue:

For those brand-owner clients that do decide to try to do communications planning themselves, trying to create the right internal environment will be all important. And looking at how some big brand-owner clients have done this in the past is interesting. For example, when IBM first developed the

PC in the early 1980s, it used its new facilities at Boca Raton in Florida to create a separate environment that would foster innovation. There should be a parallel in media planning that can create game changers.

Apple has an internal environment that allows creative, eccentric people to live there; so do Diesel, and Benetton. Benetton for example created Fabrica in 1994 as an artistic laboratory or, as the company describes it, a 'communication research and development centre'.

This underlines the fact that manufacturers are actually more fluid structurally than agencies, so agencies shouldn't underestimate their ability to create the right environment. Maybe in the future, for example, General Motors might have its main operation in Detroit, but its marketing and communications planning might sit in New York. Grant Millar of British Telecom agrees:

One of the important things that you've absolutely rumbled is that marketing organisations are much more flexible structurally and organisationally than agencies. Agencies are extraordinarily conservative.

In fact, I think that these issues of internal environment are already starting to be addressed in many client organisations, as Tony Regan of Nylon confirms:

I wonder if the balance of 'environmental appeal' between client and agency isn't changing. Historical wisdom has said that agencies were the fun place to work, whereas client companies were often a miserable 'office above the factory'. I think this is changing. Many client companies seem to be introducing a pioneering culture of creativity and ideas. And while agencies are cosmetically appealing environments, in reality all the anecdotes suggest that agency life is not really that appealing – it's much harder and more demanding than it ever was.

The time it takes to brief

The notion of clients expanding their scope also works because it is so time consuming for them to brief people. In the future, clients will get a vast amount of information from research and data consultancies and so will have a more 360-degree view of consumers than their given specialist agencies. And if you're the client, if you are going to ask an agency of some sort to do the communications planning, you have to brief out all the information you have access to, in order to inform the agency to the degree that it can start to bring value to your business.

This problem will be compounded by the need for strategy to be very fluid in future. In other words, with all the effectiveness feedback coming from data on a continual basis, we won't have one annual strategy that remains static all year long. It will be constantly evolving and changing.

So in a way, it makes sense for a lot of clients to use the data to do the communications planning themselves, before briefing implementation to the agencies. For those clients that choose this route, it will make their agencies more implementational and will lock them into specialist roles.

Clients dealing with big media owners directly

I mentioned that client in-house media departments are a growing phenomenon. And I believe that these same departments will prove to be the vanguard for client communications planning endeavour in the future. At the moment these departments focus on ensuring that they get the best value out of their budgets with their media agencies, but they also do other things.

One of the things they do is help build and manage relationships with media owners or vendors and they don't just rely on their media agencies' own relationships with media owners to serve their best interests. This can spill over into the client in-house media department, striking deals up directly with media owners or vendors, and even into doing their own buying. This is relatively commonplace, particularly in the United States.

Anheuser-Busch in Europe has created its own internal planning and buying subsidiary, called Busch Media Group (BMG). This is managed by Mike McGough. He writes:

The in-house structure allows our media buyers and planners to work hand-in-hand with brand marketing, sponsorship and promotions departments to create integrated marketing programmes for our brands. This allows our planning and buying to be more cohesive and gives us better control of all media spend.

So we may see this trend continue, and we may see in-house media departments slowly morph into client communications planning entities.

This point was picked up on by Reg Lascaris, Regional CEO, TBWA Group and co-founder of Hunt Lascaris TBWA, when I spoke to him:

I think you're right about clients. They want to get their hands on this stuff, they want to get their hands dirty again and they want to control communications planning. There's no doubt about it. In fact in some companies now they're already putting in a media specialist inside. This person could easily translate into a communications planner in the future.

Writing strategies that actually happen; and making the idea bigger than just communication

A last, slightly cynical and tangential take on the whole thing, to support my view that clients will now start doing communications planning themselves.

How often does an agency planner ever write something that actually happens first time? My view (and I happen to be one!) is not often. All too often we write strategies that never happen, and a large element of this is because the whole planning exercise is subjective, however we choose to look at it. In other words, a client will only ever instigate a fraction of what you write, because they don't write it themselves. And when as a planner you do get the strategy finally approved, it is only after a lot of 'toing and froing'.

So if a client writes the communications strategy, it has a much higher chance of actually happening first time! It makes the strategy function more meaningful and, in terms of manhours, a heck of a lot more efficient. Furthermore, if part of communications planning is in the area of solution-neutral ideation, then if this is internalised in the client organisation and the idea is created by a cross-discipline group of people, there is also a better chance that the organisation will see the idea as bigger than just communication. It will become part of packaging and new product development. It will have a better chance of becoming a real business idea.

The implications

Some clients will choose to do it and some won't

Despite all the good reasons we've just looked at, there will be a significant body of clients that will not want to do communications planning. The complexity of the function will put them off. And they will see the alternative – the agencies doing it on their behalf – as perfectly acceptable.

Much will depend on the client's internal culture, on the category and how much communication influences its business. In many categories, it will quite simply not be worth it, because of the generally low proportion of revenue that is spent on communication. It may also turn out that local clients in some markets choose to 'go for it' and some don't.

Furthermore, it also might depend on the role of marketing and communications within the organisation. Companies that tend to drive their businesses without much reliance on traditional marketing or communication might not really see much need to do communications planning at all.

This point was made to me by John Griffiths, a UK brand consultant:

There is a new breed of company like Amazon, eBay, Ryan Air and Starbucks who are managing to become leaders in their categories without spending much money on marketing and communication at all.

So there won't be any hard-and-fast rules about which clients want to do communications planning and which don't. We could argue that there might be a tendency for smaller clients to do it themselves. For within smaller companies, there will not be as strong a need to keep down staff numbers and there will be a more natural tendency for marketing individuals in these companies to be good generalists who have always seen communication from a 360-degree perspective.

But then again, we could also argue, conversely, that it will be the big client companies that will do it. Talking to John Partilla of Time Warner Global Marketing, he was right to point out that

one key consideration is how a client would stay connected to the opportunities of the marketplace – in the same way as media planners generally are. So potentially it'd be only the biggest clients who would be important enough to media owners/vendors to ensure they'd be tripping over themselves to get in the door with opportunities.

Data will still be imported

If we think about the basic constituent parts of communications planning in 2015, they might look like a triangle with the largest part at the bottom being data (or knowledge from data). To make this dovetail with the Strategy Map, where data is on the left, we can lay the triangle on its side, as in Figure 9.2.

Those clients that decide to do communications planning themselves will actually not do it all and they will still choose to import the data piece. I can see them saying, 'I want someone to get all my data

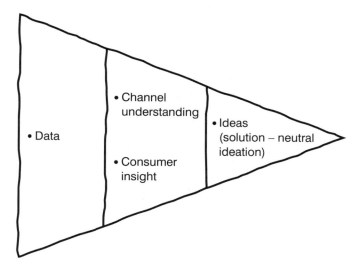

Fig. 9.2   Constituents of communications planning in 2015.

together and I want them to give me insight and understanding of what that data means.' This will be for a couple of reasons.

First, because of all the constituent parts, this is the one that will involve the most people. So with pressure to keep numbers down, the data part of communications planning will be too labour intensive, particularly for big clients with lots of brands. Unilever has about 20 people at Port Sunlight in the UK who do some data modelling. Their job is to look at around 100 countries and 30 brands per country. Because of the breadth of the job, they only look at things like what should the advertising to sales ratio be in Spain. Should this be different in Italy? And how about South Korea? They can't drill down to the area of which communication channels Unilever should use, because they'd need more than 20 people to do so. In fact, they'd probably need more like 1000 people! So this area, quite simply, involves too many people.

Then there is the issue of brand priorities if it's done internally. If two marketing directors come along and want their brands analysed

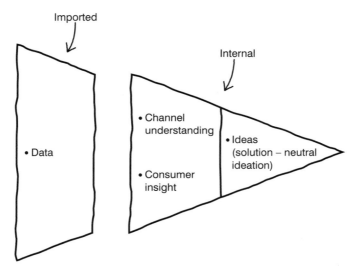

Fig. 9.3 Clients who 'do it' will import the data.

simultaneously, what happens then? The one who is de-prioritised will more often than not go to an outside supplier to get the job done immediately.

And last, there is the argument about 'marking your own homework'. If marketing directors are increasingly to be judged according to the ROI of communication, then surely the 'judge' (the person analysing the data) should sit outside the client organisation.

Having established that clients are still likely to import the data piece, is this all they will import? What about ideas, from the ad agencies? My view on this is that by this stage client organisations (who want to do communications planning) will have people who are highly capable of solution-neutral ideation. So these clients will need to rely less and less on ad agencies or other types of agencies for this input.

Clients will grow; agencies will lose ground

I believe that by 2015, communications planning – wherever it is done – will be getting more complicated. As a result, no one individual will be a communications planner on a brand. Rather, there will be a blend of skill sets: some analytical, some insight and ideas based, and some around motivating others.

In terms of the size of the communications planning business and the relative shares, I am going to assume that clients will by now get into doing communications planning wholeheartedly. This will continue to fuel its further growth and will also mean that they make serious inroads into the agency share of the 'doing' pie.

For those clients that, by 2015, are still reliant on agencies, the business will probably gravitate further towards the integrated BTL agencies, media agencies and communication independents, as the agency types that are the best stand-alone providers and that can simultaneously embrace the ROI and the ideas/insight cultures.

Ad agencies will be hanging in there by the skin of their teeth. There will still be some clients who ask them to do communications planning on their behalf. But as we've established, for clients who are choosing to do communications planning themselves, they will now have become proficient enough in the area of ideation not to need this input from ad agencies.

All of this can be seen in Figure 9.4.

On the Strategy Map in Figure 9.5, there will be a further drift to the left.

Conclusion

Those clients that choose to take on communications planning themselves will increasingly come to see it as the heart of the marketing function. They will see it as something that has a liberating effect on communication, but also on things like NPD and distribution. This represents a paradigm shift from where we are now; at the moment, most clients think that communications planning is just another take on existing processes.

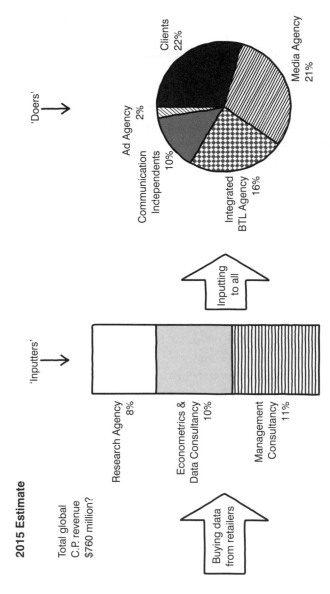

Fig. 9.4 Communications planning estimated size and share – 2015.

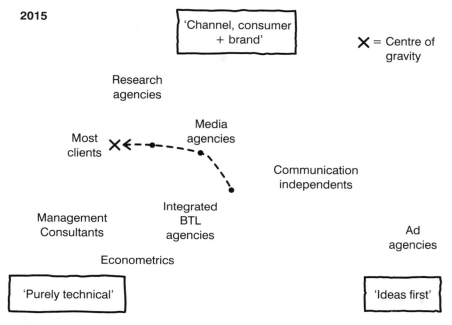

Fig. 9.5 The Strategy Map: 2015.

In such companies, marketing will increasingly deliver a new definition of media to the business – a definition more removed from CPP (cost per rating point) and GRP (gross rating point) and based much more around Hollywood and content. It will be dynamic and interesting. The communications planners in client organisations will be highly empowered individuals who can and will genuinely transform brand communications. This will also have a very positive effect on the relationship between marketing and trade marketing. Because both sides will be heavily involved in the process, the bonds between these departments will form naturally, and it will become necessary for them to sit next to each other within the organisation.

So in the future, for those clients that decide to do it themselves, marketing (and communications planning within it) will be very different from today. It will become a hugely desirable, empowered and even 'sexy' function!

For these clients, the future of marketing is communications planning.

◆

Key points made in this chapter

2015

- At the moment, manufacturing clients are not really trying to do communications planning because:
  - there are headcount issues and it's easier to outsource it;
  - they don't really have the right skill set;
  - most clients aren't thinking like this yet;
  - there is a perceived 'in-house' problem, that in-house departments can get stale.
- That said, in the period around 2015, clients will increasingly take communications planning back from agencies and start doing it themselves. This is because:
  - they always used to do it;
  - the 4 Ps and marketings' declining role in this context;
  - as marketing directors get increasingly responsible for the effectiveness/ROI of communication, so too will they want to control it more tightly;
  - corporate governance will spill over to brand governance;
  - many clients will want more control over their brands at an emotional level; they'll also want to start getting their hands dirty again;
  - the client environment will become more appealing to agency people;
  - briefing will take a lot of time and it will be inefficient to brief out all the information/data-based knowledge;
  - clients are already dealing with big media owners/vendors directly.
- Not all clients will choose to do communications planning. Some will, some won't. Much will depend on internal culture, category and geography.

- But because a sizeable number of clients will want to do communications planning themselves, clients' share of communications planning will obviously grow, and agencies will lose some ground.
- For those that do decide to do it themselves, data-based knowledge will still be imported.
- For those that do decide to do it themselves, marketing will become more sexy. And for them, the future of marketing will be communications planning.

10
The Twin Achilles' Heels

Developments 2015–2020: ad agencies starting to split in two

Production

Production has long been at the heart of ad agency and integrated BTL agency remuneration. It is the 'engine' that makes the real money and it is indeed a massive machine. Even with the introduction of fees, the more these agencies produce, the more they generally get paid. But it is also one of their two big Achilles' heels.

Although today many ad agencies talk a good 360-degree game, the reality is that TV still drives the agenda, because this is where most production money is involved. Yet another shoot in Cape Town or Bermuda, with the accompanying drama and extended production schedule, is their meat and drink.

But production no longer depends on highly complex, expensive analogue studios. Outside the big production companies, there are many smaller companies that can develop and produce good-quality, inexpensive digital material, across channels and disciplines – above-the-line, below-the-line but also in digital interactive channels. Indeed, digital production has become so much more fluid and inexpensive that advertising clients and some media agencies now have their own production capabilities, and produce 'infomercials' for example.

So if this is the situation today, where will things be tomorrow? My view is that in the future we will see a couple of developments.

First, we will see the ad agency (and to a lesser extent the integrated BTL agency) production income come under fire. Talking to Reg Lascaris of TBWA, he remarked:

I think ad agencies will try to defend production, but I think production will increasingly be going to specialist companies. There will also be a lot of production that's done by clients themselves. At the end of the day, in future this will be an area where client procurement departments will drive a lot of the decisions.

In my opinion, it will not just be specialist companies and manufacturing clients that try to get their teeth into production, but also the media agencies. As communication channels increase, so the expertise for production will drain out of the ad agency. In areas like interactive TV (iTV), mobile telephony or in-store plasma screens, traditional ad agencies are already struggling to get their heads around it all. So as communication channels fragment and multiply, the logic will be that those who are most in touch with the channels will be able to produce the content most effectively. Beyond TV and outdoor, beyond the main media types of today, there will be an ever-extending 'tail' of channels that will require specialised knowledge in terms of what can and can't be done. And the media agencies will be closest to all the communication channels.

This will be the main reason why the media agencies may try to get involved in production. But also, with an explosion in communication channels, production income is going to show growth in the near future, whereas media is in a sense commoditised and a category that isn't really growing substantially.

Ten or twenty years ago, full-service agencies had two money-making engines: media and production. Media has since left the nest and ad agencies really only have production left to make any profit. But production is now under huge threat.

Client procurement departments are starting to wade in and scrutinise production costs. In some cases, this has gone a step further to them starting to control it. I believe that the Central Office of Information (a big UK advertiser) is now starting to ask ad agencies to pitch creative ideas, then procuring the production itself (albeit with input from the ad agencies).

Media agencies — if they do decide to enter this space — will be able to afford to loss-lead on it and undercut other suppliers. They will be able to become (again) the 'disruptive technologies' — but this time of production. They will potentially be cheaper, quicker and more user-friendly to clients. They will be able to loss-lead the same way as the full-service creative agencies used to on creative and strategy, with the massive back-end media and production function.

I talked to Martin Thomas, one of the founders of Nylon, about production. His view was this:

Many media agencies could open a production division tomorrow. In fact, I don't know why they don't, although it would probably be at the non-glamorous end of things. Because the production grunt work is certainly going to increase thanks to the proliferation of channels, the growth of retail, and all the rest of it. When you think about the sixty-second film, you have to conclude that the cost of execution is going to come down. In ten years' time will we still be spending £500k on a film? It's difficult to see why we would. The economics just don't stack up, especially as the real opportunities are in much more interactive, engaging content. There's real potential for economies of scale in production; that'll be the next big commoditisation.

For example, we're trying to create a unit for retail strategy and execution at the moment. In places like Tesco and Wal-Mart, you have to create content that works in the new mediums, but creative agencies turn their nose up at it and sales promotions agencies can't quite do it. In future, you'll need a way of generating effective content for this kind of thing — an engine that takes an idea and delivers pieces of content as efficiently as possible.

It's perhaps a bit like the way media changed from being the office at the grubby end of the agency corridor to becoming quite pre-eminent. The next will be the studio. They'll say, hang on, we're the people that make the money, we're the people who make the trains run on time. We want to be treated with a bit of respect here.

A second development in the production arena will be the increasing importance of content to brand-owner clients. According to PHD (a UK media agency), which has a specialist content subsidiary called Drum, the UK branded content market will be valued at around £100 million by 2010 – and that's just in the UK. By 2020, worldwide, it'll be massive.

Branded content and advertiser-funded programming (AFP) have come a long way recently. Increasingly we're seeing opportunities to develop communication strategies by putting content at the centre of things. For example, in the US, Campbell's tomato soup struck a deal with NBC over the critically acclaimed prime-time drama series *American Dreams*. The series is all about family values, depicting a more innocent America in the 1960s as seen through the eyes of the Pryor family from Philadelphia. Campbell's integrated its brand into six episodes of the script in an ingenious way. It created a Campbell's tomato soup essay contest that Patty Pryor, the youngest daughter, wants to enter. 'How does your American Dream differ from that of your parents?' is the subject matter. There then follow many scenes in which Patty buys lots of cans of soup to answer the contest, with the storyline showcasing many 'possibilities' of tomato soup. Campbell's paralleled the AFP content with a real-life contest, via a consumer promotion, in the in-store, home and school classroom environments. This shows how AFP is increasingly being used as the central hub from which other communication elements feed.

Looking forwards, clients are increasingly going to want to develop AFP and content that sits as the central element, as brand consultant John Griffiths underlined in our conversation:

In the future, intermediaries are going to be increasingly asked for content development strategies to forestall the duplication of content for different purposes by different suppliers – by advertising, direct marketing, design and web agencies.

Furthermore, only a few years ago, TV stations' programming direc-tors and commissioning editors would turn their noses up at AFP, but this is also changing based on new circumstances. In the UK the 2004 Communications Act took programme rights out of the hands of the TV stations and gave them back to the production companies. This meant that TV stations lost a lot of revenue from things like DVD sales, which meant that they could afford to fund fewer programmes of their own. So now there is a far greater willingness among TV stations to embrace AFP.

Looking at the future, what is interesting is that there will be several types of organisations battling it out to help create this AFP content. Obviously the production companies will be important players. They have existing relationships with TV station commissioning editors. And increasingly we'll see production companies that just specialise in AFP emerging. But the media agencies will also be heavily involved in AFP content development. Their claim will be that they under-stand and can evaluate the currency of AFP, and that they can under-stand the media market, the production market and the broadcast market. Furthermore, media agencies will in the future be acquiring the rights to content beyond AFP. In other words, they will be devel-oping independent relationships with production companies through which they develop content or acquire the rights to content. They will then use this to leverage deals and sell programming to media owners, in return for commercial space for their clients. And the ad agencies will also be involved in this area, as they will see themselves as experts in all forms of content, and they will have the ability to create big, engaging AFP programming ideas.

To quote Mark Boyd, director of content at BBH in the UK:

Media agencies will find the pull to content irresistible: they have the rela-tionships with media commercial departments and are staring at declining margins. Specialist AFP agencies will struggle with credibility, weight and retained clients and will have a tough two years before they can build a business in a new industry. Longer term, creative agencies will have a strong claim on realising this space.

The really important thing for communications planning is that in future, who wins a pitch may depend on who owns the rights to, or who has the ability to access or create, the best content.

Ideas

Having established the fluid nature of production and content creation among agencies and the Achilles' heel that this represents to ad agencies in particular, let's go on to look at the second Achilles' heel of the ad agency — ideas.

First, let me say that ad agencies are, on the whole, experts in ideation. It is a huge strength of theirs and, increasingly, they are happy to be paid for ideas, rather than just for production execution. This is because they feel it is here that they truly add value. Furthermore, as MT Rainey has pointed out:

a dependence on [monthly] fee income fosters a preoccupation with new business as a revenue and growth driver and, in turn, an obsession with publicity that is unhealthy in a professional business.

She goes on to say that

the reality is that strategically-informed creativity, resulting in a communications idea for the brand which forms the centre of gravity of a client's marketing programme, must be a core deliverable for today's agency. Who would disagree? I believe, however, that it must be a core 'product' . . . produced, packaged and sold separately from the execution of advertising or any communication, and certainly from its distribution and administration.'

MT Rainey and her partners founded RKCR Y&R on the premise of asking clients to pay separately for ideas, which is what it still does.

Since RKCR Y&R positioned itself in this way, more and more ad agencies have gone down this route. Although this system is still in its early days, and the commission system still lingers, this is a good development.

This system also seems to suit clients who want to circumvent the situation in which they are 'owned' by agencies. Clients want cleaner relationships and they want the ability to use ideas globally, without the need to be tied to one agency around the world.

But this development will make it harder for ad agencies to compete effectively in communications planning in future. That's because in 2020 or so, if a client is going to pay $250 000 to an agency for a communication strategy, yes they will want a media-neutral or solution-neutral idea, but they will also want a lot of rigour, understanding and knowledge derived from the data and then applied to the brand. An idea on its own will simply not cut it. So 'just ideas' in future is going to be limiting.

But the Achilles' heel of ad agencies goes beyond this, into questioning whether the type of idea that clients are increasingly going to want will also work against them. As Jonathan Dodd points out:

I think ideas are a strength and a weakness for ad agencies. They are good at ideas, but they have a funny relationship with 'media-neutral' or 'solution-neutral' ideas.

Although ad agencies are certainly good at ideas, I think that they tend to default to ideas that are more creative than strategic and that tend to be rooted in above-the-line execution. This is for two reasons. First, culturally ad agencies think that the best ideas come from execution up – from bottom up; whereas they see the 'top-down' approach running the risk of producing dry, boring, strategic ideas. Secondly, within ad agencies ideas are briefed into the creative department. Unfortunately this approach fails to take account of the type of ideas that are increasingly needed by clients in a world of multiple communication channels, and more and more digital, interactive content.

Of course, I'm generalising when I say that ad agencies tend to default to ideas that just happen to be much easier to express above-the-line. Not all do, by any means. TBWA is a network that has some offices that are very good at through-the-line ideation, such as its Swedish, French and South African offices. In my limited experience, Ogilvy, Fallon and Euro RSCG are also good.

Talking to MT Carney of Ogilvy New York, she outlined why Ogilvy tended to be good at 'solution-neutral', 360-degree, strategic ideas:

Whereas most ad agencies put the brief for the brand idea straight into the creative department, at Ogilvy we share responsibility for its origination between the strategic planners, senior creatives and client service. This ensures that the brand idea is driven by the brand and its objectives, top down. And only after we have a brand idea do we brief out the execution of this idea into the wider creative pool.

There are also other kinds of agency that have got their heads around the type of strategic communication idea needed today, like Michaelides & Bednash. To remind you, this is a communication independent; in fact the world's first. And it is positioned around creating communication ideas that are originated top down, and rooted in an understanding of audience, brand and culture. The cultural piece is important; if you can tie a brand to an emergent cultural trend, it gives your communication natural 'legs' as well as a tendency to attract PR. My view is that Michaelides & Bednash is a lot better at coming up with communication ideas than many ad agencies.

Integrated BTL agencies are becoming very good at coming up with solution-neutral ideas. Media agencies are also fast becoming experts at ideas. Even brand consultancies like Added Value are getting good at this.

So if they are to defend this Achilles' heel, ad agencies need to understand ideas beyond advertising much better than they currently do. But at this point, they still have the upper hand. This is in part because they have the advantage in selling ideas via storyboards. It has become a sales game. They sell through the 'back end', through showing how an idea would look, whereas other agency types, such as communication independents or media agencies, sell an idea through insight – through the front end. At the moment the back end wins nearly every time!

Ad agencies transforming

In the future, let's say between 2015 and 2020, ad agencies are going to be under huge competitive pressure on three fronts: communications planning, creativity/ideas and production.

We've seen that communications planning at this time is likely to be far more rigorous than it is at the moment. To compete will demand a real understanding of communication channels and linkage to data. We've also seen that the media-neutral or solution-neutral ideation piece will increasingly be done by the communications planning 'doers', those more at the centre of things – the integrated BTL agencies, media agencies and communication independents, as well as the clients, who will also increasingly become masters of ideation. And we've seen that production is going to be fluid and done in many places.

Talking to Reg Lascaris of TBWA, he reiterated these concerns:

The problem is that if the ad agencies start losing communications planning and production, a lot of their traditional income will disappear. Then the big fight will be how to value an idea; because in the end you're going to have to charge good fees for that. That's why the agency business is going to get tougher and tougher. And if they are in effect just left with ideas, it's going to be hard to have successful agencies.

So ad agencies will be defending communications planning and the ideas piece that is wrapped up in it, as well as production of communication material and content in a broad sense. Faced with this, I believe it's inevitable that ad agencies will start to go down two routes and that they will have a choice to make: either to focus on creativity/ideas + communications planning, or to focus on creativity/ideas

+ production. In other words, creativity/ideas will be a given, but they will have to choose between communications planning and production. To try to maintain any sort of competitive advantage on all three fronts – communications planning, creativity/ideas and production – will be untenable. It will be to fail at all three. So I believe that we will see a splitting or bifurcation in ad agencies.

To compete at communications planning will demand real focus and investment and with tight margins it will be impossible to be good at this as well as everything else. Tony Regan of Nylon thinks that the split I've outlined is indeed coming, as he remarked to me:

I think ad agencies have already been thinking about which of those two roads they want to go down for the last few years.

That takes us back to Chapter 4 and Nitro. If you remember, Nitro is an ad agency group that is emerging at the moment. Its key proposition is creativity/ideas + planning. It is lean, keeps down the client service element and puts senior people in clients' offices for extended periods – much like the management consultants do. Talking to Paul Shearer, its global creative director, he believes that a more honest relationship with clients is going to be key here.

The way forward is to be transparent in every sense. It's time for our business to stop telling and start showing.

As I mentioned, I see Nitro as an 'agency of the future' – the first of a wave of ad agencies that is more focused on creativity/ideas + planning than on production. This obviously dovetails with the split in ad agencies that I see starting in this period between 2015 and 2020. There will be an existing precedent for the creativity/ideas + planning route. Furthermore, by this time communications planning will be well paid, and the creativity/ideas + planning route will be financially very viable.

So those ad agencies that go the 'strategy' route will now become communications planning 'doers' and will move towards the centre of things. They will become agencies that develop communication strategy, with ideas at their hearts, and they will know how to demonstrate to clients how to execute the strategy in creative terms. This ability to go beyond a strategy with an idea, and actually bring the strategy and idea to life, will give them a good competitive advantage that compensates for any initial weakness in rigour.

This advantage comes back to a point made by Bruce Haines when I spoke to him:

It's very difficult to come up with a 'working' communication strategy in isolation from creative execution. It might be the most rational strategy on Earth, but to be really workable, it needs the creative and strategy relationship.

So the ad agencies that in future go down the strategy route will have an advantage in bringing strategy to life and creating very workable strategies.

Maybe with the emergence of these new strategy-focused ad agencies we will finally come to see the type of thing that John Harlow of Naked talked about at an IAAA Conference recently:

The agency of the future that we're talking about [as an upstream central marketing partner to clients] can only make the move upstream if it can find a way to move out of the 'production ghetto'.

On the flipside, those agencies that go the 'production' route will find themselves in a position where they can be competitive at content across the board. They will be better able to defend against the muscling in of the media agencies in the production arena and better able to defend against the TV production companies.

So the splitting of the ad agencies will be the start of better times to come for them. It will be the start of a brave new future, and a better future. It will also allow them to leverage their historical USP in the creativity/ideas area on one focused front: either on the communications planning front or on the production front. It will give them far more focus, which will mean revenue growth. But as Paul Shearer suggests, the ad agencies of the future will have a different ethos. They will be more genuinely through the line, and there will be more transparency in the system.

What might stop this happening?

While I do believe that ad agencies will start to split in around 10 to 15 years' time, I absolutely acknowledge there are good reasons why this might not happen. Here I pass over to Peter Walshe, global account director of Millward Brown:

I think the power of creativity will always have to be reckoned with and thus will always have an important part to play as an essential ingredient in getting brand messages to consumers. But creativity in a vacuum is not effective. The difference in sales effects are far greater because of variation in creative than for media laydown. And when these come together the prize is great indeed. The actual production of communications needs to be a part of this process otherwise a further 'gap' appears where the idea and strategy can be diluted.

The implication for the future in harnessing relevant creativity that actually works for the brand is that production for production's sake (i.e. divorcing the actual making of communications from the creative process) is less likely, because the need to integrate strategic thinking in the production process will become more essential than ever. The idea of shipping out the idea once it has been creatively developed to a film director with no accountability or insight into the development process potentially adds another barrier to effective communication with the consumer. Which is why I believe the smart creative agencies will ensure that their strategic offering continues to encompass production and that pure production houses that take any creative script thrown at them and churn them out will not be sustainable even if it is cheaper. There will need to be a connection to communications creative development and channel planning that relates to the strategy for the brand. Without this the centre falls apart.

My view is that Peter is underestimating how impossibly stretched agencies will be (at this point) in trying to be good at the strategy, the ideation and the production pieces.

Fusion

In the period 2015–2020 we will start to see some fusion of agency types, but it will be 'fusion among equals'.

Communication independents

In a communications planning sense, ad agencies will be reborn. Those that are liberated from production will become more independent minded, more strategic and very much business partners of clients. They will also come to look more like the existing communication independents that had their roots in media agencies.

So ad agencies in the communications planning arena will become ad agency-based communication independents and they will take their place alongside their media agency-based cousins. Both will be competing in the 'doing' area of communications planning with the integrated BTL agencies and media agencies, servicing those clients that do not choose to do communications planning themselves.

Which agencies will go down this route? It's very hard to say, but my guess is that those agencies that seem most determined to keep hold of the strategy piece today will also be as determined to keep hold of it tomorrow. So TBWA, for example, might well be one of these strategy-oriented agencies.

When I spoke to Rod Wright of TEQUILA\ and TBWA, this was certainly the impression I got:

Part of the thought process is to say, 'What is the business space in which we exist?' You've got a bunch of agencies that have gone into the marketing communications area and then another bunch that have gone into the ideas area, saying ideas are bigger. This is still limiting, because this assumes the answer to a question. So the last space, where we at TBWA are trying to move ourselves, is to say, actually what we have that clients need is creativity in its broadest sense. And therefore we can find our space by giving clients business creativity. It doesn't mean at the moment we can deliver any of that, but that is the best possible space in terms of being able to offer value to clients, whatever the question is. If you start your relationship based on the broadest sense of creativity in business, that then allows you to come up with better ideas. It's a much broader-based relationship and a much deeper role.

Looking further at potential agency positioning in the future, we can create a 'strategy and execution' map of sorts to try to make sense of which direction the different agency types might go. Figure 10.1 shows where they are today.

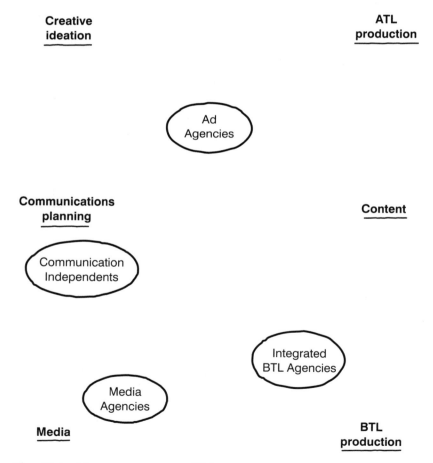

Fig. 10.1   Key agency types – 2005.

Let's have a look at the picture as it will probably be in 2020. It becomes apparent that there will be increasing overlap between a couple of agency types: first, between the media agency-based communication independents and the new ad agency-based communication independents; secondly, between the media agencies and integrated BTL agencies. This is shown in Figure 10.2.

What this will mean is that there will inevitably be some fusion between them. You will find acquisition and mergers between the

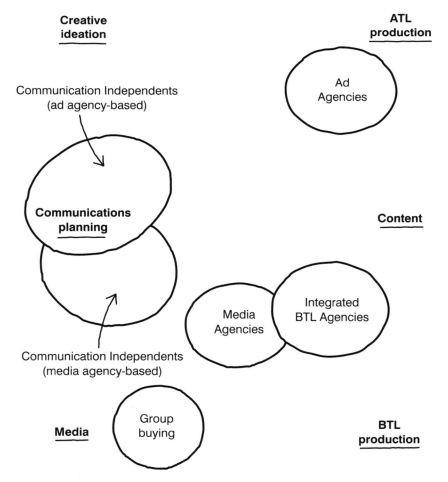

Fig. 10.2   Key agency types – 2020.

media agency-based communications independents and the new ad agency-based cousins. This will really be with a view to building some scale in a competitive sense, to rival the competition – namely the media agency and integrated BTL agency networks. It will also be so that the ad agency-based communications independents can benefit more from the rigour and back end of the media-based guys.

But don't forget that by this stage, it is likely that most of the media agency-based communication independents will be owned by the big agency holding groups (they'll have had to sell up themselves to obtain access to the rigour in the back end). So really, the fusion, acquisition and mergers that take place will happen within the agency holding groups, rather than across them.

This fusion of new ad agencies focusing on strategy (or what I now see as ad agency-based communication independents) and the media-based communication independents will mark another turning point in the communications industry. It will be the return to the media/creative marriage that everyone wants to happen, but it won't happen before this point while media and creative are both so implementation bound. So, rather, it will come out of strategy and creativity/ideas, and an equality between them. It will come out of agencies that look very similar and have a similar 'shape' saying let's combine forces.

When I spoke to Kees Kruythoff of Unilever, his feeling was that the ultimate 'product' from a client perspective was communications planning and creativity joined up, and that this would indeed be best delivered through a fusion of 'strategic' agencies in future:

We need more and more creativity, joined up with communication strategy. We need creative directors to engage in the 360 strategy process. Ultimately it'll be about creativity and strategy together as equals and it'll all go back into one agency, but within that agency, you'll need to have the understanding of the complexity of channels, and that's where specialism comes in; but also to have the spirit, creativity and free flow to come up with great communication ideas.

Grant Millar of British Telecom, in a very similar vein, had this to add:

There's lots of talk about going back to full service. But I don't think that can succeed unless the ad agencies shed their back end. You need integration of media and creative, when they are equals. Pulling media back into an ad agency [as they are today] won't do it.

Media and integrated BTL agencies

There might also be fusion, mergers and acquisitions between media agencies and integrated BTL agencies over this period. This would make sense. They are both comfortable with data and rigour, but each side can add a missing dimension to the other. From the media side, integrated BTL agencies have a creative capacity (they produce creative). From the integrated BTL agency side, media agencies have an understanding of channels, how to use them and what they cost. It would also make sense culturally. Both have mutual respect; and both have increasing strategic capabilities. So all in all, they'd make good bedfellows.

Any other possibilities?

Will any other kind of fusion be going on in the period 2015–2020? Well, maybe. There is also the potential for management consultants and media agencies to create JVs. Whether this develops will very much depend on the stance taken by clients towards management consultants getting involved in the 'doing' side of communications planning; in other words, whether they'll see 'doing' as well as the inputting of econometric-based knowledge and judging of communication ROI as mutually exclusive.

To quote James Walker of Accenture:

I think for smaller clients there is a very appropriate argument for having ROI linked to implementation, a virtuous circle of implementation and ROI. But for major global players, that's always going to be an important business for we management consultancies, because you'd be mad to give the ROI evaluation to a company within a holding agency group who does your media planning and creative. I've been in those organisations, and you do have pressure to come out with the right answers.

So assuming that clients on the whole see the two sides as mutually exclusive, media agencies and management consultants might see JVs as a way of working together and circumventing client sensitivities – putting business into something and sharing profits. For management consultants, it would be a way to get financial benefit from the 'doing' of communications planning and implementation; and for media agencies, it would be a way to profit from the management consult-ants' client relationships.

Conclusion

In the future, communications planning and creativity will converge. They have to, because at the end of the day clients will really want them to do so. The fusion between communication independents – the media agency-based ones of today and the ad agency-based ones of tomorrow – will make this happen and will mark the start of a renaissance in the strength of 'ideas-first' communications planning. It will also mark the start of a move on the Strategy Map from the left – the technical, dry side – back towards the middle – towards a point of equilibrium between ideas and ROI. For the ad agencies, it will be a turning point in their fortunes in the strategy game.

◆

Key points made in this chapter

2015–2020

In the period between 2015 and 2020, ad agencies will be seriously struggling on two fronts:

- First, in terms of production:
  - ○ Production is at the heart of ad agency remuneration. It's the engine that makes the real money.

○ In future, production expertise will be more fluid. Already we are seeing expertise in terms of content creation, across a range of suppliers.

○ In future, with communication channels fragmenting and multiplying further, we can expect to see the production 'tail' getting much longer; and the cost to clients of production will increase.

○ The media agencies will feel they can compete on price, and will see themselves as those who can best understand many of these channels; and they will therefore try to get into the production game themselves.

○ AFP expertise will be a further area where media agencies try to get involved.

• Secondly, in terms of ideas:

○ With communications planning at this time, clients will be looking for 'rigour plus'; a reliance on 'just ideas' will not cut it.

○ And while today ad agencies are still seen as the best purveyors of communication ideas, this will be less so in future. In a world of multiple communication channels and increasingly digital, interactive content, clients will need genuine solution-neutral, strategic communication ideas, and these will come from many suppliers.

○ Clients will even be creating communication ideas themselves.

• Faced with these threats, ad agencies will not be able to defend on all fronts and will be forced to choose between two routes:

○ creativity/ideas + communications planning;

○ creativity/ideas + production.

• Those that go down the former route will metamorphose into ad agency-based communication independents, and will sit alongside their media agency-based cousins.

• Among the agencies doing communications planning (servicing those clients that choose not to do it themselves), the competitive environment will result in some fusion between agency types.

Part IV
Weightlessness

2020 onwards

A period where ideas make a comeback; where their ROI value is 'outed'

A period where communications planning is liberated

A period of 'unconscious competence'

11
2020 Vision

A summary of where we end up at in 2020 and how each of the players will have done over the period 2005–2020

I set out at the beginning of this book to try to predict what would happen to communications planning up to the year 2020. Having now gone through how I see things evolving over the years, here's where we arrive at in 2020.

Those at the centre of things will be the big winners

Being in a central place is always a good idea in business. This is partly about ensuring that you do not become too specialised in one area. Here we can take a lesson from the big retailers like Wal-Mart, which provide everything under one roof, as cheaply as possible.

It is also about reconciling different cultural tensions. For most of the years 2010–2020, we can expect to see data and ROI as the biggest drivers in communications planning. While those companies that can embrace this data reality will do well, nevertheless doing communications planning will always demand a balance in perspective. You might recall that in the Foreword Ken Sacharin talked about the two types of people that inhabit the marketing and communication world – the artists and the engineers – and communications planning will demand the skill sets of both. Therefore those organisations that end up as the primary 'doers' will be those that become adept at both the insight/ideas side of things and the ROI side of things – those that can reconcile the polar cultural tensions under the same roof and create conditions that enable mutual respect of the two, while never favouring one over the other.

As I've indicated several times, those that can best do this over the period 2005–2020 will be clients, media agencies, integrated BTL agencies, and media agency-based communication independents.

And as I mentioned in the last chapter, in the period between 2015 and 2020, some significant ad agencies will start to abandon production in favour of strategy and communications planning. Here they will metamorphose as ad agency-based communication independents. They will beef up their strategy credentials and find ways of obtaining access to tools, data and rigour; and they will also join this group of key players at the centre of things.

By 2020, we will start to see the effect of the new ad agency-based communication independents, in terms of their share of the communications planning pie. Compared with the picture in 2015, when ad agencies had just about slid off the communications planning map, we can see that they will have reversed the declining fortunes of the ad agencies in this area (Figures 11.1 and 11.2).

Coming back to the Strategy Map, you can see the effect of the new ad agency-based communication independents in moving the pendulum back towards the middle again (Figure 11.3).

How will the individual players have fared over the years?

For everyone, 2020 will be a better place in terms of communications planning revenue. Everyone will be earning more than they were in 2005 – and by 2020 communications planning will be approaching the norm in terms of communications process.

Reflecting on the growth of the market as a whole over the 15-year period, you can see in Figure 11.4 how revenue is likely to evolve. It will show slow growth, until the pivotal point in 2010. After this

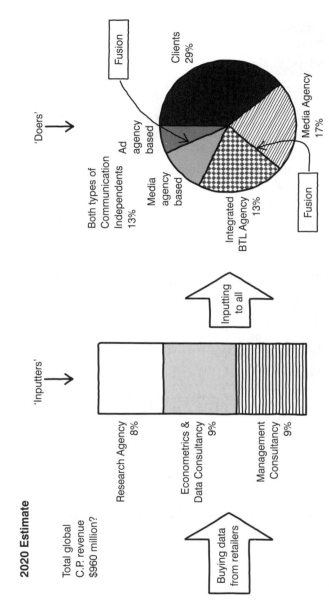

Fig. 11.1 Communications planning estimated size and share – 2020.

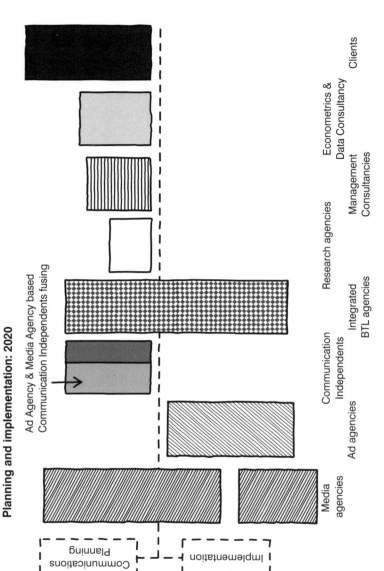

Fig. 11.2 Planning and implementation – 2020.

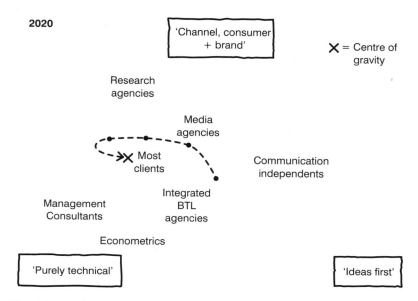

Fig. 11.3 The Strategy Map: 2020.

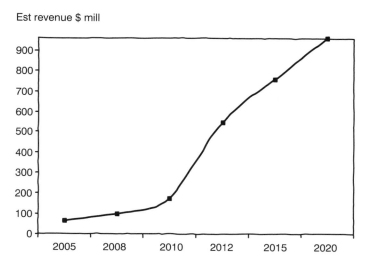

Fig. 11.4 Projected revenue – communications planning: All.

it will boom, thanks to a much increased demand for communications planning from clients (who will now fully understand its advantages) as well as the ability to link it to ROI effect, and thus get paid well for it.

But some players will have gained share and will have outpaced the market. Others will have lost share and will have been outpaced by the market. Figures 11.5–11.12 show my thumb-suck estimates of the projected fortunes of the eight main players in the Space Race – ad agencies, media agencies, integrated BTL agencies, communication independents, clients, research agencies, econometrics/data consultancies and management consultancies.

In 2020, what will life be like?

Let me speculate . . . Asia will be more important than North America; and more and more client companies and agencies will be moving their head offices to places like Shanghai and Mumbai.

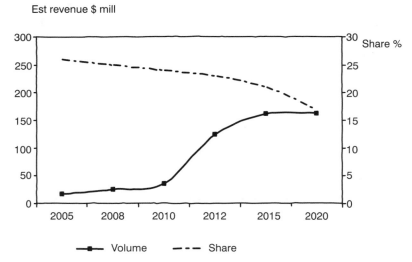

Fig. 11.5 Projected revenue – communications planning: Media Agencies.

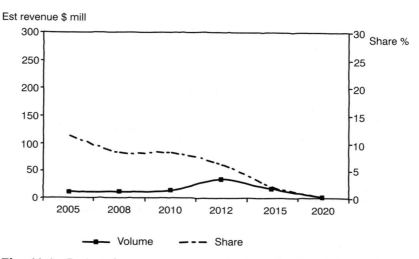

Fig. 11.6 Projected revenue – communications planning: Ad Agencies.

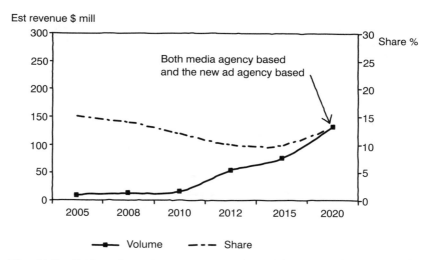

Fig. 11.7 Projected revenue – communications planning: Communication Independents.

Est revenue $ mill

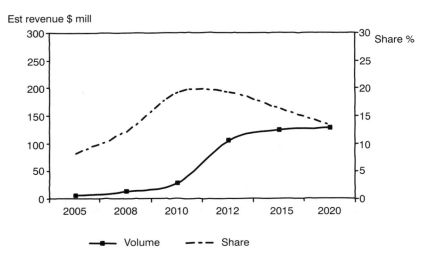

Fig. 11.8 Projected revenue – communications planning: Integrated BTL Agencies.

Est revenue $ mill

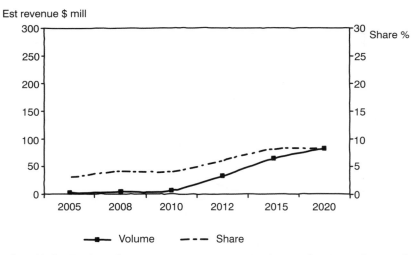

Fig. 11.9 Projected revenue – communications planning: Research Agencies.

Est revenue $ mill

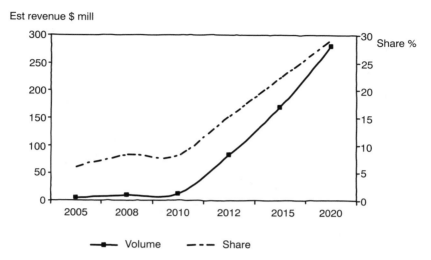

Fig. 11.10 Projected revenue – communications planning: Clients.

Est revenue $ mill

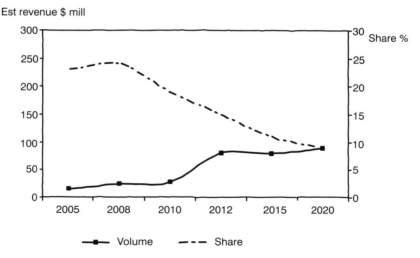

Fig. 11.11 Projected revenue – communications planning: Management Consultants.

Est revenue $ mill

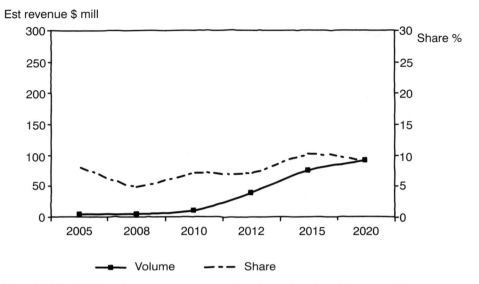

Fig. 11.12 Projected revenue – communications planning: Econometrics Data Consultancies.

Hillary Clinton might still be in power, but running for re-election against Kurt Russell (the ex-actor). P&G will have opened its first international retail supermarket chain, called All-in-one. The mobile phone will be the new TV, the top of the hierarchy of communication channels. And marketing directors will be the second most highly paid individuals in client companies, after the CEO.

Of course, none of these things may happen, but one thing is sure. Fifteen years is long enough for there to be some significant changes in the world. What's the quote about overestimating short-term change and underestimating long-term change? Well, 15 years is long enough for there to be some big changes.

So if you feel that my vision of 2020, in terms of communications planning, is quite a jump away from today's reality, think about the timescale. It's a decent amount of time. How old will you be in 2020?

But then, given the rate of change in a technological sense, there may be those among you who feel that by 2020, the outcome should be more radical and decisive. So although I've outlined some big changes, perhaps you think there should be some more clear-cut winners and losers – and that I haven't been brave enough in my thinking.

Well, that may be so. But I've resisted the temptation to create a series of potential models or scenarios, which ultimately would have been fence sitting and frustrating for you to read. I've tried to be logical and objective. I've tried to look at the changes that I believe will occur at a macro level and how these will play out, without favouring anyone in particular.

Based on all the developments we expect to see, we know that this 'road' up until 2020 will be a difficult one for clients and agencies. There will be a lot of pressure, and a lot of tension.

In the period between 2010 and 2020, where change is happening fastest and where we are, in effect, cutting through the Earth's atmosphere, the ad agencies in particular will be under immense pressure. For them, in a defensive position and with extremely tight margins, change will be very traumatic. Within client organisations marketing will have a new-found sense of responsibility, but there will be a lot of pressure to drive sales through communication.

I think that where we arrive at is potentially realistic and broadminded. And in its own way, it is a very different place to where we are today; in particular, a place where the client is far more the driver of things and not just the recipient.

◆

Key points made in this chapter

2020 vision

- Looking at developments over the period up until 2020, those at the centre of things will be the big winners: clients, media agencies, integrated BTL agencies and communication independents.

- Part of their success will have been in their ability to move to the left – to embrace ROI, rigour and data – while nevertheless still providing some sense of balance between the left and right, between ROI and ideas.
- Those ad agencies that metamorphose into the new ad agency-based communication independents will also become increasingly successful, and central in the game going further into the future.

12
Beyond 2020: The ROI of Snow

A look at the future beyond 2020, where ideas start to drive communications planning

There is a lot of talk today about ideas, innovation and creativity at the CEO level in business. In the US there is a new breed of CEO emerging – ideas champions like Edwin Land of Polaroid, Joe Wilson of Xerox, Michael Dell of Dell Computing and Steve Jobs of Apple (and in fact Steve Jobs credits Land as the inspiration behind Apple in the early days). They are having an infectious affect on other CEOs, like Sam Palmisano, who has recently taken over at IBM and is now driving ideas and innovation throughout that business.

But despite all the talk about ideas and creativity at the CEO level of business, my view is that in the next 15 years, further down the food chain in marketing – which is supposedly the more ideas-oriented part of client companies – there will be less focus on ideas and more on return on investment.

Around 2010, communication will take a very necessary leap forward, and we will finally be able to link communication exposure through to sales. We will be able to tell the effect that a piece of communication has had, down to the level of which communication channels and disciplines have had the biggest effect for the least money.

This will be a very necessary prerequisite in marketing communications. But because marketing will suddenly be held more responsible and accountable for the sales effect of communication, then the decade that follows will be all about driving sales; and modelling the past to predict the future will become the overpowering modus operandi in marketing and communications planning.

Short-term measures – that is, sales – will dominate over intermediate or longer-term measures, such as brand saliency or brand momentum. We will lose some of the ability to look at the longer term.

In the years preceding and after 2020, I believe that things might start changing again. We will go into a new chapter. Ideas will come back 'in' again. Whereas the previous decade will have been characterised by our ability to link communication in general to return on investment, the next decade will be all about our ability to link ideas to return on investment. The economic argument behind ideas will be 'outed'.

Like many things, you need to go through a tough spell to come out at a better place. You need increasing agency specialisation to get to discipline equality, the precursor for real communications planning. So too you need to go through the dark days of data to get to a place where ideas are liberated again.

As I write, it's snowing outside. This might play havoc with the trains, but I really like snow; in fact, most people do. There is something magical about it; something slightly other-worldly; something that transforms our lives for the odd day. It brings with it a sense of possibilities.

Snow and rain are essentially the same thing – water in the air. And to me, communication is similar. It is the equivalent of water in the air. This communication can be 'rain' – just another ad, just another bit of communication drizzle. Or it can be snow. And to me, ideas are the 'snow' of the world of communication. They transform it into something magical.

They are things that humans respond to, a little like jokes or humour somehow: they provoke a positive reaction inside our brains. They engage emotionally and rationally. They hold a kind of promise of a slightly better world, an altered perspective. They are things that humans remember. In a world of oversupply, sophistication and attention deficit, ideas attract us like beacons; and consequently, often they produce the biggest jumps in return on investment. These are not incremental, small efficiency steps that we might get by moving a bit of money here and there, between brands, geographies, channels and disciplines, but big leaps.

The real issue is that past performance is measurable. We can use this measurement to create improvements in planning and implementation; we can even respond and create very rapid feedback loops, so that learning gets acted on very quickly. But – and it's a very big but – past performance is not a prediction of future success. Modelling the past will only make the future a little better. It will not produce the leaps. It will not get us beyond 'good'. So how do we look forward while not ignoring backwards? How do we look both ways simultaneously?

In the past, implementing new ideas has always involved a leap of faith. That is why you see so few ideas implemented. For every 100 ideas generated, probably only one is ever implemented. In business, we are uncomfortable with leaps of faith, because business has a responsibility to shareholders to be responsible! Ideas are scary, disruptive things in business. Not so in our personal lives – everyone who gets married takes a leap of faith. We do it all the time as kids, growing up; we do new things – things for the first time – every day. But ideas in business? It's easy to talk a good game and agree with their importance; less easy to sign them off.

So to sell ideas, we always come back to case studies of how ideas have transformed things for others. For example, a few years ago BMW in the US took its ad budget and redirected it into producing films with famous directors, which it then showed on the internet. But it promoted them so well, that test drives – the most important KPI in this case for BMW – went up tenfold. We've all played the case-study game, and unfortunately, putting up 20 case studies doesn't ever really prove anything.

Andorra

Post 2020, we will be able to start to sell ideas on more than leaps of faith or case studies – because, I believe, we will start to see the serious pre-testing of ideas. In much the same way as we meticulously test an ad before executing it today, we will do the same with ideas tomorrow. This will mean that we can predict the ROI effect of an idea before we roll it out. We will be able to give it a 'return on an idea investment' figure (an expression I pinched from an article by Sam Rudder, 2001).

How will we do this? How will we be able to look forwards and backwards simultaneously? Well, let me introduce you to Andorra. Andorra – in case you don't know – is the little country that sits in the Pyrenees mountains between Spain and France. It's small, beautiful and relatively isolated. And it's the sort of place that might, peculiarly, have an important role in communications planning post 2020. The thing about ideas is that they generally travel. They need local interpretation, but a good idea is a good idea is a good idea.

Looking forwards and backwards in future may mean putting ideas discretely into little markets (or regions) to see if they work; testing ideas, but in a confined geography that limits the economic risk, then analysing how well they work. For a global brand, this might mean running 'normal' communication around the world, while simultaneously testing three possible 'future communication ideas' at one time, in three tight geographies. Testing tomorrow, today, quietly.

The differences in sales effect between two separate communication ideas is potentially quite large. Granted, execution of an idea is as important as the idea itself. But the fundamental truth is that two communication ideas will always have very different 'return on an idea investment' figures. And if ideas can truly be applied around the world, the amount of money it would cost to run and test a communication idea in a country like Andorra, relative to the potential global payback if it's a great idea, is peanuts.

This is nothing new, let me add. Clients already run test markets for new product development. In the UK, the city of Newcastle is the test bed for the nation. It's relatively compact and socially representative. As a consequence, lots of brand-owner clients test new products there and there are often products in the shops that you won't find elsewhere. But as yet, clients have not applied this type of thinking to the business of global communication ideas.

A couple of people I interviewed for this book thought that the real-world testing of ideas could indeed be a possibility in the future.

Coming at it from an advertising point of view, Reg Lascaris of TBWA remarked:

Clients at the moment would test an idea using consumer research. But if an idea is totally unique, you can't really judge its effect in the marketplace using existing research techniques. So I like the real-world idea testing notion.

And coming at it from a researcher and econometrician point of view, Nigel Foote, group strategy director and managing partner EMEA for Starcom, had this to add:

Judging future performance from what consumers say [in pre-test groups, for example] is going to be increasingly unreliable. We need more effective test and control to drive communications effectiveness – and we need to look at what people do, not what they say. The problem with test and control approaches in the past was delays – by the time you get a clear read your competitors are alerted and can copy you. In the future, through better data understanding and behavioural metrics, we will be able to learn from test cases much quicker. You'll be able to understand if an idea was good, very quickly, and then have the confidence to go with it. The future will all be about parallel testing and refining multiple strategies in-market, rather than the consumer group 'pre-test' and gradual roll-out we tend to have today.

To summarise . . .

Post 2020, we will all have developed a sense of basic skill with communications planning. We will be competent. And we will want to go further. Linking return on investment beyond past performance of channels and disciplines, and applying it to future-facing ideas, will be the next big breakthrough.

Ideas, just as strategy before them, will have to make a pact with measurement in order to take a big jump forward. This will be a pact with the 'devil', some may feel. But inevitably, it will be the only way that anyone will ever be truly paid for ideas. For how else can we, as agencies, expect a manufacturing client to shell out, say, $1 million for an idea, unless we all have some way to really value it?

Talking to Rob Hill from Ogilvy South Africa, he made an interesting observation about this:

There's a traditional paradox between ideas and measurability. Solving it, maybe we need to think laterally, as you are doing. I'm reminded of the famous Einstein quote . . . where he talked about paradox. In his view, you could only solve a paradox by elevating your thinking to a higher level. He had the view that at a higher level, all paradoxes blend.

Real-world idea testing may well be one way to do this. And the ROI of ideas, or the ROI of snow, will be the new driver of communications planning post 2020.

So the balance between the left side and the right side of the Strategy Map will come back from over on the left into the middle. And the 'shape' of communications planning will go from a pyramid on its side to an hour-glass on its side. This is shown in Figure 12.1.

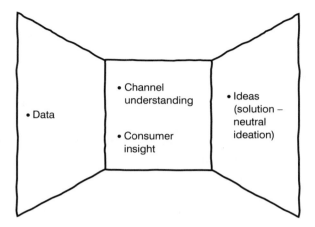

Fig. 12.1 Constituents of communications planning post 2020.

◆

Key points made in this chapter

- Ideas are the 'snow' of the world of communication. They transform communication into something magical.
- In the past, selling ideas has always relied on case studies, and implementing ideas has always involved a leap of faith.
- In future, we will increasingly apply ideas globally, and we will start seriously pre-testing ideas. We will use discrete, small countries like Andorra to do so.
- This is because the amount of money it will cost to run an idea in a small country like this is a relatively small investment, compared to the potential global payback if it turns out to be a great idea and the idea can be applied globally thereafter.
- Post 2020, we will increasingly be able to determine the 'return on an idea investment'. And the ROI of ideas will be the new driver of communications planning.

Last Words

This is a book about marketing. It takes a broader, more holistic view, beyond a navel-gazing agency view and beyond the situation today.

This is also a book about hope: hope for our collective industry. It tells the tale of how, in these years after the break-up of the full-service agency, communications planning has come along to turn things on their heads once again; but coming out of which, in 15 or 20 years down the line, we will all be in a better place.

It takes us through the dark days of data, but then gives us a glimpse of a future beyond this, where ideas make a comeback and can be tied to return on investment; and where marketing has embraced communications planning and ideation, empowering itself in the process.

It shows us how ad agencies – when it comes to communications planning – will struggle for many, many years; but ultimately they will metamorphose into entities that are much more competitive again.

It demonstrates how integrated BTL and media agencies will grow up alongside each other, competing but with a sense of mutual respect. It also shows us how communication independents will flourish over the years.

It's all about the agency business growing up and coming to a better understanding of and respect for data. It's about how we will come to a far more sophisticated view of mixing data-based knowledge with consumer insight, understanding of communication channels and ideation; and of what will drive decision making. As a by-product, the agency business will come to see itself as an equal to management consultancies.

So while there will be ups and downs for all of us along the way, this book sees the future as a place where communication is more sure of itself and its contribution to brands, brand valuation and sales.

When I spoke to Rob Hill of Ogilvy South Africa, he shared this view that communications planning would help the industry grow up:

In a way, the industry needs to take another step forward in terms of maturity. And I think communications planning will do this. It will become a fundamentally strategic lever, and not just a lever that has a lingering question mark. It will drive accountability in the industry which will see a second revolution. It will drive forward what you could call the 'professionalisation' of marketing.

Many people have talked about us going from the 'marketing age' in the late twentieth century and into the 'creative age' in the twenty-first century. But to me, they are not mutually incompatible. In my view, we will never really leave the marketing age; it's just that marketing will have to change; it will have to become more creative itself. And communications planning will be what empowers it to do this.

For some client companies, this will be extraordinarily difficult. Internal 'corporate' culture often hampers innovation and creativity. So too does the high people churn – I think the average length of time that marketing people spend in a job is only around nine months, which is even less time than it is on the agency side. Nevertheless, marketing within client companies will get there, and will be more empowered in the process.

How much do I believe what I've written? Well, I do have a few core beliefs.

First, I think that the future of communications planning will depend on how far the industry can measure communication activity and link it to behaviour and sales.

Secondly, I believe that there's an inevitability about clients, at some point, getting to grips with communications planning themselves and coming to see it as a core competency.

Thirdly, I believe that there's an inevitability about ideas coming to drive communications planning down the line, but only after we've gone through a period of modelling data and 'backward-facing' planning.

The detail in this book is simply wrapping around these views.

Funnily enough, even with the core beliefs, I acknowledge that the outcome in terms of agency shares could be quite different to the one I've detailed in the book. There could absolutely be an element of fluke or luck in it all. If the clients who drive the whole thing in the next few years take a certain view that it should go one particular way, then this will steer the development of communications planning, regardless of other forces or logic. Which clients commit first will be important.

Furthermore, the ad agencies might do a lot better than I envisage – if clients choose to help them to do so. If you're talking about FMCG clients, most see their most senior relationships still with the ad agencies. So these clients might take a long-term view and say, let's have a bit of protectionism. They might say, 'I want to retain the ad agency as my most senior agency partner long term. I know they're not perfect in terms of today's changing world. But they will get there eventually. And it is my responsibility to help them to do this; to help them evolve, to help change their model.' So you might see some ad agencies coming through this smoothly, because they'll have the support of clients.

I can also envisage two other potentially big variations on what I've written.

First, the chief 'doer' in the future (alongside the client itself) might not be the group of agencies that I have written about so often – the integrated BTL, media agencies and communication independents – but rather, some form of agency holding group entity. Secondly, the retailers may also become 'doers'. In this case, if a manufacturer wanted to communicate in-store with its customers, it would just have to give the retailer a brief and budget and let it do the communications planning for the brand, in its own environment.

So there we are. One thing's for sure: there is going to be plenty of competition in the 'doer' space, and even in the 'inputter' space. There will be no simplistic outcomes.

Recently, at an American Association of Advertising Agencies' Media conference, they asked attendees in the opening session what was the most important industry trend at the moment: 38% of them said it was communications planning. The next highest (quite a way behind) was cross-media measurement at 21%; then came econometrics/market-mix modelling at 19%; single-source measurement initiatives like Project Apollo at 10%; and branded entertainment/product placement at 10% as well.

The interesting thing from my point of view is how our industry seems to see communications planning and measurement as both highly important but somewhat intertwined. This goes some way to vindicate my core beliefs. Together, communications planning and measurement will form the backbone of marketing in the future.

Interestingly, the same attendees were asked to vote on how the agencies were doing to facilitate communications planning. The consensus was poorly, with the media agencies being seen as the least constructive of everyone. So while our industry can clearly see the importance of communications planning, we're at a loss on how best to take it forwards. I hope this book helps.

And in fact, this book in its broadest sense is all about my desire for our industry to fly, which I believe it truly can. And therefore as a

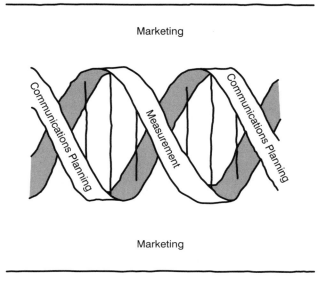

Fig. 12.2   Communications planning and measurement are interwoven.

metaphor I've shown the developments that I foresee as a journey from wanting to fly to learning to fly to cutting through the Earth's atmosphere and becoming weightless. A hundred years ago such a journey would have seemed incredible and the state of weightlessness unthinkable. Most people looked up at space with their boots planted firmly on the ground and scoffed at the insane few who dared to dream that one day someone would fly to the moon. But just as the smart application of ideas and technology has put men and women into orbit and beyond, so over the next few years communications planning looks set to propel the marketing and communications industry into a completely different dimension. No doubt there will be some difficulties on this journey, but at its end I believe that the industry has the ability to produce something extraordinary – as extraordinary as floating in the sky or, indeed, holding a snowflake in the palm of your hand!

Profiles of Interviewees.

Paul Alexander, vice-president, global advertising, Campbell Soup Company

Based in Camden, New Jersey, USA

Paul Alexander is vice-president, global advertising for the Campbell Soup Company and is responsible for all advertising, media and commercial production. He started with Campbell's in February 2001. Prior to that, he spent 15 years in brand management and advertising development with Procter & Gamble in Cincinnati, Ohio and London. Paul serves on the board of directors of the Ad Council and is a member of the ANA. He received his undergraduate degree from Harvard College and his MBA from Harvard Business School.

Paul Baker, managing director, Ohal Limited

Based in London, UK

Paul joined Ohal in 1975 when it was a small company exploring – and also leading – in the area of 'how advertising works on sales'. Innovative companies – such as Beecham, Brooke Bond Oxo, Bowater Scott and Pedigree Petfoods – were keen to learn in this area and duly commissioned projects to evaluate their media spend. Initial agency 'hostility' has now changed such that forward-looking agencies now see 'accountability' as a positive element of their relationships with clients, and econometrics as the most effective way of carrying this out. The IPA Awards are a major proof of this. Ohal is now the largest econometrics group in Europe with a significant office in the US and has recently become part of WPP.

Stephan Bruneau, managing partner, Mediaedge:cia EMEA

Based in London, UK

Stephan started his career at P&G where he gained experience in marketing, media, business analysis and knowledge management over 10 years. In 2001 Stephan joined Accenture's Marketing Sciences team in London, where he advised global companies on ways to improve the effectiveness and efficiency of their marketing investments. Since 2004, Stephan has been a managing partner at Mediaedge:cia, based in London. He is heading MediaLab for EMEA, Mediaedge:cia's insight and ROI unit specialising in consumer, market and media research, tools supporting the communications planning process, as well as consultancy projects in the ROI area.

Marie Therese Carney, senior partner and worldwide planning director, Ogilvy

Based in New York, USA

Marie Therese (or MT) started her career in the media department of Ogilvy & Mather in London, where she developed award-winning work for Guinness and Ford. After moving to Ammiratti Puris Lintas, she moved into account planning, where she worked on many accounts including Unilever and Iridium. On arriving in New York, she worked for Michaelides & Bednash before taking the role of worldwide director of strategic planning for Universal McCann. Returning to her first agency, Ogilvy & Mather, in 2004, MT has been given global responsibility for 360-degree communications planning, as well as a five-person global planning management team.

Will Collin, co-founder, Naked Communications

Based in London, UK

Will began his career at BMP DDB as a trainee account planner in 1989. There he worked on clients such as H.J. Heinz and Alliance & Leicester, for which he won an IPA Effectiveness Award in 1992. In 1997 he moved to media specialist PHD as communications strategy director, then in 2000 he founded Naked Communications with Jon Wilkins and John Harlow. Will is a regular speaker and commentator on communications issues, for example with the Account Planning Group, the Marketing Society and the Advertising Association. He is a member of the IPA Strategy Committee and IPA Council, and a module editor for the IPA Excellence Diploma.

Charles Courtier, worldwide executive chairman, Mediaedge:cia

Based in New York, USA

Charles has worked in the media world for over 20 years. He is currently worldwide executive chairman of Mediaedge:cia and was instrumental in the development and rollout of the company around the world. He moved to New York in 2001 and holds the additional responsibility for Mediaedge:cia's North American operations. Prior to this he was CEO of The Media Edge across Europe, Middle East and Africa and successfully launched the company in 37 countries in the region. His advertising roots are through Young & Rubicam, where his final role was European media director before the creation of The Media Edge beckoned.

Jonathan Dodd, executive vice-president, G2 Worldwide

Based in London, UK

In the early 1980s, Jonathan joined Grey in the UK. He was a founding partner of Joshua, now a top three integrated communications agency in the UK, and more recently of Geometry, a brand design consultancy. In 1999, Jonathan was one of the original founders of G2, Grey Global Group's international branding network. His most recent client responsibilities have included being global brand director for British American Tobacco. At the beginning of 2004, Jonathan was also asked to lead the group's 'First Moment of Truth' and Shopper Marketing initiative, working with P&G to meet its growing needs in this important area.

Nick Emery, chief strategy officer, MindShare Worldwide

Based in London, UK

Nick is currently chief strategy officer for MindShare Worldwide. He is responsible for global client service and product development as well as working with the WOW Factory on idea generation. He also works with the British government on the advisory committee for the National Grid for Learning.

Nigel Foote, group strategy director and managing partner EMEA, Starcom

Based in London, UK

Nigel is responsible for the strategic resources across the Starcom Group, namely the Starcom Intelligence Unit, and the Contact Innovation and Media Systems teams. Having over 16 years of experience in senior and board-level management roles across the disciplines of media strategy, planning and research, Nigel was most recently MD of TNS Media Intelligence. Prior to that he was managing partner of the marketing analytics consultancy Hudson River Group in the US, and deputy MD of a leading internet and new technology research consultancy.

John Grant, brand marketing consultant

Based in London, UK

John Grant has written several highly acclaimed books on the future of brand marketing and has advised prominent international organisations on brand strategy and communications, including IKEA, Diageo, Coca-Cola, the BBC, Napster, Nokia, the Government of Sweden, BT, Heidrick and Struggles and the Ministry of Sound. Before becoming an independent consultant, John worked in advertising from 1987 to 1999. He was planning director of Chiat/Day London as well as a co-founder of St Luke's.

Bruce Haines, group chief executive, Leo Burnett

Based in London, UK

Bruce began his advertising career in 1973 at Garland Compton. He moved to Young & Rubicam and then to Abbott Mead Vickers, becoming its first head of client services. Following its purchase by AMV, Bruce moved to Leagas Delaney as managing director, subsequently becoming CEO and chairman of the agency, where he worked on clients as diverse as Harrods, Tanner Krolle, Nationwide, BBC, Hyundai, Adidas and Pepe Jeans. In 2001 he was elected president of the Institute of Practitioners in Advertising (the industry's trade body), a position he held until April 2003. In 2002 he joined Leo Burnett as group chief executive.

Rob Hill, national strategy director, Ogilvy South Africa

Based in Cape Town, South Africa

Rob began his career in communication as a copywriter, first for the IMA, then for O&M. For the last 16 years, he has worked as a strategic planner on a diverse range of accounts, including SAB, Old Mutual and VW. Rob has a particular interest in corporate brand development, the increasing importance of branding in corporate strategy, 360-degree communication, internal brand management and ethnographic research.

Chris Ingram, founder, The Ingram Partnership

Based in London, UK

Chris Ingram started in advertising in 1960 and worked in several agencies before founding the media specialist CIA in 1976. CIA was floated on the London Stock Exchange in 1989 and by 2000 the holding company, Tempus Group, was a marketing and media communications group with 67 offices across 29 countries. In 2001 it was sold to WPP for over £430 million. In 2002 Chris launched Genesis Investments, a private equity business, and in July 2003 he launched The Ingram Partnership, a strategic brand-building and communications consultancy. He is deputy chairman of London Business School's Foundation for Entrepreneurial Management and chairman and owner of Woking Football Club.

Reg Lascaris, regional CEO, TBWA Group & co-founder, TBWA Hunt Lascaris

Based in Johannesburg, South Africa

TBWA Hunt Lascaris was formed in 1983 with Reg Lascaris as managing director. Today he is responsible for the Africa, Middle East and Mediterranean regions and is head of business development for the worldwide group. He is also one of 12 main board members of TBWA Worldwide. TBWA Hunt Lascaris is widely recognised as one of the most creative agencies in the world and it has won countless awards, including *Financial Mail*'s Agency of the Century and recently Agency of the Decade. Reg is also the co-author of five bestselling books, *Third World Destiny*, *Communicating in the Third World*, *Revelling in the Wild*, *Fire and Water* and *The South African Dream*.

Kees Kruythoff, chairman, Unilever B.R. South Africa

Based in Durban, South Africa

Kees joined Unilever Rotterdam in 1993, and worked for the Spreads business in several different marketing and sales jobs. In 1999, he moved to South Africa as brand development director. Then between 2002 and 2004 he moved to Asia, where he helped build up the foods business, in particular with N.E.A. Lipton in China. Still in love with Africa, however, Kees returned to South Africa in 2004 and was appointed chairman.

Richard M. Metzler, executive vice-president, marketing, DHL Express

Based in Florida, USA

Dick Metzler has 25 years of transporta-tion and logistics marketing experience. He spent close to two decades as a senior leader in FedEx's marketing depart-ment. More recently, Dick was at APL Logistics, a $1 billion global third-party logistics and supply chain management company, where he served as chief executive officer. He joined DHL in September 2003, and is responsible for overseeing all of its marketing activities in North and South America, including advertising, customer acquisition and retention and market research. In his time at DHL, he has raised its brand awareness in the US and has driven new product development and pricing strategy.

George Michaelides, co-founder, Michaelides & Bednash

Based in London, UK

George Michaelides created the concept of media strategy at UK creative hot-shop HHCL, going on to co-found the world's first ever media strategy agency, Michaelides & Bednash. The company has grown to include offices in London and New York, and counts Unilever and Channel 4 among its clients. In recognition of his track record for innovation, *Campaign* magazine named George 'Media Pioneer of the 1990s', as well as listing him as one of advertising's 10 leading shapers.

Grant Millar, head of media in group marketing and brand, British Telecom

Based in London, UK

Grant Millar started out in media in the UK with a year at Haymarket Publishing. This was followed by four years as a media planner at MediaVest in the UK. Grant joined BT in October 1998 and is responsible for the BT Media Team, which has raised the profile of media as a strategic item within BT by revealing the business impact of effective media planning and buying, and demonstrating that media innovation and creativity can build brand and business results. In 2004 his role extended to include heading up the communications planning team: in combination with media to enable through-the-line media and messaging strategy for all BT communications.

Guy Murphy, deputy chairman, Bartle Bogle Hegarty

Based in London, UK

Guy is a director of the advertising agency Bartle Bogle Hegarty, which he joined in 1991. His background is in account planning. In 1997 he moved from the London office to BBH in Singapore to be head of planning for the Asia Pacific region. Four years later he returned as head of planning for Europe, and was promoted to deputy chairman in 2004.

Damian O'Malley, executive planning director UK and Ireland, McCann Erickson

Based in London, UK

Prior to joining McCann in 2004 Damian ran a successful international brand architecture consultancy with offices in London, Dublin, New York and Los Angeles. Between 1977 and 1997 he worked as an account planner at Gold Greenlees Trott, Woollams Moira, Gaskin O'Malley and DDB (London and New York). Damian is an honorary life member of the APG and a founder member and former chair of the AAAA's US Account Planning committee. In 1998 he was named as one of the two planners in *Campaign* magazine's fantasy agency of the last 30 years.

John Partilla, president, Time Warner Global Marketing

Based in New York, USA

John joined Time Warner in 2004 and is responsible for driving global marketing in its mission to work with major advertisers and help drive the growth of advertising and marketing revenue across all of Time Warner's businesses. Prior to this, John spent 18 years at Young & Rubicam and amassed an extensive roster of brand development experience, having worked across most of Y&R's businesses including Campbell's, Colgate, Kraft, Sony and Viacom. He managed dozens of brands globally across these client portfolios, particularly for Colgate's international business units. Notably, in 2000, John was founder and CEO of Brand Buzz, a $100 million billing creative solutions agency within Y&R Inc.

John Preston, founder and director, Match Integration

Based in Sydney, Australia

Initially John worked for J. Walter Thompson and Bartle Bogle Hegarty in London, specialising in media. He moved to Australia in 1990 and has made major contributions to Ogilvy & Mather, Campaign Palace (Melbourne), Mojo and Optimedia (where he was managing director). Recent experiences have been as founding partner, regional media director and subsequently managing director of Whybin Lawrence TBWA. Under John's term as managing director the agency was voted Sydney agency of the year and the fastest-growing communications company by BRW 'fast 100 companies'. John has now established an integrated multi-channel planning company, Match Integration.

Tony Regan, co-founder, Nylon

Based in London, UK

Tony is regarded as one of the pioneers of communications planning in the UK. Since 1990, when he joined HHCL to initiate the controversial new discipline of 'media strategy', he has continued to develop the specialism, in 1994 as a founding partner of Michaelides & Bednash and then in 2001 as joint managing director of PHD. His early career was in research and advertising planning, and he has since been a champion of insight-led communications planning.

Paul Shearer, global creative director, Nitro

Based in London, UK

Paul started in the business in 1989. He worked for many years at Bartle Bogle Hegarty with John Hegarty as one of the creative heads, and then went on to work at Wieden and Kennedy Europe as executive creative director, where he directed many famous Nike commercials. He has won a bunch of awards, from five Cannes Lions to eight D&AD pencils. However, Paul is genuinely more motivated by sales results than awards.

Martin Thomas, co-founder, Nylon

Based in London, UK

In 2004, Martin co-founded Nylon, the communications planning JV that is owned by Y&R, Wunderman and Mediaedge:cia. Prior to this, Martin had in fact worked for Mediaedge:cia for five years, heading up communications planning and advising clients in the particular areas of sponsorship, media relations, presence marketing and brand experience. Before Mediaedge:cia, Martin had been UK managing director for Cohn & Wolfe, one of the world's leading PR consultancies, working on brands such as Coca-Cola and Absolut.

James Walker, partner, Accenture Marketing Sciences

Based in London, UK

James Walker is a partner in Accenture's CRM practice, where he is the EMEA lead for Accenture Marketing Sciences. James joined Accenture when it acquired his company, Edge Consulting, in 2002. Previously, James was a director of Edge Consulting, chairman of Brand Science, worldwide chairman MindShare ATG, media development director at J. Walter Thompson, and director of market modelling at the Henley Centre. At Edge Consulting, James developed new tools and processing for marketing–mix/portfolio optimisation analyses and worked with major multinationals in various industries on projects across many different countries.

Peter Walshe, global account director, Millward Brown

Based in Warwick, UK

Peter has been at Millward Brown for the last 15 years and is responsible for developing and running several key global accounts, including SportZ and BrandZ (the WPP worldwide brand equity study covering more than 22 000 brands and delivered to over 2500 clients via the internet). He is a winner of a recent Atticus Award for a paper on measuring the effectiveness of PR. He originally trained and worked as an actor (appearing in several TV commercials as well as famous shows such as *Dr Who* and *The Naked Civil Servant*).

Rod Wright, worldwide CEO, TEQUILA\

Based in London, UK

Rod is worldwide CEO of TEQUILA\ and has also been director of development for TBWA Worldwide since 2001. He has been part of the worldwide operating group of TBWA since it was formed in 2000. His career has taken him to work in London, Hong Kong, New York and Paris. He ran BDDP Europe from 1995–98 before doing a similar role for TBWA after the merger of the two companies. Prior to that he worked for Ogilvy & Mather in New York – as ADC to the chairman & CEO and responsible for Ogilvy & Mather Direct North America – and was in Hong Kong running Asia Pacific from 1990–95. He started his career in London, becoming managing director of Ogilvy & Mather Direct in 1997.

References

Preface

Dawson, Neil & Ellyatt, Michael (2003) 'What's the big idea?', The Account Planning Group, www.apg.org.uk.

Chapter 1

Sherrington, Mark (2003) *Added Value: The Alchemy of Brand-Led Growth*, Palgrave–Macmillan.

Chapter 2

AdAge (2004) 'McDonald's pulls further away from mass marketing', *AdAge*, 16 June.

Austin, Mark & Aitchison, Jim (2003) *Is Anybody Out There? The New Blueprint for Marketing Communications in the 21st Century*, John Wiley & Sons Ltd.

Business Week (2004) 'The vanishing mass market', *Business Week*, 12 July.

Duffy, Neill & Hooper, Jo (2003) *Passion Branding: Harnessing the Power of Emotion to Build Strong Brands*, John Wiley & Sons Ltd.

Earls, Mark (2003) 'Advertising to the herd: How understanding our true nature challenges the ways we think about advertising and market research', *International Journal of Market Research*, Vol. 45, No. 3.

Economist (2004) 'The harder hard sell', *Economist*, 26 June.

Financial Times 21 September 2004.

Grant, John (1999) *The New Marketing Manifesto: The 12 Rules for Building Successful Brands in the 21st Century*, Texere.

Grant, John (2002) *After Image: Mind Altering Marketing*, HarperCollins.

Marketing (2004a) 'Confused' , *Marketing*, 24 June, p. 86.

Marketing (2004b) 'Supermarket, banker . . . lawyer?', *Marketing*, 30 June.

Saunders, Julian (2004) 'Drowning in choice: The revolution', *Market Leader*, Spring.

Watts, Kate (2003) 'The power of influence in the age of reference'. *Admap*, September.

Chapter 3

Bullmore, Jeremy (2004) 'Who's going to sit at the client's top table?', *Admap*, October.

Sorrell, Martin (2002) 'Composing for the orchestra', *Marketing Week*, 29 October.

Chapter 4

Campaign (2004) 'New-model planners', *Campaign*, 3 December.

Chapter 5

Surowiecki, James (2004) *The Wisdom of Crowds: Why the Many Are Smarter Than the Few and How Collective Wisdom Shapes Business, Economies, Societies and Nations*, Random House.

Chapter 6

Malcolm, Rob (2002) '100% marketing', speech to British Brands Group.

Wood, John (2005) 'The impact of technology on integrated marketing', *Admap*, March.

Chapter 7

Baker, Paul (2004) 'Multimedia and multi-channel effects', *Admap*, October.

Christensen, Clayton (2000) *The Innovator's Dilemma: When New Technologies Cause Great Firms to Fail*, Harvard Business School Press.

Chapter 8

Aufreiter, Nora, Elzinga, David & Gordon, Jonathan (2003) 'Better branding', *McKinsey Quarterly*, November.

Chapter 9

Hill, Rob (2005) 'Isn't it time for brand governance?', Bizcommunity.com, www.biz-community.com, 19 January.

Chapter 10

Campaign (2005) 'Who is the best for branded content?', *Campaign*, 11 March.

Chapter 12

Rudder, Sam (2001) 'What future for ad agencies?', *Admap*, May.

Index

3G services 141

4Ps 183–4

360-degree communications planning 4–15, 47, 90, 188, 191, 194, 203, 210, 218, 257, 265

360-degree planning, contrasts 7–8, 90

2000–2005 period ('unconscious incompetence') 1–114

2005–2010 period ('conscious incompetence') 115–55

2010–2020 period ('conscious competence') 157–221, 225–6

2020 onwards period ('unconscious competence') 223–43

a

Abbott Mead Vickers BBDO 71

ABC process 4–5

above-the-line (ATL) 21–6, 29–30, 39, 58–60, 88–90, 209–10, 216–21

see also TV . . .

ad avoidance trends 24–5, 35–6, 80, 134–5, 159–60

dwindling importance 22, 26, 29, 58–60

fusion prospects 216–21, 245

overreliance 22–3, 209–10

Accenture 9, 73, 89, 105, 164, 171, 187, 219–20, 253

account management 66–7, 72–5

accountability issues 73–5, 115, 184–7, 238, 255

Achilles' heels 203–21

ACNielsen 142

ad agencies 4, 8–16, 20, 46–69, 74–5, 85, 88–113, 117–35, 170–4, 177–8, 196–9, 203–21, 226–31, 245–8

see also agencies

advantages 88–92, 111–13, 208–9, 226–35

change 211–21, 226–35, 245

dwindling importance 15–16

fusion prospects 215–21, 245

future prospects 111–13, 117–35, 170–4, 177–8, 196–9, 203–21, 226–31, 245–8

'generalist' requirements 66–7

'insurance' 54

legacy problems 95–6

major players 66–8, 88–92

networks 65–8, 88–92

P&L units 64–9, 96, 107–8

problems 15–16, 85, 88–92,
  94–103, 177–8, 196–7, 204–5,
  208–12, 245
production remuneration
  203–14
revenue streams 89–92, 175–6,
  203–14, 226–31
roles 14–20, 47–50, 59–68, 74–5,
  85–99, 105, 111–13, 133–5,
  170–8, 196–9, 203–21,
  226–31, 245–8
sense of purpose 94–7
split 212–21
types 65–8
ad agency-based communication
  independents, concepts
  218–21, 226, 231
ad avoidance trends 24–5, 35–6, 80,
  134–5, 159–60
Added Value (Sherrington) 4
Admap 47, 120–1
advertiser-funded programming
  (AFP) 25, 206–7
advertising strategy 20, 88–92,
  94–7, 102–4, 127, 165–79,
  192–7, 212–21
Aegis 69, 125
AFP *see* advertiser-funded
  programming
agencies
  see also individual types
  advantages 83–114, 124, 127–35,
  141–2, 176–7, 184–5, 197,
  208–9, 210–11, 226–35
agency–agency relationships
  44–56, 90–2, 169–70,
  172–5
alternative ideas 104–13,
  181–201
'bullshitting' agencies 48, 54

change 43–56, 57–81, 83–114,
  117–35, 211–21, 226–35,
  245–9
client converts 188–9
client relationships 44–56, 60–81,
  86–7, 104–6, 120–35, 168,
  181–201, 205, 209,
  246–9
criticisms 44–56, 72–5, 83–114,
  127, 175–6, 209–10, 216–21,
  240–1
cultural issues 15, 45–8, 70,
  85–92, 94–7, 210, 225–6,
  246–7
execution criticisms 45–8, 72–5,
  85–6, 94–7, 102–4, 106–8,
  127, 175–6, 209–10, 216–21,
  240–1
fusion prospects 215–21, 245
future prospects 111–13, 117–35,
  141–2, 159–79, 184–5, 196–9,
  203–21, 223–43, 245–8
holding groups 105, 106–8, 125,
  248
implementation 45–8, 94–7,
  102–4, 127, 128–35, 175–6
JVs 64, 67, 71, 74–5, 88, 149,
  177, 219–20
location considerations 127–8
major players 13–17, 63–4,
  88–92
media owners 102–3, 108–9,
  191–2
politics 48–51, 91
problems 44–56, 83–114, 196–7
responsibilities 14–15
revenue streams 5–7, 45, 73–5,
  89–92, 95, 168, 175–6,
  203–12, 226–35
sense of purpose 94–7

strategy 45–9, 87–92, 94–7,
102–4, 127, 165–79, 212–21
structural issues 45–8, 57–81,
87–114, 211–21
'toe-dipping' restructuring
57–81, 248
types 14–16, 46, 59–61, 62–81,
98–104, 120–1, 215–21
aisle displays, in-store
communications 36–7, 123
Aldi 141
Alexander, Paul 15, 53, 98, 260
aliases, communications planning
7–8
Allnut, Tim 71
alternative ideas 104–11, 181–201,
242
Amazon 194
ambassadors, Red Bull 26
American Association of Advertising
Agencies 248
American Dreams (TV programme)
206
Andorra 240–1
Anheuser Busch 189, 192
annual objectives, communications
planning 21–2, 62–3, 75,
94–7, 103, 128
Antarctica 181–201
'Antes', McKinsey grid 165
Apollo rockets 57, 155
Apple 3, 77, 190, 237
Aprimo 167
Arbitron 138, 142–7
architects 99
Argentina 181
art, ideas-first school of practice
11–13
Asia 7
'associative networks', brands 69

Atkins, Robert C. 26–7
ATL see above-the-line
attitudes, consumers 120, 137,
171–2
Australia 7, 63–5, 78, 87, 128,
149–50, 181
authoring aspects, brands 37–8
awareness-based communication
models, concepts 28

b
'backward-facing planning' 247
Baker, Paul 143–4, 146, 255
balloons 19–20, 43
The Bank 70
banks 60
Barclays 162
barcodes 142, 148
Bartle Bogle Hegarty (BBH) 8, 29,
66, 80, 87–8, 153, 207–8, 253,
264
Baumgartner, Felix 26
BAV & BrandZ 93
BBC 77
Beattie, Trevor 187
Beechwood 120–1
behaviour, consumers 120, 137–55,
164–79, 247
Belgium 138
Bellamy Hayden 63, 65, 171
below-the-line (BTL) 13–30, 39,
59–62, 70–5, 88–93, 100–3,
118–35, 166–76, 184–5,
197–9, 203–21, 226–32
see also integrated BTL/direct
agencies
fusion prospects 216–21
trends 26, 29–30, 39, 59–62
types 26, 30, 39, 62, 70–1
Benetton 190

Berry, Norman 39
Betamax 3
BMW 239–40
The Body Shop 26
Bognor Regis 19
'bogof' *see* buy-one-get-one-free
    deals
bombardment problems, consumers
    24
Boots 36
bottom-up approaches,
    communications planning
    11–12, 16, 209–10
Boyd, Mark 207–8
BP 162
brand activation 64
brand engagement, BBH 8
brand governance, concepts 185–7
brand managers 29
brand plans, communications
    planning 6–7, 30–7, 41–2,
    50–1
brand switchers 163
'brand-centric' planning 11
branded content market 206–8
brands
    see also products
    'associative networks' 69
    authoring aspects 37–8
    budget allocations 9, 29–31,
        36–7, 41–2, 50, 99–103,
        165–6, 183–4
    channel-consumer-brand school
        of practice 9–12, 76–81,
        98–104, 128–35, 169–70,
        197–9, 226–9
    choice 23–7
    communications planning
        3–17
    corporate governance 185–7

differentiation benefits 11–12,
    34, 165–6
flexible aspects 37–8, 41–2
ideas-first school of practice
    11–12, 17, 54, 61, 76–81,
    98–104, 128–35, 169–70,
    197–9, 220, 226–9
influencing era 27–8, 41–2, 45
journalism approach 38
market valuations 168–9, 246
political influences 27
proposition 6–8, 31, 165–6
retail industry 30–7, 91, 101–3,
    120–5, 197–8, 234
segmentation 164–79
store environment 30–7
Branson, Richard 110, 139
Brew, Alan 186
briefs 4–7, 22, 39, 46, 49–50,
    190–1
British Brands Group 119
British Telecom (BT) 117, 167–9,
    219, 261
broadband 153, 169
Bruneau, Stephan 164, 184, 262
BSkyB 152
BTL *see* below-the-line
budgets 7, 12, 15–16, 29–31, 36–8,
    41–2, 46, 50–1, 85, 99–103,
    165–6, 183–4
    ideas 15, 29, 38
    'out of the store' marketing
        budget options 30–1, 33,
        36–7, 99–103
    purely-technical school of
        practice 9, 29, 50–1, 76–81,
        98–104, 128–35, 165–6
Bullmore, Jeremy 47
'bullshitting' agencies 48, 54
bundling 105–6

business models 99, 168
business strategy 20, 64, 77–8,
    87–8, 94–7, 102–4, 127, 192–7
business-to-business brands,
    communications planning 5–6,
    146
Butterfield 864
buy-one-get-one-free deals
    ('bogof') 31

c
cable suppliers 153
Cadbury 34
CAGR *see* compound annual
    growth rate
call centres 9
Campaign 188–9
Campaign Manager 148–9
Campbell Soup Company 15, 53,
    98, 206, 260
Canada 70, 138
    future prospects 118
Cap Gemini 9
Carat 7–8, 60, 68–9, 77
Carney, Marie Therese 28, 40, 51,
    53, 210, 265
Carrefour Bio 34, 162
cars 143–6
case-study game 240
Catalyst, MPG 69
Central Office of Information
    205
Central Planning Group,
    Mediaedge:cia 69
change 23–4, 29, 41–2, 43–56, 58,
    83–114, 117–35, 181–201,
    211–21, 226–35, 239–40,
    245–9
    ad agencies 211–21, 226–35,
        245

agencies 43–56, 57–81, 83–114,
    117–35, 211–21, 226–35,
    245–9
clients 43–56, 58–61, 117–35,
    181–201, 205, 233–5, 246–9
conservatism 52–3
consumers 23–4, 29, 117–35
cultural factors 94–7, 210,
    225–6, 246–7
digital technologies 23–4, 29,
    41–2, 60–1, 69, 86, 117–35,
    203–5, 209–10
four internal factors 94–7
future prospects 111–13, 117–35,
    211–21, 223–43, 245–8
internal factors 94–7
leaps of faith 239–40
media buying 55, 124–35
rigour 94–7, 118–20, 128–35,
    226
skill factors 94–7, 182–3,
    189–90, 197, 242
social change 29, 41–2
structural factors 57–81, 94–7,
    211–21
'toe-dipping' restructuring
    57–81, 193–4, 248
uncomfortableness aspects 43–4,
    83–4
channel neutral planning, Millward
    Brown 8
channel planning 8, 68–70, 112–13
channel-consumer-brand school of
    practice, communications
    planning 9–16, 76–81, 98–104,
    128–35, 169–70, 197–9,
    226–9
ChannelConnect tool, Millward
    Brown 10–11
Checkmate, OMD 68

chief executive officers (CEOs) 51,
119, 147, 170, 185, 234, 237
Chile 181
Chime Communication 28, 70
China 80
choice, brands 23–7
Christensen, Clayton M. 139–40
CIA 254
Circus 70
Clark, Chris 71–3
Clemmow Hornby Inge (CHI)
71
client silos, US 51
clients
see also manufacturers
agency relationships 44–56,
60–81, 86–8, 104–6, 120–35,
168, 181–201, 205, 209,
233–5, 246–9
agent converts 188–9
alternative ideas 104–6, 181–201,
205
annual objectives 21–2, 62–3, 75,
103, 128
bundling 105–6
change 43–56, 58–61, 117–35,
181–201, 205, 233–5, 246–9
commitment 57–81, 128–35,
168, 182–201, 247–9
communications planning 5–6,
9–17, 20–42, 44–56, 58–61,
86–8, 104–6, 127–35, 168–79,
181–201, 205, 233–5, 246–9
control needs 187–8, 205
core competencies 183–4, 247
corporate governance 185–7
criticisms 44–56
cultural issues 193–7
data 184–5, 191–201, 238–9
emotional issues 187–8

future prospects 120–35, 168–79,
181–201, 205, 233–5, 246–9
globalisation trends 187–8
imported data 194–7
information shortfalls 48
mixed messages 55–6
outsourcing 182
ownership issues 181–201
politics 49
problems 182–3
procurement departments 205
revenue projections 233–5
skills shortfalls 182–3, 189–90,
197, 242
strategies 192–7
streamlining trends 182
'toe-dipping' restructuring
57–81, 193–4
Clinton, Hillary 230, 234
Clubcard scheme
see also loyalty . . .
Tesco 150–5, 163
Coca-Cola Company 7–8, 27, 50,
59–60, 64, 149
cognitive learning styles, consumers
22–3, 25–6, 69
Cold War 154
Coles 150
Colgate Palmolive 32
collaboration 109–11, 125, 162–3
collectivist approaches 44–56
Collin, Will 15, 52, 64, 85–6,
89–90, 258
Columbus, Christopher 3
commitment, communications
planning 57–81, 127–35, 168,
182–201, 247–9
communication channel planning
concepts 7–8, 68–70
Unilever 7–8, 59–61

communication channels 7–8,
9–16, 22–42, 46, 68–70,
76–81, 98–104, 128–35,
165–79, 204–21, 237–46
see also individual types
budget allocations 9, 29–31,
36–7, 41–2, 46, 99–103,
165–6, 183–4
channel-consumer-brand school
of practice 9–16, 76–81,
98–104, 128–35, 169–70,
197–9, 226–9
concepts 7–8, 21, 22–42, 204–5,
237–8
digital technologies 23–5, 29,
41–2, 60–1, 69, 86, 117–35,
203–5, 209–10
influencing era 27–8, 41–2, 45
interlinked usage 21, 22–42
types 21–42, 99–103, 204–5
communication independents
11–16, 45, 62–6, 74–5, 93,
100–3, 118–35, 141–2, 170–7,
184–5, 197, 203–31, 245–8
ad agency-based communication
independents 218–21, 226,
231
advantages 93, 141–2, 176–7,
184–5, 197
cultural issues 15, 45, 210
'disruptive technologies' 141–2,
205
fees 45, 168, 226–31
fusion prospects 218–21, 245
future prospects 118–35, 141–2,
170–7, 184–5, 197, 203–21,
226–31, 245–8
major players 63–5
problems 93, 100–3, 128–9,
176–7

revenue streams 45, 168, 226–31
roles 15–16, 45, 62–6, 74–5, 93,
100–3, 124–35, 141–2, 170–7,
184–5, 197, 203–21, 226–31,
245–8
start-ups 177
communication strategy, importance
20–42, 49, 63, 71–3, 77–8,
87–8, 94–7, 102–4, 127,
165–79, 192–7, 212–21
Communications Act, UK 207
'communications agencies' 68–70
communications industry, empty
spaces 3–4, 248
communications planning
aliases 7–8
annual objectives 21–2, 62–3, 75,
94–7, 103, 128
channel-consumer-brand school
of practice 9–16, 76–81,
98–104, 128–35, 169–70,
197–9, 226–9
concepts 3–17, 19–56, 98–104,
242–3, 245–9
data-driven prospects 160–79,
184–5, 191–201, 238–9,
242–3, 245–9
definition 3–7, 29–30
first-mover competitive
advantages 3–4, 7, 41–2, 83–4,
247
flying analogy 20–42, 249
funding issues 84
future prospects 111–13, 117–35,
159–79, 181–201, 203–21,
226–31, 245–9
hindrances 43–56
historical background 4–5
holistic plans 5–6, 8, 28–30,
38–9, 41–2, 44, 48, 144, 245–9

ideas 5–6, 11–17, 29–30, 38,
  45–8, 54–5, 76–81, 89,
  98–111, 128–35, 160, 196–7,
  208–21, 225–6, 237–49
improvement methods 98–113,
  119–20
international comparisons 78–81
naval analogy 57–8, 83–4
origins 4–5
players 12–17
popularity 42, 76
pull/push forces 61–2, 134,
  172–5
purely-technical school of
  practice 9–13, 29, 50–1,
  76–81, 98–104, 112, 128–35,
  142, 169–70, 197–9, 226–9
reasons 19–42
responsibilities 14–15
schools of practice 8–17, 61,
  76–7, 98–104, 128–35,
  169–70, 194, 220, 226–9
skills needs 77–81, 94–7, 182–3,
  189–90, 197, 242
Strategy Map 11–13, 61, 76–7,
  98–104, 128–35, 169–70, 194,
  197–9, 220, 226–9
top-down/bottom-up approaches
  11–12, 16, 209–10
competition
  competitive instincts 3–4, 57–8,
    83–4
  first-mover competitive
    advantages 3–4, 7, 41–2, 83–4,
    247
  retail industry 30–2, 101–3,
    123–5, 248
  winners 111–13, 225–36
competitive advantages 3–4, 7,
  41–2, 83–4, 124–5, 212

Compose tool, TGI 10–11, 120,
  166
compound annual growth rate
  (CAGR) 32
computer games 23, 91
computers, developments 23, 58
confectionary marketing 122–3
confidentiality issues, data
  disclosures 162
connections planning 7–8
'conscious competence' period
  (2010–2020) 157–221,
  225–6
'conscious incompetence' period
  (2005–2010) 115–55
conservatism 52–3
consultants 45–7, 62–7, 93, 98–9,
  118–35, 154, 164–71, 176–8,
  197–9, 226–33
  see also communication
    independents; management . . .
  fees 45, 73–5, 168, 226–33
consumers
  see also human beings; shoppers
  ad avoidance trends 24–5, 35–6,
    80, 134–5, 159–60
  attitudes 120, 137, 171–2
  behaviour 120, 137–55, 164–79,
    247
  bombardment problems 24
  change 23–7, 29, 117–35
  channel-consumer-brand school
    of practice 9–12, 76–81,
    98–104, 128–35, 169–70,
    197–9, 226–9
  cognitive learning styles 22–3,
    25–6, 69
  collective IQs 24, 25–6
  communications planning 5–16,
    22–42, 53

data 111–13, 117, 120–1,
138–55, 159–79, 184–5,
191–201, 238–9, 242–3, 245–9
demographics 98, 120–1, 164–79
herd instincts 27–8
ideas-first school of practice
11–12, 54, 61, 76–81, 98–104,
128–35, 169–70, 197–9, 220,
226–9
influencing era 27–8, 41–2, 45
insights 10–16, 86, 98, 120, 161,
164–79, 195–7, 225–6, 242–3,
246
loyalty schemes 34, 142, 150–5,
161–3, 165–6
needs 22–7, 53, 68–70, 86–7, 98,
120–3, 137, 140–1,
164–79
PPMs 60, 138–47
segmentation 164–79
'The Soul Meter' 137–55, 168
understanding 53, 68–70,
119–20, 164–79
content
fusion prospects 216–21
production arena 206–14
continuous improvements 22,
119–20, 166–7
control
client needs 187–8, 205
feedback loops 166–7, 239
Cook-It 35
core competencies
clients 183–4, 247
research agencies 75
corporate governance, brands
185–7
corporate social responsibility
(CSR) 186
cost per rating points (CPPs) 199

couponing, mobile phones 23,
148–50
Courtier, Charles 15, 76–7, 111–13,
260
'creative age', 'marketing age' 246
creative agencies 49–50, 59–61, 85,
88–93, 102–3, 111–13, 177–8,
208–21, 246–9
Creative Artists 89
creative brief 4–5, 22, 39, 46,
49–50, 190–1
creativity 29–30, 39, 45–8, 71–3,
88–93, 102–3, 111–13,
208–21, 237–43, 246–9
see also ideas
crises 20–1, 42
cultural issues
agencies 15, 45–8, 70, 85–92,
94–7, 210, 225–6, 246–7
clients 193–7, 246–7
communication independents 15,
45, 210
sense of purpose 94–7
customer relationship management
(CRM) 7, 23, 30, 33, 39, 60,
69, 148, 150–5, 164–6

d
Daley, Lee 25
dark days, data 159–79, 238–9, 245
d'Arlandes, Marquis 19
data 111–13, 117, 120–1, 138–55,
159–79, 184–5, 191–201,
238–9, 242–3, 245–9
clients 184–5, 191–201
communications-planning driver
160–79, 184–5, 191–201,
238–9, 242–3, 245–9
confidentiality issues 162
dark days 159–79, 238–9, 245

databases 111–13, 117, 120–1,
138–55, 159–79, 184–5,
191–201, 238–9, 242–3,
245–9
deception dangers 159–60
future prospects 159–79,
191–201
knowledge conversion 150–5,
161–71, 184–5, 245–9
loyalty schemes 34, 142, 150–5,
161–3
ownership 160–3, 184–5
sales of data 161–3, 194–5
segmentation 164–79
storage issues 111–13, 117,
120–1, 138–55, 159–79
uses 150–5, 161–7, 184–5,
191–201
Data Protection Act, UK 162
data warehouses 160–1
DaVinci 63, 65, 106
see also Omnicom
DDB 66
Debenhams 162
deception dangers, data 159–60
Delaney, Tim 189
Dell, Michael 237
demographics, consumers 98,
120–1, 164–79
deployment strategies,
communications planning
5–6
DHL Express 48–9, 183, 189–90,
256
Diageo 63, 119
Diesel 190
diets 26–7
differentiation benefits, brands
11–12, 34, 165–6
digital photography 141

digital technologies
developments 23–5, 29, 41–2,
58, 60–1, 69, 86, 117–35,
138–55, 159–79, 203–5,
209–10, 234
PVRs 24–5, 35, 80, 134–5, 137,
142
direct marketing (DM) 22, 36, 46,
66–7, 77–8, 97, 102–4, 120–5,
176–7
direct-based agencies 11–15, 17, 22,
62, 70–1, 97, 120–5
discounts, media discounts 55, 124–5
Disraeli, Benjamin 160
'Disruption Consultancy' 67
'disruptive technologies' 139–42, 205
'distributed communications
planning' model, alternative
ideas 109–11
Dixons 36
Dodd, Jonathan 93, 209, 257
Dove 39–41, 163
'Drivers', McKinsey grid 165
Drum 206
Duffy, Neill 38–9
Dunn, Edwina 150
dunnhumby 150–5, 164
DVD sales 207

e
Earls, Mark 27–8
eBay 194
econometrics 9–13, 29, 76–81,
98–104, 112, 128–35, 142,
164–75, 197–9, 226–35, 241,
248
EDLP 184
'effectiveness bingo' 54
Einstein, Albert 242
Element Communications 71

emails 23
  viral marketing 23, 28
EMEA 241, 262–3
Emery, Nick 4, 183, 263
emotional issues, clients 187–8
employees
  talented people 46, 69, 74–5,
    87–92, 94–7, 189–90, 195
  turnover levels 246
empty spaces, human instincts 3–4,
  248
engineers 225–6
Enron 185
EnterpriseIG 186
episodic marketing 37–8
EPoS systems 148
Esso 27
Eurisko Media Monitor 147
Europe 7–8, 24, 63–5, 77, 122,
  124–6, 134, 141, 149
  see also individual countries
European Commission 126
Eurostar 53
events 30, 33, 36–7, 67, 70, 166
execution criticisms, agencies 45–8,
  72–5, 85–6, 94–7, 102–4,
  106–8, 127, 175–6, 209–10,
  216–21, 240–1
Experience 63, 65
experiential marketing, Starbucks 26
extreme sports, Red Bull 26

f

Fallon 7–8, 71
FCB 67
FedEx 256
feedback loops 166–7, 239
field-marketing agencies 101
finance directors, marketing
  directors 184–5

first-mover competitive advantages
  3–4, 7, 41–2, 83–4, 247
'fish' process, concepts 4–5
fleet analogy 57–8, 83–4
flexible aspects, brands 37–8, 41–2
fluid identity, brands 38
flying 19–42, 249
FMCG manufacturers 32–3, 40–1,
  149, 152, 163, 247
Foote, Nigel 241, 263
Forato, Marco 172
France 65, 87, 118, 181, 210, 240
Freud Inside 71
Friends (TV programme) 37
full-service agencies 46–7, 58, 67,
  111–13, 204–5, 219, 245
  resurgence 67, 111, 219
  roles 46–7, 58, 67, 111, 204–5
  unbundling 46–7, 58, 105–6
funding issues, communications
  planning 84
Fusion 537
fusion prospects, agencies 215–21,
  245
future prospects 111–13, 117–35,
  141–2, 159–79, 181–201,
  203–21, 223–43, 245–8
  2005–2010 period ('conscious
    incompetence') 115–55
  2010–2020 period ('conscious
    competence') 157–221, 225–6
  2020 onwards period
    ('unconscious competence')
    223–43

g

G2 Worldwide 70, 93, 101, 257
Gagnon, Rich 67
Galileo Galilei 159
games 23, 91

Gargarin, Yuri 154
The Gathering 64
gender issues 98
General Motors 42, 59–60, 97, 190
'generalists', requirements 66–7,
    77–8
geographies
    budget allocations 9
    purely-technical school of
        practice 9–10
George 32
Georgiadis, Phil 86–7
Germany 118, 141
Gfk/Telecontroll 147
Gharekhan, Nikhil 172
GlaxoSmithKline 189
globalisation trends 187–8
gondola-end displays 101, 138
Good Stuff 65
Grant, John 24, 37, 77, 87, 90, 103,
    111, 259
gravity 43–56, 128–35, 248
Grey Global 70, 126
    see also Joshua
Griffiths, John 194, 206–7
grocery retail area 31, 122–5,
    148–55
gross rating points (GRPs) 101,
    199
GroupM 125
groups see teams

h
Hackworthy, David 66
Haines, Bruce 66, 213, 255
Harley Davidson 140
Harlow, John 64, 102, 213
Hayward, Martin 153–4
helicopter views, benefits 117–18
The Henley Centre 153

herd instinct 27–8
HHCL 63
Hill, Rob 39, 95, 186, 242, 246,
    257
hindrances, communications
    planning 43–56
The Hive 70
holding groups 105, 106–8, 125,
    248
holistic plans, communications
    planning 5–6, 8, 28–30, 38–9,
    41–2, 44, 48, 144, 245–9
Homebase 36
Honda 140–1
hope 245
HSBC 107
Hudson River Group 164
Hull, Light 150
human beings
    see also consumers
    competitive instincts 3–4, 57–8,
        83–4
    empty spaces 3–4, 248
    herd instinct 27–8
    humour 239
    messaging systems 160
    'The Soul Meter' 137–55, 168
Humby, Clive 150
humour 239
Hunt Lascaris TBWA 192, 252–3

i
IAAA 213
IBM 164, 189–90, 237
ideas 5–17, 29–30, 38, 45–8, 54–5,
    76–81, 89, 98–111, 128–35,
    160, 196–7, 208–26, 237–49
    see also creativity
    alternative ideas 104–11,
        181–201, 242

budgets 15, 29, 38
concepts 238–43
measurability paradox 242
quantification 54–5
'return on an idea investment'
    figures 240–1
ROI 11, 98–104, 238–43
testing 240–2
ideas-first school of practice,
    communications planning
    11–17, 54, 61, 76–81, 98–104,
    128–35, 169–70, 197–9, 220,
    226–9
'I'm Lovin' It' idea, McDonald's 38
implementation 6–7, 45–8, 71–3,
    94–7, 102–4, 127, 175–6
    agencies 45–8, 94–7, 102–4, 127,
    128–35, 175–6
    briefs 6–7
improvements
    communications planning
    98–113, 119–20
    continuous improvements 22,
    119–20
in-store communications 7, 23,
    30–3, 35–7, 68–9, 99–103,
    120–5, 138–47
    concepts 7, 23, 30–3, 35–7,
    68–9, 99–103, 120–5
    forms 23, 35, 68, 101–3, 121–5,
    128, 138–47
in-store TV plasma screens 23, 35,
    101, 122–3, 128, 142, 204
influencing era, concepts 27–8,
    41–2, 45
'infomercials' 203
Ingram, Chris 64, 84, 108, 254
The Ingram Partnership 12–13,
    63–5, 84, 254
Initiative Media 125

The Innovator's Dilemma
    (Christensen) 139–40
insights, communications planning
    10–16, 86, 98, 120, 161,
    164–79, 195–7, 225–6, 242–3,
    246
Institute of Practitioners in
    Advertising (IPA) 255, 258
'insurance', research 54
integrated BTL/direct agencies
    13–17, 20, 62, 70–1, 74–5,
    88–9, 92–3, 100–3, 118–35,
    166–76, 184–5, 197–9,
    203–21, 226–32, 245–8
    advantages 92–3, 124, 128–35,
    197, 210–11
    fusion prospects 216–21, 245
    future prospects 118–35, 166–70,
    172–6, 184–5, 197–9, 203–21,
    226–32, 245–8
    major players 70–1
    problems 88–9, 92–3, 100–3
    production remuneration 203–8
    revenue streams 203–8, 226–32
    roles 14–16, 62, 70–5, 88–9,
    92–3, 100–3, 120, 125,
    166–76, 184–5, 197–9,
    203–21, 226–32, 245–8
integrated communications
    evaluation (ICE) 69–70
integrated marketing
    communication (IMC), Coca-
    Cola Company 7, 50
Integration, MCA tool 10–11, 79,
    93, 120, 166
integration contrasts,
    communications planning 7
intelligent fridges 145
interactive advertising 25, 204
Interactive Africa 38

interactive TV (iTV) 204
interlinked usage, communication
    channels 21, 22–42
international comparisons
    see also individual countries
    communications planning 78–81
Internet 23, 27, 36–7, 120–1,
    142–3, 147–8, 194, 239–40
Interpublic 106, 125
interviewees, profiles 251–65
investment decisions 55–6
IQs, collective IQs 24, 25–6
ISBA 117
Italy 24, 147

j
Japan 52, 64–5, 97, 140–1
Jobs, Steve 237
The Joined-Up Company 23
joint ventures (JVs) 64, 67, 71,
    74–5, 88, 149, 177, 219–20
Joshua 70
    see also Grey Global
journalism approach, brands 38
judgement 159
JWT 8

k
Kennedy, John F. 154
Kenyon, Tony 125
key performance indicators (KPIs)
    167, 240
knowledge
    data conversion 150–5, 161–71,
        184–5, 245–9
    power 34–7, 62, 75
    retail industry 34–7, 161–3
Korea 187, 195
KPMG 161
Kroger 150

Krushchev, Nikita 154
Kruythoff, Kees 22, 58, 168, 218,
    261

l
Land, Edwin 237
Lascaris, Reg 192, 204, 211, 241,
    252–3
lateral thinking, alternative ideas
    109–11, 242
Leagas Delaney 189
leaps of faith 239–40
learning 22–3, 25–6, 69, 239
Leo Burnett 66, 255
Lewis, Marc 147–9
Lidl 141
lies, statistics 160
Light 147–50
Light, Larry 38
lip service 21–2
Lipton Ice Tea 26
location considerations, agencies
    127–8
long-term measures, short-termism
    238
'loop team' concept, Leo Burnett
    66
L'Oréal 184
'low-carbohydrate' diets 26–7
loyalty schemes 34, 142, 150–5,
    161–3, 165–6

m
McCann Erickson 85–6, 254
McDonald's 36–8, 46, 112, 169
McGough, Mike 192
McKinsey 165, 185
magazines 23
Magna 125
Malcolm, Rob 119

management consultants 13–16, 45,
47, 73–5, 98–104, 118–35,
154, 164–71, 178, 197–9,
226–33, 246
agency relationships 169–70
fees 45, 73–5, 168, 226–33
future prospects 118–35, 154,
164–71, 178, 197–9, 226–33
revenue streams 45, 73–5, 168,
226–33
roles 73–5, 98–104, 118–35, 154,
164–71, 178, 197–9, 226–33
value chains 73–5
manufacturers 30–7, 118, 161–3,
190–201, 247
see also brands; clients
retail industry 30–7, 123–5,
161–3, 197–8, 234, 248
market valuations, brands 168–9,
246
'marketing age', 'creative age' 246
marketing brand plans,
communications planning 6–7,
30–7, 41–2, 50–1
marketing channels
budget allocations 9, 29–31,
36–7, 41–2, 46, 99–103,
165–6
channel-consumer-brand school
of practice 9–12, 76–81,
98–104, 128–35, 169–70,
197–9, 226–9
communications planning 5–9,
21–42, 59–61, 237–43
purely-technical school of
practice 9–10, 29, 98–104,
128–35, 197–9
selection issues 7
marketing directors 21, 51, 119,
125, 184–5, 195–6

communications planning 21, 51,
125, 184–5, 195–6
inertia 21
marketing disciplines
budget allocations 9, 46
communications planning 5–6, 9,
29, 70, 77–8, 237–43
purely-technical school of
practice 9–10, 98–104, 129–35
marketing function, lip service
21–2
Marketing Management Analytics
164
marketing mix 7, 143, 248, 253
marketing resource management
software 167
Marketing Society 117
marketing strategy 20, 64, 71–3,
77–8, 87–92, 94–7, 102–4,
127, 165–79, 192–7, 212–21
Mars 72
mass customisation 151
mass media 121
mass sampling, Red Bull 26
Match Integration 63, 65, 87, 90,
264
MCA tool, Integration 10–11, 79,
93, 120, 166
measures, performance 44–6, 56,
60, 98–104, 111–12, 118–20,
138, 160, 167–9, 171–8,
196–7, 219–20, 225–43, 247–9
media, digital technologies 23,
41–2, 60–1, 69, 86, 117–35,
203–5, 209–10
media agencies 10–14, 48–70,
74–88, 92–135, 141–2, 160,
166–7, 172–6, 184–5, 197–9,
203–21, 226–30, 245–8
see also agencies

advantages 68, 84–8, 111, 124, 128–35, 141–2, 184–5, 197
'disruptive technologies' 141–2, 205
fusion prospects 216–21, 245
future prospects 111, 117–35, 141–2, 160, 166–7, 172–6, 184–5, 197–9, 203–21, 226–30, 245–8
major players 68–70
networks 68–70, 74–5, 84–8
problems 84–8, 89, 94–5, 100–3, 160
production remuneration 204–5
proprietary tools/techniques 68–70, 79, 86–7, 120, 166
revenue streams 69, 84, 168, 175–6, 203–5, 226–30
roles 14–16, 48–9, 54, 58–62, 67–70, 74–8, 84–8, 94–5, 105, 111, 125, 141–2, 160, 166–7, 172–6, 184–5, 197–9, 203–21, 226–30, 245–8
sense of purpose 94–7
structural issues 87–8
techniques/tools 68–70, 79, 86–7, 93, 120, 166
vision 68
media buying, changes 55, 124–35
media discounts 55, 124
media holding groups 105, 106–8, 125, 248
The Media Kitchen 63, 65
media neutral planning 7
media owners
alternative ideas 108–9, 191–2
relationships 102–3, 108–9, 191–2
The Media Palace 63

media strategy, concepts 20–3, 71–3, 77–8, 87–92, 94–7, 102–4, 127, 165–79, 192–7, 212–21, 251, 259
MediaCom 125
Mediaedge:cia 7–8, 15, 25, 63, 67–9, 76–7, 111–13, 125, 164, 184, 258, 260, 262
see also Nota Bene; Nylon
messaging systems, human voice 160
Metzler, Richard M. 48–9, 183, 189–90, 256
Michaelides & Bednash 52, 63–5, 210, 251, 259, 265
Michaelides, George 52, 64, 96–7, 251, 259, 265
Microsoft 3
Miles Calcraft Briginshaw Duffy 67
Millar, Grant 117, 118–19, 167–9, 190, 219, 261
Millward Brown 8, 10–11, 172, 214, 256
ChannelConnect tool 10–11
Mindset, MindShare 68–9, 139
MindShare Worldwide 4, 68–9, 77, 125, 139, 183, 263
mission 101
mixed messages, clients 55–6
MMS services 141
mobile marketing companies 147–50
mobile phones
couponing 23, 148–50
developments 23, 141, 147–50, 204, 234
SMS technology 141, 148–50
movie business, communications planning 12–13
MPG 69

MTN 63
multi-format portfolios, Tesco
31–2
multiple channels, importance
22–42, 209–10
Murphy, Guy 29, 80, 87–8, 253

n
Naidoo, Ravi 38
Naked Communications 15, 52,
63–5, 71, 85–6, 89–90, 102,
112, 171, 213, 258
naval analogy 57–8, 83–4
Navigator system, Mediaedge:cia
68
NBC 206
Nectar 162–3
Nestlé 122
Netherlands 34–5, 65
networks
ad agencies 65–8, 74–5, 88–92
media agencies 68–70, 74–5,
84–8
new product development (NPD)
26–7, 197
new rigour, change factors 94–7,
118–20, 128–35, 226
Newcastle upon Tyne, UK 241
newspapers 23, 33
Nike 60–1
Ninah 164
Nitro 71–5, 212, 264
North America 7, 51–2, 60, 63–5,
77, 118, 149
future prospects 118
Norway 65, 181
Nota Bene 49, 63, 65, 95
see also Mediaedge:cia
Nylon 67, 71, 85, 90, 93, 112, 190,
205, 212, 258, 259

o
objectives-driven approaches,
communications planning
21–2, 62–3, 75, 94–7, 103, 128
Ogilvy & Mather 4, 27–8, 39, 40,
51, 53, 66–8, 70, 95, 111, 177,
186, 210, 242, 246, 252, 257,
264, 265
Ohal Limited 143–4, 146, 164,
255
O'Malley, Damian 85–6, 98, 254
OMD 7–8, 68–9, 125
Omnicom 63, 106, 125
see also DaVinci
OPera 125
operating systems 68
opportunities 3–4, 84–114
opt-ins 121
Optimedia 7–8
original communications 38–41
'out of the store' marketing budget
options, concepts 30–1, 33,
36–7, 99–103
outsourcing, alternative ideas
110–11, 182
own-label brands 30, 33–4
ownership issues
clients 181–201
data 160–3, 184–5

p
P&L units 64–9, 96, 107–8
packaging 36–7, 58, 101
Palmisano, Sam 237
Partilla, John 56, 109, 194, 262
Passion Branding (Duffy) 38–9
perfect structure 98–111
performance measures
concepts 167, 225–43, 247–9
KPIs 167, 240

ROI 44–6, 56, 60, 98–104,
111–12, 118–20, 138, 160,
169, 171–8, 196–7, 219–20,
225–45
personal digital assistants (PDAs)
68–9, 139, 145
personal video recorders (PVRs)
24–5, 35, 80, 134–5, 137, 142
PHD Media 71, 125, 206
Philips 59
Pinnington, Danielle 122–3
place, 4Ps 183–4
placement, products 25, 248
players, communications planning
12–17
Plus 34–5
Pointlogic 164
Polaroid 237
political influences 27, 48–51, 91
Pollard, Ivan 12–13
portable people meters (PPMs) 60,
138–47
portfolio optimisation 34, 172, 253
power
knowledge 34–7, 62, 75
retail industry 30–7, 41–2,
123–5, 161–3
PowerPoint documents,
communications planning 6
PR 7, 22, 26, 30, 46–7, 58, 66–71,
102, 210
pre-testing, ideas 240–1
Preston, John 87, 90, 264
price, 4Ps 183–4
problems, agencies 83–114
Procter & Gamble (P&G) 34,
60–1, 77–8, 104, 138, 143–4,
163–4, 187, 189, 234
procurement departments, clients
205

production arena 203–14, 239–40
products
see also brands
4Ps 183–4
placement 25, 248
Project Apollo, Arbitron and VNU
138, 142–7, 248
promotion, 4Ps 183–4
promotions 7, 26, 36–7, 46, 62,
66–7, 70, 101, 142, 148–51,
166
Pronk, Casey 122
proposition, brands 6–8, 31,
165–6
Proximity 70
Publicis 106, 125
pull/push forces, communications
planning 61–2, 134, 172–5
purely-technical school of practice,
communications planning
9–13, 16–17, 29, 50–1, 76–81,
98–104, 112, 128–35, 142,
169–70, 197–9, 226–9

q
qualitative research 11, 112, 144–6,
171–2
quantification, ideas 54–5
quantitative research 11, 112, 144,
171–2

r
race issues 98
racing instincts, humans 3–4
radio 23, 102–3, 134, 143–5
Radio Frequency IDentification
(RFID) 144–5
Radio Joint Audience Research
(RAJAR) 147
Rainey, MT 208

RAJAR *see* Radio Joint Audience
  Research
real-world ideas testing 241–2
reasons, communications planning
  19–42
Reckitt Benckiser 189
recruitment, talented people 46, 69,
  74–5, 87–92, 94–7, 189–90,
  195
'Red Adair'-style teams 110
Red Bull 26–7
Regan, Tony 84–5, 190, 212, 259
research 9–12, 54, 112, 119–35,
  138–55, 164–72
  see also data . . .
  channel-consumer-brand school
    of practice 9–12, 128–35,
    169–70
  'insurance' 54
  knowledge/data conversion
    150–5, 161–71, 184–5
  types 11, 112, 119–21, 137–55,
    171–2
research & development (R&D)
  184
research agencies 4, 13, 16, 73–5,
  100–3, 119–35, 142–7,
  164–70, 171–4, 197–9, 226–32
  communications planning 4, 13,
    16, 73–5, 100–3, 119–35,
    164–70, 171–4, 226–32
  core competencies 75
  future prospects 119–35, 164–70,
    171–4, 197–9, 226–32
  revenue streams 226–32
  roles 75, 100–3, 125, 133–5, 155,
    164–70, 171–4, 197–9, 226–32
respect 46
responsibilities, communications
  planning 14–15

retail industry 30–7, 69–70, 91,
  101–3, 120–5, 138–47, 150–5,
  161, 197–8, 234, 248
  in-store communications 7, 23,
    30–3, 35–7, 68–9, 99–103,
    120–5, 138–47
  knowledge 34–7, 161–3
  loyalty schemes 34, 142, 150–5,
    161–3
  manufacturers 30–7, 123–5,
    161–3, 197–8, 234, 248
  own-label brands 30, 33–4
  power 30–7, 41–2, 123–5,
    161–3
  trade funding 32–3
retail media 35–7, 101–3
'return on an idea investment'
  figures 240–1
return on investment (ROI) 11,
  20–1, 44–6, 56, 60, 98–104,
  111–20, 138–9, 160, 169,
  171–8, 185, 196–7, 219–45
  future prospects 237–43
  ideas 11, 98–104, 238–43
  importance 11, 20–1, 44–6, 60,
    98–104, 111–12, 118–20,
    138–9, 160, 178, 196–7,
    219–20, 237–45
  lip service 21
revenue streams
  ad agencies 89–92, 175–6,
    203–12, 226–31
  agencies 5–7, 45, 73–5, 89–92,
    95, 168, 175–6, 203–12,
    226–35
  communication independents 45,
    168, 226–31
  future prospects 226–35
  integrated BTL/direct agencies
    203–8, 226–32

management consultants 45,
    73–5, 168, 226–33
media agencies 69, 84, 175–6,
    203–4, 226–30
research agencies 226–32
revenue-protection practices,
    communications planning 5–7,
    89–90
RI/Kantar 101
rigour, change factors 94–7,
    118–20, 128–35, 226
Rise Communications 63, 65
RKCR Y&R 208–9
Rozier, Pilatre de 19–20
Russell, Kurt 234
Russia 154–5
Rutherford, Alan 59–60
Ryan Air 194

s
Saatchi & Saatchi 25
SABMiller 4, 43–4
Sacharin, Ken 225
Safeway 161
Sainsbury's 23, 123, 148–9, 162
Sainsbury's@Jacksons 148–9
St Luke's 259
Samsung 107, 187–8
Sanlam 63
Saunders, Julian 23
Scandinavia 65, 78
    see also individual countries
schools of practice, communications
    planning 8–17, 61, 76–7,
    98–104, 128–35, 169–70, 194,
    220, 226–9
science, purely-technical school of
    practice 9–13, 29, 76–81,
    98–104, 128–35, 169–70,
    197–9, 226–9

Seddon, Joanna 172
segmentation, future prospects
    164–79
self-scanning devices 143–7
sense of purpose, cultural issues
    94–7
share prices 20–1, 55–6
shareholder value 22, 55–6, 119
Shearer, Paul 71–3, 212, 214, 264
shelf-level interactive devices 123
Sherrington, Mark 4
Shoppercentric 122–3
shoppers
    see also consumers
    in-store communications 7, 23,
        30–3, 35–7, 68–9, 99–103,
        120–5, 138–47
    loyalty schemes 34, 142, 150–5,
        161–3
    PPMs 60, 138–47
    'The Soul Meter' 137–55, 168
short-termism 117, 238
Singapore 78
single-source data 137–55, 248
skills needs, communications
    planning 77–81, 94–7, 182–3,
    189–90, 197, 242
Smoothies 104
SMS technology 141, 148–9
snow 238–9, 242, 249
social change 29, 41–2, 186
Sorrell, Sir Martin 45–6, 49
Soul 67
'The Soul Meter' 137–55, 168
The Source, OMD 69
South Africa 7, 22, 63–7, 78, 95,
    163, 186, 210
Space City, Russia 154
space race 154–5
spaces, human instincts 3–4

Spain 24, 240

Spar 36

special placement, in-store communications 36–7

specialisms 46–7, 58, 66, 238

sponges, flying analogy 19–42

sponsorship 22, 25, 30, 33, 36–7, 50, 69, 206–8

spreadsheets 182

Starbucks 26, 194

Starcom Group 60, 77, 125, 241, 263

statistics

see also data

lies 160

stereo 23

storage issues, data 111–13, 117, 120–1, 138–55, 159–79

store environment, importance 30–7

strategies

agencies 45–9, 87–92, 94–7, 102–4, 127, 165–79, 212–21

clients 192–7

types 20–3, 63–4, 71–3, 77–8

Strategy Map, schools of practice 11–13, 61, 76–7, 98–104, 128–35, 169–70, 194, 197–9, 220, 226–9

'strategy team for hire' idea 110–11

straw, flying analogy 19–42

Street Support 60

structural issues

agencies 45–8, 57–81, 87–114, 211–21

perfect structure 98–111

'toe-dipping' restructuring 57–81, 193–4, 248

supermarkets 31–2, 34–6, 101, 138, 142–8, 150–5, 161, 205–6, 234

see also individual supermarkets; retail . . .

supply chains 119

Surowiecki, James 109

'sustaining technologies', concepts 139–42

Sweden 87, 210

Switzerland 147

t

T-shirt logos 138

talented people 46, 69, 74–5, 87–92, 94–7, 189–90, 195

TBWA Group 7–8, 66, 67, 70, 90–1, 177, 192, 204, 210–11, 215, 241, 252

teams, alternative ideas 109–11

technologies

see also data . . . ; digital . . .

developments 23–5, 29, 41–2, 58, 60–1, 86, 117–35, 138–55, 159–79, 203–5, 234

disruptive/sustaining technologies 139–42

future prospects 117–35, 137–55, 159–79

loyalty schemes 34, 142, 150–5, 161–3

mobile phones 23, 141, 147–50, 204, 234

'The Soul Meter' 137–55, 168

telco market

brand market valuations 169

winners 111

telephone 23

Tempus 64

TEQUILA 20, 62, 70, 88–9, 177, 215, 252

Tesco 31–2, 34–6, 142, 150–5, 163, 205–6

test markets 240–3

TGI, Compose tool 10–11, 120, 166

Thomas, Martin 67, 90–3, 205, 258

through-the-line planners 60–1, 66–7, 70–1, 101–3, 146, 210

Time Warner 56, 109, 112, 194, 262

timescales, communications planning 6–7

'toe-dipping' restructuring 57–81, 193–4, 248

tools/techniques 10–11, 68–70, 79, 86–7, 93, 120, 166, 226

Top Gear (TV programme) 144

top-down approaches, communications planning 11–12, 17, 209–10

total branding, JWT 8

total communication planning 7

Toys 'R' Us 32

trade funding, retail industry 32–3

trade-marketing brand plans, communications planning 6–7, 30–7, 41–2, 50–1, 119–20

transparency requirements 185–6

trust 28, 31, 46

turnover levels, employees 246

TV 21–35, 46, 58, 92, 102–3, 122–3, 128, 134–5, 142–4, 150, 153–4, 203–14, 234
  ad avoidance 24–5, 35–6, 80, 134–5, 159–60
  AFP 206–7
  declining trends 24–6, 29–30, 33, 58
  developments 23–5, 122–3, 128, 134–5, 142, 150, 153–4, 203–14, 234

in-store TV plasma screens 23, 35, 101, 122–3, 128, 142, 204
  poor quality 21
  PVRs 24–5, 35, 80, 134–5, 137, 142
  sponsorship 25, 30, 206–8

Tylee, John 188–9

u

UK 24, 31, 63–8, 70–3, 78–9, 87, 108–9, 122–6, 148–50, 161–2, 181, 195, 207, 241
  Communications Act 207
  Data Protection Act 162
  grocery retail area 31, 122–5, 148–55
  PVRs 24

unbundling, full-service agencies 46–7, 58, 105–6

uncomfortableness aspects, change 43–4, 83–4

'unconscious competence' period (2020 onwards) 223–43

'unconscious incompetence' period (2000–2005) 1–114

understanding, consumers 53, 68–70, 119–20, 164–79

Unica 167

Unilever 4–5, 7, 22, 32, 34–5, 37, 39, 42, 49–50, 58–61, 63, 72, 77–8, 148, 168, 187, 189, 195, 218, 261

Unity 63–4

Universal McCann 125, 265

UPS 111

US 24, 51–2, 63–5, 78–9, 118, 122, 124–5, 134, 138, 140–1, 150, 191, 237, 239–40
  client silos 51

future prospects 118, 125, 126, 134
Japan 52, 97, 140–1
PVRs 24, 134–5
Russia 154–5

v
value chains 73–5, 119
venture capitalists 177
Veridiem 167
VHS 3
viral marketing, emails 23, 28
visibility techniques, Lipton Ice Tea 26
vision 6, 14, 68, 225–36
Vizeum 7–8, 69
VNU 138, 142–7
Vogel, Peter 63

w
Wade-Gery, Laura 31–2
Wal-Mart (Asda) 31, 32, 34–6, 101, 142, 162, 206, 225
Walker, Christine 125
Walker, James 73, 89, 91, 105, 187, 219–20, 253
Walker Media 86–7
Walshe, Peter 214, 256
water in the air 238–9
Watts, Kate 28
WCRS 71
web-linked kiosks 23
  see also Internet

weightlessness 223–43, 248
Whybin Lawrence TBWA 264
Wieden, Dan 187
Wilkins, Jon 64
Wilson, Joe 237
winners, competition 111–13, 225–36
Wood, John 120–1
workshops 109–10
WOW Factory 263
WPP 45–6, 71, 101, 106–7, 112, 125, 126, 153, 188, 254, 255, 256
Wright, Rod 20, 62, 88–9, 91, 215–16, 252
Wunderman 67, 70

x
Xerox 237

y
Yahoo 104
Yankelovich Partners 24
Young & Rubicam (Y&R) 67, 208–9, 260, 262
  see also Nylon

z
zeitgeist 128
Zenith 7–8, 125

Index compiled by Terry Halliday